What people are saying about …

Tell Me a Story

"Wherever our ministry distributes wheelchairs, we encounter thousands of people who are hungry for the gospel—yet are not able to read. The number of people who cannot—or choose not—to read is skyrocketing; we must grasp the depth of this need as well as the importance of communicating the gospel orally. Dennis Johnson's book *Tell Me a Story* combines heartwarming stories with cutting-edge methods to help the church reach a burgeoning population of nonreaders—it's an important work for every Christian interested in reaching the lost!"

Joni Eareckson Tada, Joni and Friends
International Disability Center

"A great story about storytelling—by two master storytellers I'm blessed to have as friends and traveling companions. Denny Johnson and Joe Musser get it. They know why telling the right story the right way is so important. Read this book, and you will know too."

Lt. Col. Oliver North, USMC (Ret.), *New York Times* best-selling author-speaker

"Jesus had a heart for children that changed the world—and changes it still. You need to read *Tell Me a Story* so you can be part of the movement."

John Ortberg, Jr., author and pastor of
Menlo Park Presbyterian Church

"This book reintroduces us to Orality, the ancient secret of how to pass on God's teachings to the next generation by telling truthful stories to our children starting at two to three years of age when their character is being formed. Denny Johnson also tells how we can teach children beyond our families by first building them a playground as a demonstration of love, thereby paving the way to 'story times' about Jesus, His life, and His offer of heaven for them. Orality is the simple, practical, and effective way that Jesus taught; let us learn from the Master."

Evelyn Christenson, author, speaker, and
president of United Prayer Ministry

"Denny Johnson's love for children and the next generation is contagious! His capable storytelling helps us to understand what Orality is, how it works, and why the church is growing in the non-West."

Rev. Samuel E. Chiang, executive director
of International Orality Network

TELL ME A STORY

TELL ME A STORY

Orality: How the World Learns

DENNIS JOHNSON

with Joe Musser

TELL ME A STORY
Published by David C Cook
4050 Lee Vance View
Colorado Springs, CO 80918 U.S.A.

David C Cook Distribution Canada
55 Woodslee Avenue, Paris, Ontario, Canada N3L 3E5

David C Cook U.K., Kingsway Communications
Eastbourne, East Sussex BN23 6NT, England

The website addresses recommended throughout this book are offered as a resource to you. These websites are not intended in any way to be or imply an endorsement on the part of David C Cook, nor do we vouch for their content.

LCCN 2011941131
ISBN 978-0-7814-0807-3
eISBN 978-0-7814-0818-9

Center Spread Design: Larson Group Design Company
Cover Photo: Shutterstock

Printed in the United States of America
First Edition 2012

1 2 3 4 5 6 7 8 9 10

103111

DEDICATION

This book is dedicated to my wife, Evie, and to our children, Tonya, Cary, and Rynn, and to our family members—who like Kevin have accompanied me on trips and who may have discovered themselves as one of my illustrations of this "storytelling" book.

I also wish to dedicate this book to our Kids Around the World president Jim Rosene and his wife, Denise; our Kids Around the World staff; volunteers; and our phenomenal board of directors. Their diligence, vision, and dedication to the cause of Christ helped to give me the inspiration for this book through experiences that offered a great many of the anecdotes and illustrations in this book.

ACKNOWLEDGMENTS

In addition to my recognition of my family members in my dedication, I also want to mention my gratitude to my wife, Evie, and my daughter Tonya, and for Jim Rosene and the Kids Around the World staff members for their help with research, photos, and especially input of ideas and creativity, and for their critiques of the content and helping with the accuracy of details in this book.

Thanks also to Joe Musser, coauthor and longtime friend, for his experienced assistance and contributions. My appreciation also goes to Jeff Larsen for his creativity and intuition in the design of the book cover and photo spreads that added so much to the overall presentation.

It's impossible to thank everyone who made a contribution, but longtime friends and Christian leaders offered ideas, memories, anecdotes, and material from their own experiences. Some of those to whom I want to express my thanks include: Frank Beach; Dr. Steve Douglass and his wife, Judy; Dr. Paul Larsen; Lt. Col. Oliver

North (USMC, Ret.); Rev. Victor Kulbich; the late Dr. Avery Willis; and Rev. Samuel Chiang.

And last but assuredly not least, my thanks go to the editorial, marketing, and production teams at David C Cook Publishing for their fantastic help in putting this book together. My personal gratitude goes to Ingrid Beck (managing editor), Caitlyn York (project coordinator and copy editor), Nick Lee (designer), and Karen Athen (typesetter), for keen attention to the details of how the book was packaged, and to others whom I haven't even met but who put in countless hours and made great contributions of energy and ideas to make this book come to life.

CONTENTS

FOREWORD

I have known Denny Johnson nearly all my life. Our families went to the same church as I was growing up. His sister and I were in the same Sunday school class.

What I have seen through the years is a man who walks with God, cares for his family, and operates with integrity in his dealings with others. He has had colorful and fulfilling experiences in almost every facet of his life—as a successful entrepreneur, businessman, church leader, and board member of many religious, cultural, and political organizations.

Denny also travels all over the world. He has contributed time, money, and expertise to needy causes—particularly for schools, missions, global and local poverty, and educational needs. And at a time in his life when most other men his age have retired, Denny has taken on new tasks and challenges.

One of his endeavors is called Kids Around the World, a non-profit charitable faith-based organization that brings joy and hope to many children around the world whose lives have been devastated by war, natural disasters, or economic stress. One method they use is to build playgrounds.

Another method is to use a low-tech but highly effective approach to following up with children after they see the JESUS film. In 2003 Kids Around the World became affiliated with Campus Crusade for Christ and now partners directly with our organization in follow-up with overseas audiences who've seen the JESUS film. Audiences recognize the characters from the JESUS film in the visual stories that Kids Around the World brings to them by Flannelgraph pictures and stories. Storytelling from the Bible is an especially effective method of reaching children. This method is being used to teach almost one million youngsters every week.

A third method they use is humanitarian aid. Every minute, twelve children from around the world die of starvation. So Kids Around the World decided to become a serious part of the solution to world hunger. For example, within days of the catastrophic earthquake that hit Haiti, Kids Around the World recruited three thousand volunteers from local church groups to pack and ship two million meals for children in the midst of Haiti's recent catastrophe.

Kids Around the World also brings medical volunteers with them to overseas mission projects, adding health and surgery clinics and dental and eye clinics that address a number of medical needs.

The strategy of Kids Around the World is to share the truths of the Bible visually because, in many situations, neither the kids nor their parents can read. A little-known fact is that two-thirds of the world cannot be reached and discipled in writing.

In Ghana, Vietnam, Bosnia, Cuba, Guatemala, India, Afghanistan, China, and other countries—such as tsunami-stricken Thailand and earthquake-ravaged Haiti—there were no language barriers when the kids got their chance to play on the brand-new playground equipment and listen to Bible stories. Love is a universal language with a communication power all its own.

Nonliterate or functionally nonliterate humans have for centuries struggled through life through no fault of their own. If they can't learn to read or write, they may well die before they have the opportunity to meet Christ and have their lives changed forever.

I believe this book captures the heart of Denny Johnson's odyssey to hasten to find ways to teach the Bible through storytelling before it's too late. That is the way Jesus communicated with His followers. Jesus told stories and parables to all those who listened to Him. Most of His audience was unable to read or write. They would never have overcome the obstacle of illiteracy to understand what Jesus was saying if the Lord hadn't made it easy for them. He told them stories they could relate and respond to.

The apostle Paul also expressed the challenge of trying to communicate the "good news" to a world that has little knowledge of Jesus Christ:

> "Everyone who calls on the name of the LORD will be saved." But how can they call on him to save them unless they believe in him? And how can they believe in him if they have never heard about him? And how can they hear about him unless someone tells them? (Rom. 10:13–14 NLT)

It's encouraging to know that nearly a million kids are being "told and retold" every week just because of the efforts of Kids Around the World.

—Steve Douglass, president of Campus Crusade for Christ

Preface

MAJOR POINTS THAT EVERY CHRISTIAN OUGHT TO KNOW[1]

In my lifetime I've seen incredible changes in just about every different facet of society and culture, yet for me the most dramatic changes are those that have been occurring on the world's mission fields over the past decade. Many of these changes have taken place here in our own country, but more recently they have also spread to other nations around the globe.

I am not a sociologist or theologian, so my observations are somewhat subjective. Still, they are systemic of what's happening everywhere else, so I feel qualified to comment on them. I have also researched the subject extensively, and that information backs up many of my observations and conclusions. Whenever possible I have cited the sources where I found the information to back up what I have observed.

That's why I am comfortable in presenting the bold statement above as a lead-in to this book in this preface: major points that every Christian ought to know. These points are simply conclusions to searches and questions that I have wrestled with over the past twenty-five years or so. Perhaps you'll find resonance in what I discovered—and maybe you'll see some of your own conclusions validated. Nevertheless, these are the thoughts of the content of this book:

- Two-thirds of the people living on earth either can't read or choose not to learn that way.
- Orality (storytelling) is the way to reach those people.
- Orality is best described as storytelling: It is the way the world learns.
- Why is it so important that we understand Orality and use it more?
- Who is doing the job of reaching kids?
- Orality is a strategy that Kids Around the World uses to help children get to know God.
- Building playgrounds is a nonthreatening way to break the ice in other cultures.
- Churches seldom invest enough into children's ministry, whether in the US or abroad.
- Many churches do not understand the importance and value of "belonging" and the effectiveness of "storytelling."

- Not enough churches and Christian agencies are telling kids about heaven—"the place where they have an opportunity to spend eternity."

—Dennis W. Johnson
Rockford, Illinois

Chapter One

SMALL BEGINNINGS

Some years ago I was home when the doorbell rang, and when I went to answer it, a US postal carrier was standing outside. He had a big grin. "Mr. Johnson, you wouldn't remember me," he began after introducing himself. "You were probably just six or seven years old when you accompanied your dad and mom to the Blackhawk Court Projects."[1]

My mind went back to that time in our respective lives. I remembered how my dad took us with him every Sunday morning to the "projects," to set up for a Sunday school outreach program for the tenants and their children. My job was to sweep the floor of the activities room and help set up and arrange the folding chairs before the service. My mom would play the tinny piano, and my dad would direct the kids in singing some Sunday school choruses and present a simple story-sermon designed for their ages.

Now, many years later, here was one of the products of that work who'd attended that little Sunday school. I shook his hand, and we reminisced about those days. He told me he was a Christ follower, as were his wife and children. He was all grown up and our new mail carrier.

The man continued his story: "I don't know how I'd have turned out if it hadn't been for the Blackhawk Sunday school. I still get emotional when I remember how your dad led me to make a decision to follow Jesus. I listened to the stories and songs, and even as a young kid, your dad helped me to understand that God loved me. If that hadn't happened to me, I could have gone down a whole different path—like so many other kids in the projects—of crime, drugs, school dropouts, and the like. I just want to thank you for your dad and mom, and to let you know how much they mean to me."

I was quite moved at his story, and we became instant friends.

After our visit I still recalled those days and the satisfaction of being a part of my parents' mission of the Blackhawk Sunday school outreach of Elim Baptist Church. I felt grateful that even at age six or seven I was able to help out my mom and dad. The mail carrier's experience in the Blackhawk Sunday school was a tangible illustration of how Bible stories and songs change lives. I saw it happen again and again. I watched other kids as they were specifically invited to the Sunday school services—to hear songs and stories about Jesus and happily soak up all that they saw and heard.

Without knowing it, I first experienced the concept of Orality during that assignment at the Sunday school outreach. We didn't have printed materials to pass out. The kids didn't bring Bibles from home to read from, and most were too young to read. What was taught and what was learned was strictly done by the effectiveness of the spoken word stories—with simple Flannelgraph cutouts that my folks prepared for the children.

Now fast-forward more than fifty years. Technology has raced by as if in light-years, compared to what we had then for communicating with the kids and the few adult parents who also sat in on the Sunday worship and Sunday school services at the housing project.

The Flannelgraph and piano were the most sophisticated teaching methods outside of the spoken words that my parents used. Yet what my parents did in that simple setting still wasn't much different from what took place in the traditional churches across the city. High tech had not yet overwhelmed the churches.

Today, however, if you visit a contemporary church, you'll likely encounter some or all of the following changes in communication methodology:

- Public-address sound amplification—an old technology with new wireless microphone transmission
- Lobby electronic devices or computers for giving directions
- Stage lighting
- Musical instruments with amplification
- Film and video projectors for the sanctuary and plasma TVs for the classrooms
- TV cameras for enlarging the image of people onstage or the platform

- Bible verses couched in art projected on a wall
- Television or film clips from TV shows or movies shown as sermon illustrations
- Pagers for anxious mothers to respond to their babies if necessary
- PowerPoint projections of sermon points and announcements
- Electronic tools for teens and adolescents (via texting, Twitter, etc.)
- Electronic "urgent" notifications for adults (by Blackberries, iPhones, etc.)
- Electronic signs or projected requests for you to turn off cell phones
- Church services streamed over the Internet
- Training of pastors and teachers via smartphone apps and social sites such as Facebook

You can probably add several more examples to that list showing how the use of modern technology can enhance the worship experience and in fact enhances communications more effectively and visually—however, they also illustrate how things have changed in the past fifty years. My point is that there are countless new high-tech gizmos that convince us we can't live without them—even in church.

However, travel half a world away to Africa, India, or parts of many of the underdeveloped Asian nations where such high-tech proliferation is not as universal—yet—but it's beginning to happen there, in the urban areas, though the rest of their country is still one or two generations behind where the US stood in the 1940s in having amenities and personal accumulation.

I can remember what America was like fifty years ago. It sounds unbelievable in the twenty-first century, but I knew kids in grade school who came from neighborhoods where they didn't have running water in the house; they had a pump outside and carried water inside in a bucket.

They didn't have indoor plumbing but rather an outhouse that might get tipped over around Halloween. Moms did the weekly laundry by heating water on the stove or with a small "doughnut heater" in a washtub.

For some who lived outside the city, they didn't even have electricity—and used kerosene lamps or lanterns. Few of these families could afford a car and walked or took a bus—especially during WWII when gas and tires were rationed and hard for even affluent families to get.

Now, granted, a minority of families lived that kind of Spartan life in the 1940s. Our family was fortunate enough to have modern conveniences—but some of my childhood friends thought that people who had electricity, running water, indoor bathrooms, and a car were rich, though we never thought we were privileged or wealthy.

Ironically, even the kids that I thought were poor didn't consider themselves poor. They would be considered "poverty level" families today.

People today in rural villages in India, Africa, Indonesia, and such third-world locales are at that place where those of the Greatest Generation and some Boomers were fifty to seventy-five years ago. These third-world peoples are merely waiting and hoping to move up in social advantage with time.

In my opinion, the greatest obstacle people in other emerging countries may face in their present condition isn't necessarily poverty—although that's surely a spirit-breaker. I think it's not having any hope; they recognize their poverty and have been led to believe that there's no way out of their condition. This is especially a widespread feeling in India, where Dalits (the lowest sub-caste or "untouchables") are locked in a sorry state of existence simply as an accident of birth. The Hindu religion declares them lacking in full human status, and their dogma declares that they must serve as virtual slaves without basic human rights until they somehow find relief in another life, the "karma" of reincarnation.

While I deplore the terrible situations in which these Dalit people live, the same conditions are also in play in many other so-called third-world countries, so we can't give up hope for them. When I look at their situations, I try to look for ways to ease their suffering, pain, and hardship.

Poverty, pain, and lack of educational knowledge and vocational training is ever present in countries I've visited. Yet now I have discovered some ways to help. When we go overseas, it's to build a playground, provide food, hold a medical clinic, or teach kids and train adults to teach kids.

Samuel Goldwyn, the famous Hollywood film mogul, once said, "When someone does something good, applaud! You will make two people happy." I don't think I can recall anything else of significance that he ever said, but this statement always makes me smile, because it's absolutely true. There's nothing quite as rewarding to me than to look directly into a child's eyes and watch them light up in response to acceptance, love, attention, and learning.

I've visited disadvantaged people in scores of countries where I've gone on personal trips, church mission trips, and business and political fact-finding missions overseas. Whether participating in aspects of a Sister City program (as I did when I was a Rockford alderman and mayoral candidate), or as a board member representing a Christian service agency, or as a CEO of a group of several regional corporations, we always made a point to spend time with the local people and help where we could.

My desire was to see how we and other Americans, a traditionally generous people, might help others or share ideas and mutual solutions to problems. Sometimes we've been able to provide higher education for a young man or woman who needs that learning to become a leader in his or her country to better help his or her fellow citizens.

One case in point: The formerly Communist country of Romania had long persecuted the Christian church, even going so far as to torture and imprison their pastors and lay leaders and even execute some of them. One of their favorite tactics to silence a church group was to bulldoze their churches. It's only been about twenty years since their revolution that overturned Communism. That revolution, by the way, was begun by Christians taking a courageous stand against the tyrannical dictator Ceausescu. They were joined by students and sympathizers. Once Communism was overthrown, the iron fist against the church was partially unclenched. Church members and pastors now worship freely, and many can even get travel visas to leave the country.

One young man, the son of one of the Romanian Sunday school leaders, was eager to come to America. His father had lost his government teaching job in Romania for not renouncing his faith in Christ. My wife, Evie, and I felt led to bring the young man over to the US and pay for his education at Judson University, where he graduated number one in his class.

A man I know sponsored a student in India to get a seminary education and now supports the young man, who is now ordained as a pastor. The young man has started a church and school in northeast India. He's making a huge difference winning "untouchable" Dalits in the outskirts of New Delhi.

There are literally thousands of Americans like us who seek to help the less fortunate of other countries become educated—and then to multiply their learning by sharing their knowledge with many throughout their own land.

I'm encouraged when I see another person act on these impulses to help others. The problem is, the world's population continues to explode, and it's hard to keep up with the demand for help. We could recruit thousands more Americans to sponsor young men and women for a college or seminary education, but population growth will still outpace our good intentions.

This book is intended to give people some new considerations on how to help people in need in America and abroad. These ideas may challenge the status quo—in churches and parachurch ministries—and unsettle some of the strategies across the spectrum of evangelism through outreach organizations. It's my hope that this book will not just define problems we face today. Rather, based on statistics and insights that I gleaned from my own experience and much research, I hope this book will offer answers that I believe will address the problems that are outlined in the Lausanne

Forum of 2004 and Lausanne Cape Town 2010. Here are five major considerations:

(1) Of the seven billion people on planet earth, a majority of them can't read. Therefore, the major question for Christians and churches is, How can they "hear" the gospel?

(2) Two-thirds of the world are either nonliterate or illiterate (including up to 85 percent of Muslim women and two-thirds of Muslim men). It also surprised me that nearly half (48 percent) of adult **Americans** are functionally nonliterate or illiterate.[2] That means that two-thirds of the world's people either can't read, or choose not to learn that way. So if that's true of adults, what about the kids? How can we teach them the other things that they need to know—how can we improve their quality of life, along with sanitation and nutrition, raising a family, and securing a meaningful, productive job? And just as importantly, how can we help them get to heaven?

(3) A third of all the people in the world are children under the age of fifteen, and at least half of them, probably more, have never heard of Jesus in any context, the Lausanne Conference on Children in 2004 reported.[3] Unevangelized children generally grow up to see no relevance of

Christian faith to real life, make no contact with the church, and live and die without knowing that Jesus offers eternal life.

(4) Even in American cities there is a disconnect between traditional values and principles in contrast to the cultural and social norms of society. As a result, culture often misses the point in dealing with kids and older adolescents. Studies prove that when behavioral theories line up with actions, our results will be more in line with those theories. We can then address such serious cultural problems as school truancy, gangs, crime, and other antisocial behavior in meaningful, effective ways.

(5) Also, most churches and mission organizations across the world (including in the US) have no real strategic plans and efforts to reach and evangelize children—especially within their own congregations. Even when evangelism "outreach" programs are present, they're often merely babysitting or day-care types of activities that are understaffed, underfunded, irrelevant, and devoid of meaningful content designed to change kids' lives.

Addressing these problems will deflate some of the ideas and theories that educators and secular social scientists have used for over a half-century without seriously questioning those core values or their effectiveness. A similar flaw is present in many churches. So the question underlying this book is still: How can we reach kids around the world?

Reduced to its basic simplicity, I am convinced that it's possible to nurture children and adolescents toward Christian **belonging** (to a community of people who will also love and nurture them); then to lead them to **become like Jesus** (through the process of discipleship); then move them toward **belief** (demonstrating faith and doctrine); to ultimately help them to change their **behavior**.

During the past few years as I've measured overall effectiveness, I'm left with only one strategy that I think can keep up with population growth, and that's training teachers to multiply themselves—not only to teach but to train and disciple other teachers as well, taking advantage of the principle of compounding.

What if the teachers that we've already trained could do the same with other teachers—each new teacher recruiting and training others at the rate of a new disciple every month or even a year? As of this writing, we have trained 18,389 teachers.

My friend Rev. Samuel Chiang, executive director of International Orality Network (ION), adds a footnote to my idea. He said that besides the teachers, we should remember that it's the nature of kids themselves to tell and retell stories, and, "The power of reaching others means that the multiplicative effect is huge."

I won't argue with those who may find fault with my math or optimism, but we're going to do the job before us—the best we can, wherever we can, while we can.

But before we start, we need to know what obstacles confront us. The number and severity of worldwide threat levels have accelerated during the past twenty-five years. We have to consider these things more seriously than we ever have before.

Early in our ministry we accompanied evangelist John Guest, a powerful speaker, to participate in meetings overseas. John gave inspired presentations to Ukrainians who came to hear him (using a Ukrainian to translate his words), and many responded to his invitation to turn to God. We also brought Bill Glass, who has a successful prison ministry in America. We visited the prisons in Ukraine (some said privately to us that many of these were political prisoners). Still, many of those in prison responded in great numbers to the ministry of the American team.

However the biggest response was from the children. While the adults listened carefully to John Guest and came forward to commit themselves to following Jesus Christ—it was the kids' program leaders who saw even more incredible responses. Several hundred children wanted to pray and invite Christ into their lives. The only tools we had with us to reach them were chalk drawings, stories, songs, and puppets.

Curiously, the average age of those kids was eight—the same age I was when I responded from the balcony at Temple Baptist Church to the call of a missionary passing through our city.

While we were in Kiev, Clare De Graaf, the chairman of the John Guest Evangelical Association's board of directors, wanted to start a ministry focusing on children. He asked Frank Beach and me to interview a young man—Victor Kulbich—who was the number two man with the Baptist Union and was also the person who recorded the Ukrainian voice of Jesus for Campus Crusade's JESUS film. We discussed the ministry vision we had for his country and hired him to become the first director of the Ukrainian Center for Christian Cooperation in Kiev. Victor has nurtured this simple beginning of a ministry into something significant, and it was launched by John Guest Evangelical Association, its first major support base.

What we learned in these early days of ministry—which included ten trips to India, the Philippines, Albania, Uganda, Vietnam, Cuba, and many other countries—was this:

- Political leaders will respond to Christians who demonstrate love to their children. Then, when we have the leaders' trust, we are given permission to train their kids with biblical truth, teach them morals and character, and establish in their lives a commitment to be a Christ follower.
- We also learned that kids are the same across the world—they are eager to learn truth and values, and they respond quickly and earnestly to a gospel that makes sense to them. That's why the kids of the world, all three billion of them, have an innate openness to believing in God and accepting the precepts of His Word.
- God's Spirit is busy all around the world, touching the hearts of ready volunteers who respond to that holy call, and they're ready to help with the needs of kids.

- Missions strategies are beginning to change. They are more culturally defined and appropriate, but there is still one missing link—mission groups and denominational organizations still need to provide the national children's worker the tools that he or she needs to teach kids with stories and visuals.
- Kids everywhere love to be told stories. Even if they cannot read them on their own, they are eager to hear them from others who know them or who can read them. What engages them most effectively are the stories and lessons that they hear about a man named Jesus. And, as Samuel Chiang said, "Kids everywhere love to be told stories—but they also tell and retell the same stories to other kids, family members, and friends, so that the message truly gets out."
- Perhaps the most important tool or strategy of the past century, and particularly during the first decade of the twenty-first century, is the understanding and presentation of the fact that: Most kids learn by visual or oral methods. That fact has revolutionized our ministry.
- Orality is often perceived as a new method of communicating Christian truth. However, it's an extremely old method. Two thousand years ago Jesus used this visual-oral method of communication.

- Today Orality is also transforming the way that some churches, parachurch organizations, denominations, and even seminaries and Christian colleges are remodeling their vision statements regarding world missions. Some are beginning to see the need to make children a priority for evangelistic and missions efforts.
- It's my belief that if that happens, especially on a global scale, we might see a worldwide "Great Awakening" that can enlighten and make "new creatures" of children and young people across the planet. There are already spontaneous conversions in India, China, Africa, and many other "impossible" mission fields—most of them ignited by the Holy Spirit—in places where Americans and other Western Christians cannot go to proselytize; entire castes, tribes, and nations turn to God and become followers and disciples of Jesus Christ. Who wouldn't want to be a part of that revolution!

Chapter Two

CHERNOBYL: IS THIS WHAT HELL IS LIKE?

Kiev and Brovary, Ukraine, have been two cities that are close to my heart, and this was my first flight to the Ukraine. The pilot had just announced that we were about to land in Kiev. As we descended, I didn't know at the time what our being there would ultimately lead to. The flight itself was bizarre. The trip seemed never ending. For an international flight, the plane itself made me think of a third-world bus.

The aircraft seats were quite different from American planes with their mostly comfortable seats. In this plane the seats flipped forward to exit, like a folding chair. During the flight, the cabin was noisy and smelly, and it seemed like people had brought their meals with them and even cooked them in the aisles, which is an exaggeration, but barely.

We bounced several times when the wheels hit the runway. I strained my eyes to see what this Communist country was going to be like. I saw MIG fighter aircraft parked alongside the taxi way as we pulled up to the gate. My first impression was that the airport was old—only a few lights outside and fewer still inside the terminal. No one in our group had any idea what to expect. Would we be welcomed? It seemed that our separate heads of state were always taking verbal potshots at each other. As a result, would we as Americans be looked on as enemies or friends?

As I walked to claim my baggage, the airport people were courteous and treated us as neither friend nor enemy—mostly they just treated us as tired foreign passengers.

As our group assembled near the baggage carousel and saw that our luggage hadn't arrived, several headed for the restrooms—for the novice travelers, this would be their first experience of culture shock. These Americans were not used to Eastern European toilets.

The dimly lit men's room was old and apparently had never been painted—the finish seemed to be bare cement, and we saw several areas with shoe impressions to let you know what the center hole between the shoe impressions was for. There were no instructions, no paper to cover the seat—mainly because there was no seat. The idea was: Aim well and guard your shoes.

Instinctively your mind asks you if you have something more than a handkerchief in your pocket. There were rolls of toilet paper nearby, but its texture was like sandpaper. At a moment like this, if you carried a newspaper you were grateful.

After that experience, back at the baggage carousel, we were greeted with a warm smile from our hosts—who had now arrived and were waiting for us. Smiling, hugging everyone, and planting kisses on each cheek, they were eager and willing to take the luggage and stuff of our rather large group—and the group's excess baggage that we'd brought. We were ushered to their customs and immigration area, where they stamped our passports and cleared us for our visit.

They, too, were very polite and greeted us with a warm smile. Our Ukrainian hosts waited for us and led us outside with our luggage. I saw that they had vehicles to transport our group. The austere Communist bloc cars lacked the colorful paint jobs of today, and the vans were well worn and dull. However that was just my American pride showing. The warmth of the Ukrainian people more than made up for whatever was lacking at the airport.

We had come to the Ukraine as part of the John Guest Crusade and had helped to arrange to use the large soccer stadium near the wide main street down the center of town. The rental of the stadium came with one hitch: The officials didn't want cash—instead they wanted a coast-to-coast tour of America. We offered to host such a trip, with a stop in Rockford, Illinois, where we could discuss more ministry opportunities with them.

As our new friends from Kiev drove us to our hotel, our car passed a huge statue of Lenin overlooking the huge plaza. A few years later, I would videotape the statue of Lenin being taken down piece by piece, as the death of Communism happened in this special city in the Ukraine.

Not only would the politics change for the Ukrainians, but the focus of our lives would switch from focusing on politics—past and present—to focusing instead on the lives and well-being of children in Ukraine as well as other countries throughout the world.

Kiev is a city of nearly three million people. It's west of Russia and is divided by the Dnipro River—and with somewhat of a silent "D," Americans find it hard to pronounce; some Americans just call it the *Nipper River*.

The Kiev stadium that hosted the John Guest Crusades overlooks the "Nipper" River, and we took boat rides on it—the Ukrainian sun and looking forward to weekends enticed the families to come to the river and enjoy the water and beautiful parks. There was an abundance of parks—for older folks strolling; kids running and laughing, teasing; and young lovers holding hands, hugging—and everyone seemed to be enjoying themselves. It didn't seem to matter that they had so little money. Yet they had each other and their children. Curiously, the kids of Kiev looked and acted just like American kids.

I saw Kiev first, traveling from Boryspil International Airport by car. I'd often take that route in subsequent trips to Ukraine. My driver Igor would take Povitroflotsky Prospect highway and then turn right onto Tarasa Shevchenko Boulevard. Then he'd turn left onto Khreshchatyk (Cross Street). Khreshchatyk is the main street of Kiev. The name is from the Slavic word *khrest* (cross) and from the fact that the region lies in a valley intersected by ravines. When seen from the air, the ravines form a gigantic cross.

The entire length of Khreshchatyk was destroyed during World War II, but it was totally rebuilt in the postwar Stalin era. The street was further renovated since Ukraine's independence, and today the street is the administrative and business center of the city.

Khreschatyk is a popular destination for both locals and tourists. On weekends and holidays, the street is closed and reserved for pedestrians. This great street has all kinds of stores, cafés, and restaurants.

Khreshchatyk is sometimes a setting for outdoor concerts and festivals and street musicians. Major parades and celebrations are held on Victory Day (May 9) and Kiev Day (the last Sunday of May), replacing the former Soviet (Communist) holiday, May Day (May 1).

Tragically, on May 1, 1986, and before Ukraine declared itself an independent state on August 24, 1991, the Soviet authorities held a traditional May Day parade on Khreshchatyk to "calm the people" and "prevent panic" following the Chernobyl nuclear disaster a week earlier, when Communist authorities evacuated the entire town. The problem with that show of Communist solidarity was that thousands of Ukrainian citizens, including many children, were *already exposed* to dangerous doses of radiation and would later die or at the very least be sickened with radiation poisoning or cancers.

On a brighter side, the people of Kiev are survivors and began to work toward independence right after that. After two years or more of peaceful demonstrations, the USSR finally gave in to Ukraine's demands for freedom, which came in 1991.

Brovary is another city in Ukraine, and a Sister City to Rockford, Illinois. It likewise suffered from the effects of the Chernobyl disaster. Brovary is only sixty miles southeast of Pripyat, the actual site of the Chernobyl nuclear power plant.

That horrific Chernobyl disaster happened eighty-three minutes after midnight on April 26, 1986, after the explosion of nuclear reactor number four. More explosions and a devastating fire followed quickly. Many Ukraine first responders were killed in the aftermath of the fiery explosions and release of deadly radiation.

The fire sent a flaming column of radioactive fallout high into the atmosphere, and winds carried the deadly radiation first across a wide area of Ukraine and neighboring regions. Then it drifted across into the Soviet Union, Belarus, Europe, and even across the Atlantic to Iceland and Eastern North America, with light "nuclear rain" falling as far north as England and Ireland.

I was in a hotel in Dusseldorf, Germany, when the radioactive rain began falling. My window was open, and the misty clouds seemed to seep into the room. When I found out that radioactive fallout was in the raindrops, I became concerned about the air I was breathing.

Radioactive contamination covered massive areas in Ukraine, the small country of Belarus to the north, and Russia, (where about 60 percent of the radioactive fallout landed), resulting in the evacuation and resettlement of one-third of a million people. Scientists measured the radioactive fallout—it was *four hundred times greater than the bombing of Hiroshima.*

Russia, Ukraine, and Belarus were saddled with costs of decontamination and health care after the Chernobyl disaster—costs that amounted to $200 billion (USD). No one accurately knows how many deaths were caused from the Chernobyl nuclear event. The Soviet-era government did its best to cover up how many victims there were. Soviet authorities also ordered doctors to name other causes of death, and not radiation poisoning, on death certificates.

When Ukraine was still a part of the USSR, Mikail Gorbachev had pushed through detanté and eased in some democratic reforms. The era of Lenin ended not long after that, with the collapse of the Soviet Union, and Communism was no more. That brought new freedom to the Ukrainian people and gave us and other Christian groups opportunities to help them take advantage of these new liberties.

The police chief of Brovary told me how he was one of the first responders into the area to attempt to rescue the trapped workers inside the Chernobyl nuclear facility following the explosion. As a result he felt that he'd been exposed to deadly radiation.

We brought him to America and had him thoroughly examined at SwedishAmerican Hospital—with a number of tests to check out his organs and his thyroid glands, which would prove whether he was suffering from radiation poisoning. Fortunately, the tests proved he was not contaminated with radiation. As an expression of his appreciation, the next time we went to Brovary the police chief took our group to a special government retreat just outside of Kiev and Brovary. It was a hunting lodge, and the police chief explained to me that it was a private location used by former premiers of the USSR—a special retreat and secret meeting place for Nikita Khrushchev (Premier of the Soviet Union 1958–1964) and Leonid Brezhnev (Premier 1964–1982). There were two private villas, and they had until recent times been heavily guarded and fortified—complete with trip wires to alert the armed guards of intruders, even when we were the guests. The villas were located about halfway between Brovary and Kiev. Evie and I were given a guest room and slept in the same bed as a preeminent former Soviet premier.

Brovary and Kiev are both fewer than twenty miles from the quarantined area called the Chernobyl Exclusion Zone that still remains off limits—a quarter century after the Chernobyl incident—though most of the region is said to be "safe for living."

In 2005 a World Health Organization (WHO) report indicated that at the site of the 1986 Chernobyl explosion, fifty-six died instantly—forty-seven workers at the reactor site and nine children were obvious victims—but WHO estimated that as many as *four thousand to over nine thousand cancer deaths* occurred among the half-million people in the Ground Zero area and the surrounding radius exposed to the highest levels of radiation—although one outside estimate claimed that nearly three hundred thousand people died (or will die) from cancer and radiation poisoning.

I recall when I went to Havana, Cuba, with a delegation of Illinois state senators sometime later, we visited a government-run retreat in Havana where Ukrainian children were sent to recuperate from the effects of lung damage and radiation.

But when we were there, our hosts maintained that it was safe to visit, even though we had reservations about visiting Brovary, Ukraine, in the early 1990s (only a few years after the Chernobyl incident) when we were invited to visit. We prayed for our friends in Brovary and Kiev during that fearful period following the Chernobyl tragedy, and God was gracious to keep most of them safe from the invisible death from radiation.

Chapter Three

RIPS IN THE IRON CURTAIN

The relationship between Rockford and Brovary was proposed by a visiting soccer team from Kiev. They suggested that Rockford become a Sister City with Brovary, a city of about eighty-six thousand people. The Rockford City Council and then-Mayor Charles Box made it official in 1995.

Out of that relationship a number of specific humanitarian and ministry ventures were proposed for Brovary. We met together to discuss what type of gift we could present to them. It was during these meetings that the focus of an idea, "Kids Around the World," came into being.

Not long after the idea for starting Kids Around the World, the mayor of Brovary, Alexi Ishenko, came to Rockford to meet with

Rockford's mayor, Charles Box, and to tour the city. Alexi Ishenko was friendly, and while in our city I thought I'd take him to see the city.

Alexi and I drove around Rockford, and I showed him our schools and parks and pointed out a number of churches. Then we stopped for lunch at Mary's Market Restaurant, and as we ate, he said to me, "Why do you have so many churches in your city?"

I wasn't really sure how I should answer him. In his country, having only recently shaken off Communism, the people in Ukraine were just beginning to experience freedom. I knew that he was interested in growing his city.

"Alexi, it was the churches in America that started the major hospitals, universities, rest homes, and schools. Churches teach people how to volunteer and become leaders, and they teach the children music, drama, and morality," I explained, trying to answer his question.

After we finished our coffee, we left Mary's Market, and I drove north on Alpine Road, where we passed more than a dozen churches within just a two-mile drive. I pointed out these churches: Seventh-day Adventist, First Covenant, Mormon; and then in only a two-block section of North Alpine, a Methodist church on the right, a Catholic church on the left, and Lutheran on the right; and, as we turned onto Spring Creek Road nearing the end of our tour, United Church of Christ, Episcopal, and a Dutch Reformed church; and First Assembly across the street from my church, First Evangelical Free Church.

As if to belabor a point, Alexi repeated his earlier question: "Why do you need so many churches in Rockford?"

I told him, "Rockford is known as a city of churches—it's the same with thousands of American cities. As I said before, it was churches that built the great universities in America, as well as the hospitals, nursing homes, food kitchens, and missions to help the hungry and poor. Churches train our young people how to sing, play instruments, do dramas, and perform concerts. Churches teach morality and principles to young people. There are classes on how to treat your husband or your wife and kids. Churches teach us to respect our leaders. They train upcoming leadership for the church and give them experience. That experience and training in leadership can also be used to start industries and charitable organizations. Churches help the poor, the sick, the elderly. Every city needs churches."

I asked Alexi, knowing his town was about the same size as Rockford, "How many churches do you have in your city?"

"Two," he replied. "There is a Baptist church and an Orthodox one."

"You know, Alexi, Brovary needs *more* churches. Churches are good for a city. They can do many kinds of charity work, teach character and morality, provide schools and child care—all kinds of great works. I have an idea how you can do it. I know your city council doesn't have any money for this. But you don't need it to start new churches. All you need to do is convince the city council to donate *land* for the churches to be built. The people themselves will build them, and those works will grow and multiply."

He must have thought there was logic in my comments, for Alexi returned to Brovary and convinced his city council to give land to the churches and let them grow. He told the town council, "You must do this. It will help Brovary." And the churches *did* grow and multiply. Following our discussions on churches, and under Alexi's leadership, Brovary produced one additional Orthodox church and six additional evangelical churches.

It was interesting that when the city of Brovary gave property to the Baptist church, Pastor Lepak asked the authorities if the church could trade the large property they had given to the church for several smaller ones. That's how the Baptist church was able to plant more churches.

I remember that I also told Alexi, "The American Constitution allows religious freedom. The government has no control over religious activities and can't put a limit on how many churches we're allowed to have." I tried to explain the subtleties of our democracy compared to his new freedoms, but there were things I don't think he grasped—like the distinctions of different denominations and varied worship styles. I wasn't sure that I had clarified the disparities between our cultures—or even answered his question.

Then, nodding as if he understood, Alexi changed the subject. He said, "I want you to build a playground for our children. I know that you can do this. You can do anything." I didn't get the impression that he was simply trying to flatter me. He looked me straight in the eye and let me know his need and expressed his confidence in me to get it done.

I asked Alexi, "If we build you a playground, can we get your permission to show the JESUS film in a downtown theater and give out Bibles to all the schoolchildren?"

Alexi replied, "If you build me a playground, you can do anything you want."

As I thought of how we could get our Sister City relationship going, we concluded that a gift of a playground would be something, with the help of the local park district, we could do. We set out to do it. We planned a wooden playground, as we had just completed one in Rockford and it looked great. But after Brovary's mayor, Alexi Ishenko, took a look at it he said, "When the people get cold in the winter, they will come looking for wood and burn the playground to keep them warm. It will be stripped of wood overnight."

We scrapped that idea and chose a colorful plastic and metal one and then set out to make it all come together.

I knew such a project would involve many people and much work. I began to pray that God would bring us someone to lead this effort of building a playground. I remember writing a note in my Bible with that prayer request—the first of many more. It wasn't long before Ralph Peterson called me and said he'd head a team to build the playground. That answer to prayer was the first step toward the beginning of a worldwide ministry.

Ralph started with On Site Builders and his family to gather the volunteers, do the planning, get the playground shipped, and then travel overseas to assemble it. Such a plan was an audacious, huge undertaking. Ralph was up to the task and was the perfect guy for the job.

Ralph was also my first answer to prayer. I first wrote it down; from there the prayer went to God. Then I think He passed it on to Ralph, who shared it with what would become hundreds of volunteers for a fledgling group called Kids Around the World.

Not long after we returned from Brovary, I saw that Kids Around the World was ready to break out and become a full-fledged operation. I knew that with all of my other commitments, we needed a full-time president. I knew just the right person for the job—but I wasn't sure that *he'd* be convinced of that.

Jim Rosene was a bright, talented, and special person. For the past fifteen years or so he'd been children's minister at First Evangelical Free Church in Rockford and was doing a fantastic job there. I'd been watching him for many years and saw in him special gifts that made his work exceptional. He'd launched special programs for the church's kids, and the results were amazingly effective.

Jim has a unique love and respect for children. He doesn't patronize or just spend time entertaining them while their parents are in the worship service. He's demonstrated an ability to communicate "grown-up" ideas and truths in a manner that kids understand and can apply to their lives.

I noticed that he didn't follow tradition and have some adult Sunday school teacher stand up in front of a group of kids and drone in "reverent" tones from a lesson book or manual. Instead, Jim created excitement and expectation of fun when kids were brought together. He used storytelling, music, puppets, games, and his own mix of playfulness.

It reminded me of a technique that I'd read about called "Godly Play."[1] The program teaches children the art of learning religious content through storytelling, parables, and all the elements that Jim was already practicing.

This "playing" is a way to present the Bible-based stories of our faith, explain them, and then allow the children open-ended opportunities with crafts, songs, games, art supplies, and other creative expressions to allow kids to not only engage the story on their own terms, but to draw from it lessons to help them in their own spiritual formation.

Jim had brought a team to Brovary and did a magnificent job in presenting his style of working with children there. There was excitement in the children's eyes, and that in turn inspired the American volunteers—so much so that they started to plan the second playground to be done on the second trip in 1995.

The volunteers—and of course the kids and church members in Ukraine—loved working with Jim Rosene and were willing to do just about anything for him to bring happiness and a new sense of spirituality to the kids.

When we got back from overseas, I had long conversations with Jim and invited him to be our president. We talked about the future and what might be accomplished and dreamed together of fantastic projects. He agreed to come aboard and hit the pavement running.

When we formed Kids Around the World, we listed as its main objective, "To put as many smiles on as many faces of as many children as we possibly can." For Jim Rosene, making children smile is a full-time job. He says, "Being able to give kids something like this is great. These children, because of poor economic conditions, disasters, or war conflicts, can't experience the joy of childhood. But when we see them come onto a brand-new playground—well, that's an amazing feeling."

That next year, in 1995, Kids Around the World and Jim's team came to build another playground. This time they expanded their outreach, gave each child in the city (over fifteen thousand!) an Illustrated New Testament, and prepared special programs with puppets, staging, and sound to illustrate Bible stories for the kids.

I could see not only the energy and power of the programs, but I witnessed Jim's unswerving, unconditional love for children. He has a gift to give them, and their receiving it is a gift to him in return.

As I finish work on this chapter, I'll be meeting in Elgin, Illinois, with Victor Kulbich at The Evangelical Alliance Mission (TEAM) headquarters. He's on his way to Phoenix for meetings there. Victor is a Ukrainian pastor and Christian leader. We worked with him in Kiev to establish our work with children in Kiev and Brovary.

He began as a youth pastor in Bucha, Ukraine, which is located less than fifty miles from Chernobyl, site of the terrible nuclear reactor explosion in 1986. He was also the head of the Baptist Union in Ukraine and a seminary at Irpin. He was our first contact in Kiev. In 1990 Frank Beach and I encouraged him to consider leaving the Baptist Union to start a new ministry, the Ukrainian Center for Christian Cooperation (UCCC).

Sherry Ifft, Arlene Vanderloon, Clare De Graaf, Rich Correll, John Guest, and Evie and I were his first major supporters to get UCCC up and running.

The results of hiring Victor Kulbich and founding UCCC turned out to be pretty amazing:

- Victor started a major church in Boucha, Ukraine, forty-five miles from Chernobyl.
- Kids Around the World built a playground at his church.
- He helped start or was part of the organizing of sixty-nine Bible colleges.
- Seventeen hundred churches have been planted.

- Eighteen hundred children's teachers have been trained in ministry.
- Seven hundred youth leaders were trained.
- An association of seventeen hundred Christian doctors was formed.
- An association of two thousand Christian school teachers was formed.
- A number of Christian camps were organized, with ten thousand volunteers participating.

Through all our efforts, it was God who planted and nurtured seeds in these young lives. He guided us to appointments and divine interruptions that His Spirit used to transform lives. Sometimes, we are able to be "lucky" enough to witness the results—sometimes we can even tally results that encourage us that something significant is happening in young lives. Although it is God's doing, He sometimes brings us into the equation—which gives us such great satisfaction and real joy and delight for being part of God's plan, and for being able to rejoice at His plan in action. How amazing!

Chapter Four

SISTER CITY OPENS WIDE ITS DOORS

When a Kiev, Ukraine, soccer team came to Rockford, someone suggested that Kiev should be a Sister City to Rockford. The idea was floated through a series of conversations, but for some reason, no action was taken.

Instead, in the end it was the city of Brovary and not Kiev that became a Sister City to Rockford. That was when Frank Beach, a Rockford alderman (and a dear friend as well) and I traveled to Brovary to finalize the papers of becoming a Sister City.

Alexi Ishenko, mayor of Brovary, then came to visit Rockford and sign the documents in a formal way. That was the event that I mentioned in the previous chapter when he was intrigued by so many churches in Rockford and agreed to try planting more churches in his city by donating land for their construction.

Besides discussing property on which to build a church for Christians in Brovary, I had gotten Alexi's permission (for another trip to Brovary) to show the JESUS film in a downtown theater, and he agreed to let me give an Illustrated New Testament to every one of the fifteen thousand schoolchildren in his city.

Now it was time to see about getting those Illustrated New Testaments for Brovary schoolkids. We had also arranged for Illustrated New Testaments to be made available to us from the Bible League (where I served on the board of directors). There were hundreds of copies of the New Testament in Russian and Ukrainian languages. Then-president Dennis Mulder generously offered to donate as many as we needed for kids in the Ukraine.

Also in the previous chapter I explained how our Rockford group had traveled to Ukraine in the spring of 1994 to build the first of two playgrounds for Brovary's kids as a gift to the city.

Under the leadership of Ralph Peterson, our volunteer from Rockford, and with the help of the Rockford Park District, we built the playgrounds that included twelve swings, six slides, spring cars, a log roll, a "whirly-round," a major play structure, a teeter-totter, a volleyball court, and a half-court basketball area.

Also included were park benches, picnic tables, and landscaping for the area with trees, grass, bushes, and flowers. These two projects launched Kids Around the World, and Rockford and Brovary still maintained a strong relationship years later.

That small beginning was something God had laid out for us to focus on in the days and years ahead.

Slavic Gospel Association, an organization that was based in Chicago for many years but had recently relocated to Rockford and was devoted to helping churches struggling under Communist rule to survive the Cold War, had also taken a keen interest in helping the Slavic people of Ukraine. SGA's president at the time, Dr. John Aker, was given land from the mayor of Brovary for SGA to build a regional headquarters in the city.

Rockford resident Dave Klang took a major interest in helping cement the Sister City relationship, hoping to not just build goodwill between the cities but to take a lead in helping Brovary—the city had been suffering from the aftereffects of Chernobyl.

Brovary bore a brunt of health problems, mainly various virulent kinds of cancers, and the economic costs that the disaster showered on the city along with radiation fallout.

Dave Klang went over to visit the First Baptist Church of Brovary, Sister Church to his church, First Evangelical Free Church of Rockford. In fact, he continues his visits to assist in bringing Christmas "shoebox" gifts.

First Covenant Church of Rockford was also involved with a Sister Church—in Kalivnoka, Ukraine (just outside of Kiev). Tom Miller, First Covenant's associate youth pastor, went to Ukraine, and his trip cemented a relationship between Kalivnoka Church and his church in Rockford. Their first project was to assist Kalivnoka Church in constructing its first building for worship. First Covenant still helps its Sister Church to reach out to their village—as well as other villages around the country of Ukraine—with the Christian gospel.

Rockford residents also sent food and medicine, and area doctors visited to volunteer their services. It was a relationship that began with a small group of people in Rockford, including Alderman Frank Beach and myself representing our city government, and several from the First Evangelical Free Church in Rockford—which had by this time established a Sister Church relationship with Anatoly Lepak, pastor of the Brovary First Baptist Church.

The Sister City and Sister Church relationships offered those of us in that initial group opportunities to explore ways we could help Brovary. Almost every member of that committee took off with ideas that they, or others, had proposed—ranging from helping the churches rebuild, training pastors and church leaders, providing Bibles and training materials, and bringing volunteers from the United States to do short-term projects for the churches of Brovary.

I will always recall when Mayor Alexi Ishenko told me, “If you build me a playground in my city, you can do whatever you want to do.” He said Brovary had a “political need” for a playground to be built.

And that’s exactly what we did. Meeting a “political need” of a city—a playground for the children—set a precedent that opened up many other cities to be part of our ministry.

The same response happened in Sarajevo, with a call from USAID; it happened again in Ghana from a call from the first lady of that needy African nation; and it happened in 208 places in forty-two different countries of the world.

When we built the first playground, we discovered something that we didn’t anticipate. No one showed up to volunteer to help. It didn’t take long before we realized it was a cultural difference that stemmed from the Communist past of the former Soviet Union. In that political culture, everyone in the Ukrainian or Russian system was paid to work. Volunteerism was an alien concept. (True, some of the churches had begun to teach and take advantage of volunteerism, but the idea still hadn't gotten far in Brovary.) So we started by asking Police Chief Nicolli to help—and the schoolmaster, mayor, city councilman, and pastors. When onlookers saw their mayor and other civic leaders working on erecting a playground, they soon stepped in and said, "Please, let me do it, Mr. Mayor." All it took was one short morning for the entire community to get the point—*volunteering is good, fun, and helpful.* Building a playground provided the perfect lesson.

One day, the local *"mafia"* drove up to the site in a big black sedan. A window was rolled down, and a tough-looking face leaned out. He asked, "What are you going to charge the kids to play on your playground?"

Several adult volunteers looked up from their work and told them, "There is no charge." "Nothing," said another, while another person said, "It's true. It's going to be free for them to play here." The man in the backseat sat back and rolled up the window, and the sedan drove off and never came back.

One day while the playground was being built, I visited a nearby school. After class I introduced myself and asked, "Did I understand correctly? Was that something from the life of Jesus that was being taught?"

The teacher nodded. "Yes, I often teach about Jesus."

"Amazing. In America we can't teach about Jesus in the public schools. Our government forbids it."

The teacher seemed quite surprised. "But why not?" she asked and added, "Jesus is a famous figure in history. My children love and respect Him. It's important to me that they learn about His teaching on how to be honest, to tell the truth, to be kind and loving. He is a great example I want my children to know."

I was humiliated that I could not give her a better answer why America, a so-called "Christian nation," was not able to teach about the good things that Jesus Christ taught His followers.

Over the years we've developed a number of friends and contacts in Ukraine, and we are proud of the results we've seen there—where the playgrounds are helping to inspire Ukrainian kids to higher aspirations, and where American medical professionals volunteer to bring their medical expertise to these people. It's a greatly satisfying effort.

One of the most unusual experiences was when Stu Nelson (a former chaplain for the Rockford Police Department) and I went to a church in Brovary with two cartons of Bibles from David C Cook Publishing. They were copies of the Illustrated New Testament that told biblical stories in panels like a comic book. We got to the church a little later than we expected, and the front entrance door was locked. Stu set his carton down on the steps and knocked loudly on the door. "Maybe someone's still here," he said.

After a moment or two, someone opened the door. I told the man who later turned out to be the pastor, "We're from America, and we've brought you some Bibles to give the children."

His face lit up like a little child at a birthday party. "We have been praying for someone to come with Bibles, and now you have come!" he said, and then he grabbed my face and pulled it to him and planted a big wet kiss on my lips. Wow! That was a first—it was a tradition about which I hadn't been warned.

But Pastor Anatoly warmly took the children's Bibles and picked one out of the box to examine. He held it reverently and lovingly. "Ah …" he said, "these are wonderful. Such colorful pictures. The children will love them. Do you have more?"

"Not on this trip," I told him. "But we can get you some more. We also have Bibles for the adults, too. If you'll give me a letter telling how many you need, I'll try to get them to you." I reached out quickly to shake his hand and give him a hug—hoping to avoid another kiss as the pastor wanted to convey his gratitude.

It was always humbling to me that all of these people were always so grateful for what Americans brought to them. But *we* were grateful for the *results* those gifts brought. Many more people were becoming believers; many were taught basic doctrine and learned how to win others to Christ. Others were trained as pastors, teachers, or lay leaders. It was an exciting time and has continued to be for almost twenty years.

Chapter Five

"I'LL DO IT MY WAY"

Even though I was on the board of the Bible League, serve on the board of David C Cook, and am a member of First Evangelical Free Church in Rockford, Illinois, it's hard to totally get others "on board with your specific passion" or help others to see your vision of what's needed to reach the most people for the Lord.

People have an understandable focus, like the old Paul Anka song made famous by Frank Sinatra: "I did it my way." Sometimes even churches want to "do it their way" when it comes to building a playground or where they want to plant churches.

When it comes to missions, some churches support their own members who want to serve on a mission full-time, while sometimes a missions pastor has another focus. Some will volunteer to fill food packets in a warehouse for disaster relief, while others prefer to do it at church—"their place." Some want Sunday school curriculum material from David C Cook, Gospel Light, or a denominational publisher. Others want to develop their own materials. Some churches appoint women to their missions committee, some only men.

However, there is one focus that most churches agree on—ministries are targeted primarily to adults. There seems to be little or no serious consideration about the need for including *children* in missions outreach.

It's funny—kids are also like that; they want to do their own thing too. They want to decide who their friends are and where they want to play.

Kids want to be involved. They want better ways to learn. They want to sing and not just to be sung to. They want to choose their own clothes to wear to school and choose what fast-food restaurant to go to eat.

Kids want choices and *options*. Jesus knew that. God built His character and emotions in us, so Jesus knew that the feeling of belonging was the best way to channel kids' independent wishes and desires. But many times kids need to be guided in making decisions.

Churches sometimes need that too. Those who go it alone in their mission efforts may well miss the opportunity to be part of a larger, successful effort. Partnering with other organizations not only broadens the possibilities but may be fulfilling *God's* will.

When the disciples wrote the New Testament and told about Jesus' teaching to the crowds on the hillside, I'm quite sure that it was the women who brought their kids to the meetings on the hillside and encouraged Jesus to tell stories, so the children could understand and be enlightened when He explained the meaning of His parables.

Our Kids Around the World board is made up of husbands and wives. We felt a real need to have the women's perspective and understand their heart for children and their patience in working with children. And Kids Around the World is fortunate to have an experienced president on board who formerly headed up the children's ministry at First Evangelical Free Church in Rockford. Our board, by its focus on partnering with other organizations to reach children, was able to extend their reach by working with Rotary Club, David C Cook, World Vision, the Million Dollar Round Table Foundation, Samaritan's Purse, the Evangelical Free Church, Campus Crusade, the JESUS Film Project, Compassion International, Awana, Slavic Gospel, and hundreds of churches and other organizations.

We know that we can't do it all. Nor can you. We need each other. We need the touch of the Holy Spirit and the blessing of the Lord. Some people and organizations work with adults; some target young people. We focus on kids—almost entirely we minister to children. That's it.

And we know many of them can't read or don't learn that way. We understand that sometimes a touch, a smile, a melody, a smiley face, a text message, a "tweet," a dollar under the pillow, a hug, or even a kind word can change a kid's disposition or attitude. They feel like they belong, and they are reassured and confident as a result. Parents need to say, as God said about the Lord Jesus when He was baptized: "This is my Son, whom I love; with him I am well pleased." (Matt. 3:17).

Some sociologists tell us our world is getting better and recite a litany of examples to bolster that point of view. Others claim that the world is getting worse and we are heading for "perilous times" (2 Tim. 3:1 KJV) of imminent chaos, confusion, apocalyptic terror, economic destruction, and every other kind of imaginable ruin. So there's a possibility that both forecasts are true.

Adding to the change of the cultures and societies of the world are the wars they wage among each other. Politicians like to refer to them as "culture wars"—a clash of values and principles that neither side wants to relinquish, reducing reasonable discourse to a cacophony of yelling and screaming. So apparently, if everyone else is doing "my way," no wonder everything seems to be in chaos.

That's even happened in ecclesiastical circles. There are even all kinds of significant differences between members of the same group, denomination, church—even families. In this climate of change and resistance, how do we try to make progress in action and communication? How can we even begin to try to reach other cultures, religions, and even generations?

In a generation where serious problems are often "decided" by pollsters and radio and TV commentators, it's difficult to assess whether things are better or worse than before. This confusion is fanned by the mass media. According to the media and yearly polls from 2003 to 2008 by the Pew Forum, Fox News, Harris Polls, and Gallup, most people in America believe in God (86 to 92 percent, depending on the year and which poll).

People ask, "Why do the mainstream media so seldom report about God?" Even when the media *do* report on God or the supernatural, it's often biased or sensational—or treated from a viewpoint of skepticism or cynicism. The mass media represent and reflect a humanist, secularist, and atheist worldview. As such, they are not neutral in their reporting—they have a definite bias.

The mainstream media usually don't cover stories like the growth of Christianity in China or the explosion of conversions to Christianity in India, Africa, and South America. To most of us, these are historic events and have huge ramifications to those nations and peoples. Yet the only "religious" stories that proliferate the media and Internet are tabloid features about the fall from grace of some prominent minister or the discovery of the face of the Virgin Mary on a pancake.

While the modern mass media might be to blame for not fairly reporting events related to God's activities in the world, that blindness is not a new phenomenon. About two thousand years ago, Jesus was born into this world, and for the most part, the world ignored His life and ministry. In comparison to the world's population of the time, a scant handful actually heard Him speak, even though crowds of thousands listened to Him speak on the mountainsides. Even one commented, "No man ever spoke like that!" (John 7:46 PH).

God has intervened in human affairs—not just those examples written in the Bible, with the coming of Jesus, or at other times in world history. In the Dark Ages, superstition and corruption almost destroyed the church. In WWII, historians documented numerous supernatural interventions that helped turn the tide from the Axis powers to the Allies, influencing the outcome of the war itself.

History also records how God intervened through individuals and changed the direction of nations and global movements—when

Communism collapsed and modern murdering despots like Ceaucescu, Pol Pot, Idi Amin, and others were overthrown.

Students of history can cite many more illustrations, but the problem is that these are hardly ever noticed in the present—but rather only upon *retrospect.* We're conditioned to read about or watch and listen to the news from a viewpoint that erases God from history, so we accept that viewpoint from the media. We miss what *God* is doing in the world and so we're prepared not to see Him in world events or even local events. We often don't see God at work even in our churches, because we're not conditioned to look for it.

Is it possible to recondition ourselves to see and know what God is doing in the world and in contemporary culture and, upon reflection—in history? Can you imagine what creative, positive, affirming things might happen if we decided to be a part of God's work in the world? And can you imagine the things that could happen if we didn't always have to "do it my way," but rather let God have *His* way?

Chapter Six

GROUPS LOVE TO HEAR A STORY TOO

"You will never know that Jesus is all you need … until Jesus is all you have."

It was Mother Teresa who stated that profound truth, but she stated it so simply that each of us can grasp its depth. Mother Teresa left her native Albania and went to India and founded the Missionaries of Charity in Calcutta, India, in 1950. She ministered nearly fifty years to the poor, sick, orphaned, and dying—first in India and then in other countries. She earned international recognition in the 1980s after she was awarded the Nobel Peace Prize.

Not long before she died in 1997 at age eighty-seven, Mother Teresa spoke at the National Prayer Breakfast in Washington DC. Her speech at that gathering was deeply moving—but it was also warm and loving. She gave a biblical, simple soliloquy in which her message matched her amazing "lifestyle of service" to those in dire need. Christians as well as unbelievers in the audience respected her for living up to a moral code that she modeled implicitly. She shared a story at that prayer breakfast that every person in that audience had to have memorized. I'm sure that all of them could recall it almost verbatim after her telling, as I did.

"One evening in Calcutta," Mother Teresa said, "three other nurses went with me out to minister to people on the streets. We picked up four needy people and took them back to the hospital. Each one was in critical condition, but one was especially desperate. I said to my colleagues, 'You take care of these others. I will take care of this one.'

"I did for her all that my love could do. I put her in bed. There was such a beautiful smile on her face. She took hold of my hand, and she said, 'Thank you,' and then she died."

The audience was still for a long moment as that scene was indelibly etched into their minds. What was perhaps missing, because of Mother Teresa's humility, was the fact that her simple act of kindness for a dying patient meant so much.

I could visualize that scene perhaps as well as any in that audience. I had visited Mother Teresa's home for abandoned orphans and dying souls in the streets and gutters of Calcutta. I was with my former pastor, Dr. Lareau Lindquist, who founded Barnabas International. He'd been there before at Mother Teresa's Sisters of

Charity mission in Calcutta and invited me to accompany him on this trip. I can also remember the nuns who, like their leader, cared for the children so selflessly and lovingly.

I still remember that story by Mother Teresa—it was fixed in my mind. That's because I saw a similar scene taking place before my eyes on *our* visit, as we Americans followed the nuns from bed to bed. I recall one little boy, severely crippled. He was half-lying, half-sitting—cross-legged in his bed when we came around to comfort and touch each orphan. He smiled up at me, and he began to sing "Oh, how I love Jesus." No verse from the Bible could have been more powerfully conveyed to my mind and heart or touched me any deeper. It was a stunningly clear message that this boy sang from within his soul—*Oh, how I love Jesus.*

I wondered what the two patients had in common that communicated such intense emotional connection. The first was the woman patient that Mother Teresa brought from the Calcutta slums, who died shortly after she brought her to the mission hospital. I wondered about that person. What caused that poor soul to smile and say, "Thank you," to Mother Teresa?

I thought, maybe it was because that the person, before dying, was shown love and a sense that she belonged in that company of tenderhearted servants.

The same is true of that little boy who sang for me from his hospital bed. He was content and happy in his circumstances—circumstances that we'd probably consider as horrible. The boy, too, was in a place where he had a sense of belonging.

I believe that this quality of belonging is so important and is what the two patients had in common. There are those who make it a matter of personal choice that they have a right to *not* align with a particular group or organization—as if it were quite normal. For example, if another person is of a different color or race, then they belong to some other group. Yet distancing oneself from a group because of ethnicity or social status is a self-defeating proposition. People who are different from us can still belong with us if they are our family, coworkers, neighbors—or Christians, Rotarians, Canadians, or any group.

If people have something in common with us, then bonding with them is quicker, and our mutual relationship is fostered sooner—and therefore we "belong" to the same group.

A football team has unity—black, white, Hispanic, or Asian players can bond together despite their obvious racial *differences*—and there's a sense of belonging for all the team members. Love for a group and each individual within the group has nothing to do with color, race, or some other physical, financial, nationalist, or gender difference.

As we belong, we also "become." We learn about those things in which the group believes, and typically *these beliefs can change us*. We also discover the various kinds of things that the members of the group do. Sometimes that kind of evaluation leads us to change our interest in whether we want to "belong" to that group or organization. Sometimes people can be the reason for our hesitation to join a group or organization—or even a family. I've seen where a rebellious, troubled child can keep people at a distance, or the emotional fallout of a marriage falling apart creates chaos. There are all kinds of relational interactions that can change a person's mind about associating with a group—*Do we really want to belong with these people?*

People can change their minds as to whether they'll "become" different in order to make the requisite changes to join or stay with a group or organization to which they want to belong. Conversely, there are also situations that can chase people away from a group that could otherwise help them.

As with most groups or organizations, there's a common consensus as to the purpose of the mutual association and for maintaining that common consensus. As I see it, the first step is a need to *belong,* then to *become,* and the final step is to *behave.*

These are common qualities that I have noticed in groups worshipping God all around the world. I have been in churches in Sierra Leone, Ghana, and numerous other places in Africa. I've also been in churches in Romania, Kyrgyzstan, Estonia, China, Cuba, Honduras, Venezuela, and the Amazon highlands and basin countries, as well as refugee camps in Rwanda and Tanzania. I have sorrowed over the terrible things I saw in Delhi, Calcutta, and Sarajevo, and in Kilgali, where the refugees were ravaged by civil war, genocide, and religious persecution. I've seen people who've found God in prisons and in UN refugee camps—and in every kind of nation, including democracies and dictatorships.

Finding that special place to belong is not a "cookie cutter" formula where "one size fits all." There are probably as many options as there are people when it comes to bringing people together for a common cause or relationship.

When we build playgrounds, we offer a special place that some child can call "mine," and where that child can feel that he or she "belongs" at this playground along with the other kids who play there.

When missions groups build church buildings, they offer a similar place others can also call "theirs" and have a feeling of belonging.

And when a young couple in love finds each other and work toward that special relationship, they, too, find a place where the two of them "belong." Even counselors who try to help put a troubled or broken marriage back together can see in two people that they belong together and should try to reconcile.

When a church sponsors a backyard club, it morphs into a "small-group Bible study," and when the child becomes older, that precedent can be repeated with older teens, young adults, and even seniors. They all enjoy a feeling of *belonging*.

I can think of an even more dramatic example. I've seen major prisons in Kiev, Ukraine; Sierra Leone, Africa; Cambodia; and Joliet, Illinois. In some of these instances I was with Bill Glass, former Cleveland Brown NFL player and founder of the prison ministry Champions For Life. I was a member of his board of directors, which was why Bill had invited me to go with him to visit the two prisons.

Bill told me once, "I never met a man in prison who loved his dad." He explained that the prisoner's family somehow failed him by not allowing him to feel loved—and never showed him that he truly *belonged* to that family.

Dr. Jay Kesler, when he was president of Taylor University, offered a similar observation in a book he wrote, which also became a movie.[1] Kesler said, "This became most evident to me when I was working with young people … within the juvenile justice system. We would say things such as, 'God is your heavenly Father,' intended to invoke feelings of security, protection, nurture, provision, happiness, contentment and thoughts of a loving and caring Provider.... The problem was, it often had the *opposite* effect."

He added, "What did these kids think about when someone said, 'Father'? Maybe someone who comes home late at night, involved in all sorts of sinful, capricious and arbitrary behavior. Perhaps someone who was constantly drunk, or even abusive.... Without even realizing it, we started those kids thinking, *These people brought me here where I can get some relief from that no-good (expletive) who calls himself my father, and now they're telling me God is only a bigger version of my father!*"[2]

Kesler said that these kids wanted to bolt for the door to get away when they heard the reference to a "heavenly Father"—they weren't able to distinguish the differences between their abusive father in comparison to a God who is our heavenly Father.

Making good choices is key to life decisions—whether in choosing a life partner, or what to do if you're swayed into a life outside the law, landing you in prison. Making good choices as to what group or organization to which you'll belong can determine your future. Will it be a lifetime of goodness, positive achievement, and service, or a lifetime of failures and enslavement to addictions, conflict, breaking rules and laws, and continued submission to wrongdoing?

Most of the time, someone does not make a casual assumption that he'll be a Christian, then join the group (or church community). Rather a person decides he or she likes the group or person he or she is with. There is a group consensus as to what it means to belong to that particular group or organization—such as the group's expectation that those who are a part of the group will live according to the guidelines and expectations of the group. In the case of a church or

Christian organization, that decision to belong requires a decision from the person seeking to join the group to live according to the group consensus (in most cases that decision is presented as a commitment to first repent—to turn away from "wrong" actions and deportment and to live according to the precepts of the group. In other words, to model his or her life after Christ).

That process is not much different even with its emphasis on kids. I often repeat myself that it's important for kids to feel that they belong. Equally important is that the adults and the kids' peers invite them to a place that will be comfortable, fun, and that will bring great enjoyment—as well as inspiration, an opportunity to learn about Jesus, and opt into that process of becoming like Jesus.

The desire to belong is probably an innate instinct. Have you ever noticed the birds of the same kind sitting on a wire facing the wind? I've seen that instinct at work all over the world. I've seen birds and animals congregate in Kenya and other places just as far-flung—including the Andes Mountains, Arctic Circle, and Siberian Tundra. I've seen animals travel in herds, flocks, schools, and swarms. Is it merely a "force of nature" that compels them to integrate and swim, run, fly, or waddle together? I don't think so—it has to be an inbred instinct that God put there in the beginning.

Recently while on vacation, Evie and I watched the "Red Hat Ladies" assemble at the Cheesecake Factory Restaurant in Palm Beach, Florida. As I've noticed before—and heard from others who know more about them than I do—these ladies meet regularly for lunch. I'm told that they have no speaker, no agenda, and their purpose is to just meet to enjoy one another's friendship. As far as I can tell, the only thing that holds this group together is a red hat.

Belonging to a group, organization, or community can be just as simple as that. You can meet with others by simply wearing a red hat.

Others who get together might wear team colors of their favorite sport. Then there's all kinds of motorcycle clubs or groups. Or war veterans … bowlers … car buffs … bridge clubs … and family reunions.

Belonging is important, and it's a universal need.

When I was in the African nation of Uganda, I saw a man at the John Guest Crusade, standing in the back, at the middle of the aisle, wearing a suit and tie and wearing a badge on his coat just above the pocket. The badge declared that the man was an usher.

That man was *so* proud of being selected to serve as an usher. That task gave him a sense of worthiness and, in his mind, perhaps even status. I think he was probably wearing his only suit (in fact, it may even have been borrowed).

Except for that suit, the man was probably otherwise destitute. I guessed that when he went home that night after the crusade, it was to a simple, ramshackle hut or shack. Yet for the moment, he belonged to a special group—"ushers." True, he was a member of the church, and that gave him status of belonging. But he was also an usher—part of what he felt was an elite group that he'd never get from any other organization. That night he belonged to a special group of ushers, and it gave him such self-worth that his eyes were bright and his face beamed for the entire evening. He *belonged.*

There are many people who belong to no group or organization that gives them that kind of satisfaction. Some even end their lives in despair because they don't or can't belong. They feel as if no one likes them or cares. How unfortunate that so many people live lives of such desperation when God cares. By contrast, those of us who follow Jesus can help those desperate people by taking an interest in them and by giving them a sense they belong and are loved.

It isn't that I have some kind of obsession about this idea of belonging, but it has become a dominant part of my thinking in recent years—especially as I've been so involved in ministry to children. I've read a lot of research on how important it is for children to have a solid sense of belonging. Studies prove the significance and need of belonging to the right group or groups.

Statistics bear out the life changing (whether good or bad changes) that results when kids choose to align with positive or negative groups to which they can join or belong. Churches, Sunday schools, Boy and Girl Scouts, and similar organizations—and sometimes even a caring teacher—can have a positive influence on kids. These people and programs provide strong programming and strong one-to-one leadership and mentoring—offering multiple opportunities for kids to belong. Or, left to their own devices, without Christian and parental mentoring, they might gravitate toward a street gang.

Once kids are convinced that they *belong,* they will *become* (to be more like their mentor or like Jesus), then they learn how to *behave* (practice the values and principles of their group). These qualities are not just for kids—we see the same process with adults who are led to belong to a group such as a church, men's or women's group, or a Bible study that gives them a sense of *belonging,* and the relationships forged inside these groups encourage the members to *become* more like Jesus or Christlike mentors, teachers, or leaders who instill hope and foster the qualities and character that they seek.

I have seen firsthand how this takes place—in my church, of course, but also in a popular restaurant in Rockford: Stockholm Inn, which has a reputation for drawing people to come and "belong" with others. There are quite a few Bible studies, men's groups, women's groups, and family celebrations that come there for meetings.

During these meetings I've had a chance to overhear parts of their discussions, and it's amazing just how similar they are in format. With few exceptions within these groups—whether when "two or three are gathered" or a room full of two hundred people—there is a common thread: *stories.*

Whether large or small, the conversation centers on interesting interactions that meet all the qualities of "story." These stories or conversations are followed with interest, and you can see the good time that people are having through their fellowship.

Even in sad settings, as a funeral, for example, there are stories (eulogies) that bind the hearts and minds of those in the room as they listen to accounts that perhaps they didn't know about the departed. The absent member whom these stories are about has involuntarily brought these mourners and friends together. They feel a sense of belonging within the circle so recently vacated by the deceased, and they are there to grieve, be inspired, laugh, cry, and remember the stories.

My wife, Evie, is great at giving our family a feeling of belonging. Every birthday—all sixteen of them in our family—is recognized. Christmas, Thanksgiving, and our patriotic holidays are also made special. Sporting events (cheering for our Chicago Bulls, Cubs, and

White Sox or Blackhawks, etc.) are made into "family events," and each family member feels like he or she "belongs."

My daughter Tonya gave me another example regarding the idea of belonging. She says, "We also obtain a 'supernatural' sense of belonging when we are serving in roles where we are uniquely gifted, when we can be of service to others in areas that respond to the 'giftedness' that God gave us. I think we feel that we 'belong' even more because of that link that connects us to others and to God at the same time. We feel connected in a way that's beyond understanding.

"There's another thought that makes this supernatural. Jesus said that when there are two or more people praying—or serving, or worshipping—God is in their midst. As a result they are again connected, inspired, and energized in that unique and special way.

"Our work is important. I like to think that what we do is because of who we are. We're God-directed, and we belong to a special community that's also God-directed. This allows us to carry out God's work here on earth—in supernatural, unseen ways. We often see how He 'connects' people, circumstances, and events in unseen but remarkable ways—especially when we're serving in our areas of giftedness, walking close to Him, listening for His voice, and calling on His Spirit for our daily guidance and daily behavioral promptings. We *get to help others* feel as though they truly *belong*."

I think that Tonya's observation is quite pertinent. It underscores what I try to practice by emphasizing the importance of *helping* people (in general). By helping others, this often implies that we help other adults find direction, acceptance, or satisfaction. A single helpful action can have a ripple effect in the lives of others—ripples that extend through generations of family members. The effect can be quite profound.

I grew up in a church where the young people turned out to be major leaders over the years—Steve Douglass, John Ortberg, Jr., Gary Smalley, Ralph Veerman, and Evelyn Christenson were all members of a Baptist General Conference church on a main street in Rockford, Illinois.[3]

We often wondered how so many leaders—*godly* leaders—came out of one church.

I think it was because an early pastor's wife, Evelyn Christenson, set a tone for an emphasis on prayer. She had a dynamic ministry and practiced what she wrote and spoke about: *"Prayer makes things happen."*

She focused the energy of prayer toward certain individuals of whom she had personal knowledge of their needs as well as their potentialities, and it was powerful. It was a powerful exchange between a pastor's wife and a living God. In her prayers, she told "stories" to her heavenly Father—stories about the people and events that she was praying about. When her prayers were answered, others then carried on the process by telling "stories" about those answered prayers. And the best proof that prayer works: The kids she prayed for turned out to be powerful, fearless evangelical leaders.

Evelyn Christenson understood what it takes to help kids "make it" in life. I think she's probably the author of dozens of books. Her children's books include: *My First Journal of Prayer* and *What Happens When Children Pray.* In these books children are shown that prayer is a vital element in their lives, and it's such a powerful influence, it can actually transform a youngster from shyness, or some other stumbling block, into a dynamic leader.

Evelyn Christenson has proven that the most effective demonstration that prayer works is that so many young people from our church went on to become effective in life and leadership. It happens because we were all taught that things happen when we pray—God answers prayer.

My friends in ministry mentioned above continue to influence thousands through their continuing efforts, and I know that they do it through a dependency upon prayer.

My focus is to do likewise—and to concentrate on the importance of helping children find their way, and in the process help them to feel accepted, loved, and that they "belong."

Some additional thoughts about belonging …

Churches that are experiencing the greatest growth are the ones that, besides preaching the gospel faithfully, set up within their church the following:

- Great children's programs
- Short-term mission teams
- Outreach opportunities for kids and adults
- Small-group activities
- Church-sponsored socializing opportunities

All of these elements offer opportunities for people to "join" others within a community of common interests, offering interests and activities that provide a positive influence on one another—in other words, "belonging."

"Belonging" can add to the quality and length of life:

- It provides a support group.

- Social activities of a group help prevent depression.
- Facebook, Twitter, and other computer-based social networks can be great for those who want to share their faith or encourage others in that manner.

However, the flip side is that interaction within computer-based social networks might inhibit "real" opportunities *to belong.* Those friendships and interactions are *virtual* experiences that can easily become a substitute for *real* friendships, as well as relationships—between parents, spouses, children, neighbors, and friends.

What are sought are the genuine friendships, interactions, and relationships that lead to a tangible and real belonging. And then we must build on those qualities and interactions.

Chapter Seven

BELONGING, BECOMING … AND THEN, BEHAVING

Understanding how God is at work in the world also requires an understanding of facts and information about our contemporary world. We usually take that to mean our personal lives, the lives of our family members, church, occupation, and other organizations or societies to which we **BELONG** (as was presented in the previous chapter).

Then, when people belong to the right groups, the positive influences from such affinity associations *can have a dramatic effect upon group members and what they believe.*

It explains and reinforces ***why*** *they belong to such a group.*

To be aware of God at work in the world, one must be aware of history. Seeing how God worked in the past gives us a template for how He works today, because His principles don't change just because a new administration is voted in, or new philosophies or ethics (or lack thereof) come and go. He is the same, "Yesterday, today, and forever" (Heb. 13:8 NKJV). When we see His hand at work, we are more empowered to **BECOME** (more like Jesus)—He is real, and we can sense those supernatural activities taking place, and that we can be a party to them.

It even *affects our* **BEHAVIOR**.

I've served on the boards of trustees of at least a dozen organizations, and you probably hold—or have held—similar roles. Most of us, at one time or another, are asked to serve: at our churches, elementary schools, colleges, arts organizations, PTA, political party, Chambers of Commerce, Lions Club or Rotary, kids' ball teams, etc. The experiences give us opportunities to grow and participate in something worthwhile.

I've even thought that it'd be a good idea if every college and university have as its requirement for graduation that all students take on such an assignment—joining a group not for what they get out of it, but documenting for themselves how volunteering to help others makes a major difference in their lives. It'd be as useful as many hours of classroom learning where their experience teaches them about planning, organizing, fund-raising, recruiting, and volunteering, as well as marketing. Contributing time, energy, and creative brainstorming to help local nonprofits is excellent training for just about any kind of career.

Universally, every group has a leader in a person's first experience of "belonging," whether it's a family, a group of students, a school or neighborhood team, a political party, an ethnic group or nationality. The group is led by someone who's expected to make good choices and decisions. The leader has a clear understanding that he or she has a responsibility to be accountable to the people he or she leads.

We've already seen the many ways that adults find affinity with like-minded people and become members of groups of all kinds. Youngsters also have a need to belong, as was suggested earlier. Parents can help them to choose their affinity groups wisely. They can be involved in wholesome activities with groups—like Boy or Girl Scouts, a Sunday school class, an extracurricular school activity, or one of many positive groups. Yet, without parental care or concern, they might seek out their own place to belong, and might face peer pressure and end up in a troublesome gang.

Kids—like their parents—will find ways to be with others, and they'll seek out a place where they "feel they belong." Adult teachers, coaches, or parents can be of crucial help to children in guiding the kids' choices to positive associations—the kind that reinforce values and principles they'll need in later life. Parents who get their kids into these programs are helping them to *belong to the right influence groups* where the role models of good peers will give them behavior examples that can last for a lifetime.

Churches and parents need to focus on creating Christian "belonging" opportunities for their children, otherwise the kids will choose without particular discretion. They might choose a neighborhood gang or, as some children in the Middle East, follow a persuasive leader who wants to recruit terrorists or suicide bombers.

Bishop John Kabango Rucyahana, a Tutsi pastor and chairman of Prison Fellowship of Rwanda, decided that he'd try to bring peace and reconciliation by preaching to Hutu inmates at Gitarama Prison for their gruesome crimes in the 1994 Tutsi-Hutu civil war that generated the terrible Rwanda genocide. Bishop Rucyahana tells how he first approached his mission, telling the inmates to recall all the murderous cruelties they'd inflicted on their neighbors, where hundreds of thousands of men, women, and children were killed. "In about 10 minutes," Bishop Rucyahana said, "everyone was crying, sobbing. I said, 'Open your eyes. That which makes you cry is what God wants you to repent of.'"[1]

According to the news report, Bishop Rucyahana—whose own family was tortured and murdered during the genocide—has witnessed "thousands of searing moments of truth" as the murderous inmates come to terms with their acts of violence and bloodshed, and repent.[2]

Even those in warring groups that "belong" can make life-changing adjustments.

Or (rarely) some young people see something positive in a group that's outside the existence they're in. That was the theme of a motion picture that grabbed an Oscar for almost every film category at the Academy Awards in 2009. The film was *Slumdog Millionaire,* and a writer—who grew up in Mumbai (formerly Bombay), India, and was hired by *Newsweek* magazine as a local correspondent—wrote an account in the magazine to mark the popularity and success of *Slumdog Millionaire.* Sudip Mazumdar grew up in the same slums that were featured in the movie. Here are excerpts from what he wrote about Jamal, the slumdog in Danny Boyle's award-winning movie, for *Newsweek*:

> People keep praising the film's "realistic" depiction of slum life in India. But ... slum life is a cage.
>
> By my early teens I was running with a local gang. Membership was my source of confidence, security and excitement....
>
> I also fell in with a group of radical leftists. I didn't care much about ideology, but they offered [a] sense of *belonging*....
>
> No one wants to watch a movie about that. *Slumdog (Millionaire)* ... throbs with excitement, hope and positive energy. But remember, an ugly fact: slums exist, in large part, because they're allowed to exist. Slumdogs aren't the only ones whose minds need to be opened up.[3]

Fairy-tale endings happen mostly in movies. In real life, the experiences are usually not such a fairy tale. The writer who grew up in the India slums knows that better than we do. But did you catch the similarities in his life to those things that are universal in nearly every home? Parents and other adults who make a difference in a child's life don't always realize how important "belonging" is to children. Kids at formative ages somehow filter out logic and morality and seek out companionship—many times in the wrong places with the wrong people.

Childhood is the most formative time in a person's life, and it's a significant and critical time. It's important that parents, teachers, and church leaders focus on "creating" value-based and positive "belonging" opportunities for the children.

I've had the good fortune to be able to travel to fifty-five countries around the world, including the slums of Mumbai (Bombay). Unlike in the movie that glamorized them, *slums are horrific.*

However—whether slums are in India, Africa, Asia, or the *barrios* of Central and South America—I've seen, even in those hopeless environments, an eagerness of children to *desire something more.* When Kids Around the World comes into their slums to build a playground, it's always a life-changing event. These playgrounds help to keep kids in their neighborhoods, near the adults and friends that they know; kids are at the comfortable place where they "belong."

Once they *belong,* the next step is to help them *become,* and then to *behave* (by following the precepts of Jesus)—which leads them to being the person God wants them to be. Jim Rosene wants these principles to become primary principles for Kids Around the World in helping youngsters become Christ followers.

I've watched as they come inside the playground site and make the first tentative moves toward the slide, swings, or climbing bars. It takes only a few seconds for them to lose their apprehension, inhibitions, and shyness and begin to have fun. Then I see their potential. Looking into their shining eyes and at their bright smiles, it's easy to see why those who volunteered to come and construct the playground get such great satisfaction in helping. Just one look at a child with such pure joy on his or her face changes a volunteer's life forever.

It was this great sense of satisfaction that got us thinking of other ways to help the kids when we go overseas or even to people in needy communities in the United States—such as Katrina victims in Louisiana, or kids of poverty in Mississippi or other places.

Overseas we began taking volunteer doctors and nurses and opened clinics to operate alongside the volunteers building playgrounds. In places like Ghana, Haiti, Dominican Republic, and other disadvantaged and deprived places, our work has changed lives.

In most places like these, our volunteer medical teams are the only doctors or nurses they will ever get to see. What great satisfaction to see a child with a severe cleft palate who is given a handsome smile by an American plastic surgeon on a mission trip; or kids with bad teeth or poor vision being helped by US dentists and eye doctors.

These miracles of help—like the young man from the Mumbai slums who wrote about his own experience when *Newsweek* gave him a job—are documentary records of lives that are absolutely changed for good.

However, we also began thinking of ways to help kids learn to read and write, so that they, too, can get an education and do something substantial with their lives.

In the process of training nationals who are literate, to help teach those who cannot, we came across far too many more who are not literate. Yet we also discovered that, although they were illiterate, they're *not ignorant.* Most of them came from a visual-oral culture and society. Reading and writing to communicate knowledge wasn't as important to them in that culture.

I realized that I'd been focused on *how* ***we*** *communicate* in *our* culture, but we needed to focus on how to address these needs of people in *other cultures* by *communicating to them in their "heart" language.*

Chapter Eight

WHAT WORKS IN "THIS DAY AND AGE"?

The late Dr. Avery Willis[1] shared the story of how he hadn't really ever thought of something called Orality before the year 2000. I remember how, at the beginning of the twenty-first century, people all around the world seemed nervous about something called the Y2K "bug," which proved to be a threat that fizzled—an absolute dud. You may remember that the Y2K bug was going to affect nearly every computer in the world by causing a fatal crash because the computer software supposedly had that flaw. There were dire forecasts that airplanes wouldn't be able to fly, phone services would crash, communication satellites would go into an electronic coma—and we'd be thrown back into the caveman era.

While the Y2K "nonevent" dominated media and culture, other things were happening that got no serious attention. One of them was a meeting sponsored and convened in Amsterdam in 2000 by Billy Graham.

Dr. Willis and other ministers had gathered as part of meetings stemming from the '74 Lausanne Congress on World Evangelization to discuss a global strategy for evangelizing unreached people groups.

Dr. Willis told the group of a man who came up to him at that event and asked, "How do you disciple oral learners?" Dr. Willis thought for a while, but had no answer.

Probably half-expecting that reply, the man told Dr. Willis, "No one has done it. It's *your* job."

Jolted by the man's challenge, Dr. Willis saw the need for exactly what the man had proposed. He said, "I'd missed three-fourths of the people I was trying to reach," and added, "I realized I needed to do something."

That "something" turned out to be his answer—an ancient communication skill of the past: *storytelling*. He then put together a group of people to create a Bible storytelling program that would communicate the content of the various books and stories of the Bible through storytelling.

That initial group spent several years creating and fine-tuning that storytelling program, resulting in about four hundred stories from the Bible—translated from literate, published content into an oral, storytelling form. The group presented their ideas at the Lausanne Conference in 2004.

At Lausanne, a task force was formed to come up with an Orality project. That, in turn, resulted in the creation of the International

Orality Network (ION), with Dr. Willis as executive director. The fledgling entity was then "adopted" by a number of other groups, including Campus Crusade for Christ, Dr. Willis' own International Mission Board of the Southern Baptist Convention, and Wycliffe International.

ION became an umbrella organization that works in cooperation with those three large organizations, plus many others already involved with coming up with Orality projects. Kids Around the World president Jim Rosene was invited to join ION to focus on children. And that sharpened our own vision for teaching and training kids.

How Does Orality Work in Visual-Oral Cultures?

Communicating biblical content and principles through stories and parables is a method that Jesus used. He used visual-oral communication with His disciples and in explaining salvation (as He did with Nicodemus), grace, and forgiveness (as with the woman at the well). Jesus also used parables to teach crowds of thousands at a time on the hillsides. He told them stories about truth, about their world, about God, and about the way in which they were supposed to live.

Interestingly, Jesus didn't focus solely on Orality or storytelling. He also used literacy when it was appropriate. Even as a boy He read the Torah in the temple to the religious leaders and answered their questions about the texts. But later, as an adult, Jesus used the Bible's recorded stories and countless examples of storytelling as a means of communicating to illiterate listeners—a method that His disciples and the apostles also used with success.

Dr. Willis reminded me that Jesus' methods are the best way to communicate in a visual-oral or nonliterate culture. "All of us learned orally first," he said, "and that's why Jesus' parables were so effective."

He's right. We were taught our first words, songs, and even prayers by our mothers, fathers, grandparents, and siblings. These first words, songs, and prayers were reinforced by teachers and members of groups to which we belonged.

Dr. Willis decided that visual-oral teaching and learning would be the way to go for reaching those who can't read and thus can't learn truth from books. He decided that he had to teach teachers and preachers to use stories, drama, songs, and proverbs.

Instead of reading from the Bible or preaching a sermon, the storyteller first memorizes the content and then conveys the story in a conversational way, sharing thoughts and ideas of the passage with a friend over a cup of coffee or while sitting around a campfire. Dr. Willis told his workshop listeners to follow up their storytelling by asking questions—making sure that those who are listening understand the content of the story by interacting and "replaying" the story first in their own minds. At the completion of the interaction between storyteller and listener, the process is put to the test—after hearing the story the listener understands the content from the story and repeats its truth and content to another person.

Paul Koehler, an author and missionary in India, earned a master's degree from Fuller Theological Seminary's School of Intercultural Studies. Yet he was troubled that the church leaders he trained for ministry in India didn't seem to be using the methods and materials that he was using to teach *them*. He noticed that somehow real *understanding* of their communication wasn't getting through.

The dominant religion in India is Hinduism, followed by Islam. Interestingly, the percentage of people who claim the Hindu religion only amounts to about 20 to 30 percent of the population. Yet they have held control of the nation (except during British colonial rule) for thousands of years.

Koehler said that both Hindus and Muslims in India "have negative feelings about" foreigners who come to India with other religions, and they're especially wary of those who come to bring conversion.

As a result of fierce national pride for Hinduism and Islam, resistance to Christianity from those religions is prevalent. Preaching and the distribution of Bibles and Christian literature are prohibited in most places, but Koehler found that Bible storytelling is acceptable. What he discovered is something that I did as well in watching Jim Rosene and others in Kids Around the World. They would start this way: "May I tell you a story?" The typical response is, "Yes! Of course." And then as they listen to the Bible stories, the listeners begin to discover a God of love who cares about people just like them.

It's interesting. Some of the Christian leaders in India are literate; some are not. *Yet even those who are illiterate are able to speak many more languages than most Westerners.* There are about thirty "mother tongue" languages for the 1.1 billion people of India. Also, there are hundreds of dialects as *variations* of those languages.

If India decided that every one of its one-billion-plus citizens should be literate, imagine the task of translating, communicating, and teaching—in *thirty languages and another 1,672 dialects.* I'm even trying to imagine the impossibility of trying to *coordinate* that kind of project!

That's why, in that cultural context, visual-oral storytelling makes sense, especially in remote and hard-to-reach regions of the country and with dozens of possible dialects to master, even in the same community.

Training Christian evangelists, pastors, and teachers is complicated because the training sessions are often a two-to-three-day journey *each way*. The logistics and problems of trying to do or teach some method *other* than visual-oral storytelling to present the gospel is hard to imagine.

A common reaction, according to Dr. Willis, is that we think that stories are only for children. However, in the experience of our Kids Around the World teams, storytelling works for *both* kids and adults. Our results prove that storytelling can be tailored to any age group. Yet the argument that "stories are for children"—but *not just for kids*—is precisely why *I* suddenly became interested in Orality.

My collaborator Joe Musser and I met with Dr. Steve Douglass, and he showed us a storytelling video tool Campus Crusade was going to use in their small groups on campuses. It was an interesting, emotional visual without any dialogue. The presentation elicited viewer questions, prompted discussion, and was an absolutely groundbreaking technique.

We began to see the potential of "Orality" in communicating biblical truth to people who are unable or unwilling to read or write. It opened a brand-new door of opportunity for us.

Chapter Nine

THE ORAL MAJORITY

Webster's New World College Dictionary defines Orality as "reliance on spoken, rather than written, language for communication"; or, "the fact or quality of being communicated orally."[1]

Those who are using Orality as a means of communicating orally usually mean that they are attempting to communicate this way with those who may be highly literate, but who prefer to communicate in a visual-oral manner. That is, trying to reach those who can't, won't, or don't use literacy as a means of communicating.

Samuel Chiang is an authority on Orality, and said that there are 4.35 billion people that can't, won't, or don't use literate means to communicate.[2] That means they are unlikely to be influenced by printed materials (Bibles and Scripture portions and other literate means).

But first, some background. Some sixteen hundred leaders attended the Lausanne Committee for World Evangelization's 2004 Forum. They met thirty years after the 1974 International Congress in Lausanne, Switzerland, and challenged attendees to organize the "whole church to take the whole gospel to the whole world."

The Lausanne Congress in 1974 accepted the challenge to help the modern missionary movement evangelize the world's unreached people groups. Lausanne '74 recognized something: Four billion people—about two-thirds of the world's population—are oral learners. Writer Erich Bridges explained, "They communicate, learn, perceive reality and embrace core beliefs through orally expressed stories, narratives, songs and proverbs—not through the books, periodicals, outlines and other forms of *linear* thinking preferred by literate cultures (and churches)."[3]

Bridges reported on the Lausanne Committee for World Evangelization's 2004 Forum and later said in an article in *Baptist Press* that while two-thirds of the world's population are *oral* communicators, 90 percent of Christian workers use *literate communication styles* while working among those oral people groups. He said that Orality-based methods need to be used if the whole world is to be reached for Christ.[4]

Dr. Avery Willis, of the Southern Baptist International Mission Board, was another person who helped convene the Lausanne Committee for World Evangelization's 2004 Forum in Thailand. He also helped lay out the problems that confronted church and missionary organizations. The following points came out in the deliberations of the sixteen hundred leaders who attended:

- Of the seven billion people on planet earth, *four billion* are considered illiterate or functionally illiterate; they communicate through visual-oral means and live in an oral-based culture or society.
- As many as 85 percent of Muslim women—and 65 percent of Muslim men—are visual-oral learners and are nonliterate or functionally illiterate. Many Islamic clerical leaders in the Middle East and Africa are exclusively visual-oral communicators, based on having memorized the Quran.
- Illiteracy predominates animistic peoples—that marks much of Africa.
- Of approximately 6,900[5] languages that are spoken around the world, about 2,252 people groups (Wycliffe uses 2,100 "languages") do not have a single verse of Scripture in the heart language of the people. This represents approximately 340 million people.
- There are about twelve hundred completed New Testaments. However, there are about *two billion* people without any access to the Old Testament.
- Also, according to Wycliffe Bible Translators, about seventeen hundred more translation projects are under way, but more than four thousand languages have no translated Scripture at all—not even a portion or fragment. To me, there is an implied question with all these statistics: *Are the*

speakers of these languages to go without the gospel until we get around to them?

- Newer translations are using Orality concepts for the translations, starting with visual-oral stories of the Bible in the heart language of the people.

So how and why should we use Orality and not traditional literate methods to communicate to the two-thirds majority of the world's people who can neither read nor write?

Ironically, many have already come up with the answer. Some have hammered out the strategies in a forum, workshop, or conference like Lausanne 2004. There are others of us who have stumbled onto solutions through prayer and intuition.

I'd like to share some insights and ideas on this matter, because as my friend the late Dr. Avery Willis said in his workshop at the 2009 ION Convention about those who are *visual-oral* and *not literate* communicators/learners, "Four billion people are headed to a Christ-less eternity unless we use *culturally appropriate means* to evangelize them, disciple them, train leaders and plant reproducing churches."

To these four billion people, books, Bibles, and Scripture lessons are meaningless.

Dr. Willis and perhaps thousands of people like him have previously produced and used these written tools of communication. Yet at the ION workshop he voiced his thoughts aloud to the two or three dozen people in the classroom, *What good are those tools if the "hidden" people can't read?*

He told us that his discovery seemed to call his life's work into question. As a lifelong missionary, he had traveled around the world to teach, preach, and train those of other faiths—or no faith at all—to become followers of Jesus Christ.

And he thought that his mission to bring Christ to the world was successful. Yet Dr. Willis realized that despite all his efforts, he had somehow overlooked this "hidden people group" consisting of *billions* of individuals who had never heard of Jesus Christ. These were the functionally illiterate—the visual-oral learners.

Dr. Willis said that we are confronted with this question: *How do you make a disciple out of a visual-oral learner?* In America three generations grew up on radio and television, and two of these generations have been exposed to videos from their earliest days. These are also, in a practical sense, those who basically learn in an oral (or aural) way.

I've come to believe that Dr. Willis and other proponents of Orality were wise to target these newest generations with methods that work for these younger groups. Although they do not always use printed, literate methods to learn, they are still smart and have learned to process information through visual-oral means. For the past forty to sixty years, we who are in evangelical and missionary organizations have, for the most part, been missing the mark in trying to reach two-thirds of the world's population.

Storytelling unlocks the understanding of the New Testament Gospels. And we must recognize that Jesus is the model storyteller. He spent up to 90 percent of His time telling stories and parables and expressed great themes in strong, visual statements so that people comprehended what He had to say—but because His stories were based on typical situations that everyone understood, they *remembered* what He had said.

The Bible was printed more than five hundred years ago, and my generation believes that because we were educated with literate methods, some have assumed that visual-oral learners "think differently." But that's not a problem—it's a solution. We just need to present our message in a method and context of how they want to receive it.

Dr. Willis discovered something called Bible storytelling as a means of communicating the gospel—a new form of evangelism in 2000, as the new century was just getting under way.

Before I learned of Dr. Avery Willis, I'd heard of some mission leaders and others who were trying to communicate with people groups who could not read. They understood how a visual-oral culture functioned through traditions where stories were passed down through generations, preserving the knowledge of the clan and the history of neighboring tribes.

In that kind of environment, anthropologists measured how effective visual-oral learning was. They questioned different members of a tribe or community who had never been taught to read or write, and they were impressed at how consistent their cultural information was—their history was the same no matter who in the tribe was questioned.

I know of several Americans who capitalized on that visual-oral traditional teaching approach to communicating stories from the Bible; some mission workers and teachers had even worked to create a language for those who'd never had one before.

I also met a man—one who has become a friend of many years—who was born into a tribe with an oral tradition. Dr. Rochunga Pudaite, a member of the Hmar tribe of northeast India, grew up in that tribe that was also a former headhunting tribe with no *written* language or history.

In 1910 five members of this Hmar tribe were converted to Christianity by a Welsh missionary, Watkin Roberts,[6] who defied British colonial rulers a century ago. He was ordered to stay out of the region and to make no efforts to conduct missionary activities, especially to visit and communicate the gospel story to the Hmar tribe. He went despite the official ban.

One of his first converts was Chawnga Pudaite, father of my friend Rochunga. Chawnga sent his ten-year-old boy "Ro" some ninety miles through the jungle to be taught in a Baptist school and then go to get higher education at Calcutta University so that he could translate the Bible into the Hmar language. Sounds like quite an assignment for a ten-year-old boy!

Rochunga did get the education needed for the task, including schooling at Glasgow University in Scotland and at Wheaton College and Northern Illinois University in the US, arranged by Billy Graham and Dr. Bob Pierce (founder of World Vision and Samaritan's Purse). Ro studied Hebrew and Greek before he could translate the Bible. But there was still a major obstacle. The Hmar people were an oral society. They didn't have a *written* language. Rochunga would have to help create one before he could translate the Bible into Hmar. So that's what he did. In the late 1950s Rochunga worked with some others from his native northeast India to create a written language, and the language was used to translate the New Testament into the newly written Hmar language.

His story[7] is a remarkable one and is an inspiring account of finding ways to help communicate the gospel to a visual-oral society.

American missionary Paul Koehler—mentioned previously about his work in storytelling in India—works in India to share the gospel by using Bible storytelling. He also found that our Western style of learning doesn't always translate well in other countries—especially those who can't comprehend literacy and prefer visual-oral learning, such as in stories, drama, song, and dance. In 2001 he created and developed a pilot project in South Asia that trained more than fifty storytellers who spent two years learning how to tell, dramatize, and sing elements of a hundred Bible stories. The stories begin at creation and cover the Old and New Testament events through Christ's ascension into heaven.

Koehler reported that besides bringing a number of people to faith in Christ, more than two hundred new churches were planted in the towns and villages in the region where the pilot Orality program was tested.[8]

Recently another man I know has also been using visual-oral methods to reach illiterate people in India. Dr. Paul Larsen is the former president of North Park College and past president of the Evangelical Covenant Church of America. He is currently the Chairman of the William Carey Heritage Foundation and a consultant to another India Christian ministry that works with the "untouchables" of India—the lower-caste Dalits who are considered subhuman by the Hindu religion and thus suffer discrimination and lack of basic human rights.

However in recent years several of these Dalit caste leaders have sought out Christians in India with the idea of rejecting the idea of their subjugation to the Hindu religion. Many caste leaders are bringing their entire membership with them when they convert to

Buddhism or Christianity—especially Christianity, which the Dalit caste leaders recognize was the religion of William Carey, who fought for Dalit rights as a famous missionary to India in the early 1800s.

The leader of the Butcher Caste, who converted to Christianity several years ago, is already starting schools and churches. He's become a zealous follower of Jesus. He was originally impressed because he knew it was Christians who brought India and his untouchable caste an awareness of human rights, and it was Christians who founded hospitals and schools and made other advancements in the human condition.

Other Indian Christians with lifelong learning and spiritual maturity are mentoring this leader of the Butcher Caste, who in turn is urging others in the caste to turn to Christianity.

Dr. Paul Larsen has been an observer of rallies of thousands of people called together by this caste leader, and he tells of how thousands of people have turned to Christianity because of his influence. He reports:

> It will likely take some time before the caste leaders fully understand the gospel, but they are already responding to visual and visual-oral presentations of the gospel and are replacing the tradition of their ties to Hinduism by rejecting that religion, and turning to Jesus Christ in their own simple faith.
>
> They even have an oral *tradition of the Gospel* coming to India through the apostle Thomas. If this grass-root movement of turning to Christianity

> takes hold it will tip the balance of religion and power in India. Even now the Hindus that hold power are in the minority. The out-castes and tribal castes make up about 75 percent of the population. If they decide to seek religious freedom through Christianity, they'll be the majority in India quite quickly.

Dr. Larsen told me about something that he was part of while on recent trips to India. I asked if I could share that experience in this book, as it's a perfect example of Orality. Dr. Larsen describes his experience this way:

> In August 2008, a low-caste Indian of the Sculptors Caste showed up at Truthseekers Centre in New Delhi. Truthseekers is a Christian organization and, as one of its objectives, extends invitations to people to come to their center and compare their religious beliefs. In a nation that's seen more than its share of religious strife and confrontation over religion, Truthseekers avoids confrontation and introduces non-Christians to Jesus Christ and Christianity in a nonthreatening way. The director of the work, Sunil Sardar, is a highly educated Christian from India's lower castes.
>
> Sunil's method of exploring Christianity in a nonthreatening way is surprisingly simple and effective. The people from other religions who are

invited are asked to describe their god and what their god or gods have done for them.

After everyone listens to the different responses about various gods, Sunil shares how he met Jesus Christ and what happened to him when he responded to Christ's invitation to, "Follow Me."

Sunil tells them about the positive changes that came into his life and how Jesus Christ has made his life worthwhile and full of great blessing. Almost always the contrasts between the religions and gods of his listeners are dramatic.

The people listen politely, without heated arguments. They show intense interest and respect to Sunil as he tells them about *his* faith and points out the differences between their religious beliefs and his own faith.

Sunil's guests are inquisitive, and they ask him more questions about God, Jesus, and Christianity. Sunil patiently responds to their questions and then shares from his own experience—how God has worked in his life—and then shows them how to live by faith. He concludes with a challenge to them—how *their* lives can also be changed—and that's always followed by a universally typical response from the listeners: They pray with Sunil and turn their lives over to Christ, renouncing their other gods, and, with tearful repentance, vow to follow Jesus Christ.

Many of them also ask Sunil to disciple them, so they can live the kind of life that he models. Sunil invites these converts to Bible studies that he or his brother lead.

Vijay Paswan, Sculptor Caste leader, attended one of these Truthseekers gatherings. A clean-cut forty-year-old father of six and poor sculptor, he'd come to Delhi seeking funding for his impoverished village of six hundred. The money was to buy huge stone blocks to take back to his village, where Vijay and the other sculptors would create stone carvings. Vijay had brought with him samples of his work—and he told Sunil that it takes about six weeks to delicately carve even a simple stone figure.

Before coming to the Truthseekers Centre, Vijay had first stopped at a government office, where an official informed him that the government had no funds to loan to him for stone blocks, but later, somehow, someone sent Vijay to the Truthseekers Centre to meet Sunil.

Sunil told Vijay, "I'm sorry. I have no money either and cannot help you meet others who might fund your project, but I invite you to stay for a Truthseekers meeting." Sunil explained what the focus was for the meeting: "People come. They tell us about their god and why they worship their god. Everyone shares, and then I tell them about my God."

Sunil must have piqued Vijay's interest because he stayed for a Truthseekers meeting—though Vijay still didn't get money for stone blocks. Instead he found something greater. Sunil led him to Christ and gave him a copy of a New Testament. "You should read it through several times," he told Vijay, "and then, also read it regularly to your people."

Vijay tentatively took the book but shook his head. He admitted sadly, "I cannot read this book. I am illiterate."

"Is there not someone who could read it to you?" Sunil asked.

Vijay replied, "Well, yes, I suppose. My brother knows how to read. Perhaps I could get him to read it to me."

Sunil smiled and said, "That's good. Also ask your brother to help you gather others of your family and village to meet together regularly to hear your brother read to them from this book—and then pray together."

Three months later, I was in Delhi when Vijay returned to meet with Sunil. In those intervening months, from his brother reading from the New Testament, Vijay could recite the stories of Jesus from the New Testament—*all from memory.*

The stories included entire narratives that Vijay had memorized—and they had an effect on some *four hundred villagers* who subsequently professed

> Christ as Savior and Lord. Not only did the four hundred villagers became converts—but many more people, just traveling through the village, were drawn by the stories that Vijay told about Jesus. They added to the four hundred village converts so that soon *more than one thousand decided to convert to Christianity!*
>
> Sunil Sardar, pleased at the extraordinary progress, decided to send two of his most experienced Christian leaders to help Vijay with the evangelism and disciple-making.
>
> Vijay has a unique way of visiting. He approaches someone, introduces himself, and then hands them the booklet and asks, "I cannot read—will you please read this for me?" The practice is a humble and remarkable way to witness. Remarkably this man became a new convert to Christianity, and now he's drawing others by the hundreds—perhaps thousands—to consider Jesus Christ.[9]

The one thing that caught my interest in Dr. Larsen's article was the example of Vijay, a new Christian, who didn't know how to read, but who *memorized* content that his brother read aloud from the New Testament in a way that challenged people to repent and turn to Christ. That's definitely a spot-on example of Orality in practice.

Chapter Ten

DISCIPLING KIDS THROUGH SIMPLE THEATER

After we had created Kids Around the World as a ministry for children and had been thinking of ways to go beyond bringing joy, friendship, and influence to a community through the construction of playgrounds, we also added other ministries, such as medical and sports clinics and hunger and feeding programs, along with traditional evangelism methods. We discovered in the process that Kids Around the World was an organization that was known not only in its ministry to children; we were also becoming a major part of the Orality movement, although we didn't even know it. We used Orality for a simple reason—*it worked.*

Yet the fact was that we had to modify traditional methods to make them effective. We created a wonderful puppet program with a cast of make-believe characters and a portable stage and sound amplification so large crowds can hear in their own "kitchen" language. However, in far-flung villages, where there were no electrical sources to power the PA system, we made sure that the sound system had built-in batteries—or we used the puppets individually or took along an artist to draw pictures. As we thought more about it, these were Orality methods, and we were already using them to communicate.

Later Kids Around the World president Jim Rosene and I discovered that while our puppet programs were very effective in almost every culture and environment, we were still having to wonder about, *What happens when we leave?*

Yes, we'd made an impact while we were there. Hundreds, perhaps thousands of kids were helped or would eventually be helped by those whom Kids Around the World trained and left behind to minister to others. Even among those youngsters, adult family members were also affected by our presence and programs—but still we wondered, *What happens next?*

The answer didn't evolve all at once. We began to notice little things that were effective. When we went to places where the kids didn't understand English, we used native Christians who acted as our translators. We had them translate the stories we used with the puppets, or we made tape recordings of the stories in the language of the youngsters and played them on a portable sound system, and the kids responded.

We noticed that the translators pointed out situations in the puppet programs that were "too American" in our approach to their culture, or worse, situations that were something totally alien to their understanding or language. To get around those glitches, we saw that the translators were smart enough to improvise ways to make our stories *culturally relevant*. They didn't change the meaning or content of our stories—they simply adapted them for the audience.

Wow! Our eyes were opened. There in our midst—in Africa, Bosnia, Cuba, Vietnam, Ukraine, Bolivia, or India—there were these innovative Christians, and usually they were Christian *leaders*. The pastors had their hands full and couldn't always be available to tell stories to the children. I compared these pastors to America's early circuit riders, who cared for a number of congregations across a wide distance—that's why they (and modern "circuit riders") were too busy to minister to the kids.

In "frontier" America, since most kids in our then-primitive lands were schooled by their mothers in religion, moral principles and traditions were a part of that education. It wasn't until our modern era—at least in America—that church leaders began to notice the need for Christian education and training for children.

However, Christian leaders overseas weren't always copying American trends regarding Christian education—they were already using Orality. Overseas there are different kinds of needs, and native schoolteachers or Sunday school teachers were already finding ways to communicate the gospel to the "kids around the world" who lived in their villages. They did it mostly by storytelling.

Out of that observation, a God-inspired insight came to us: the idea of training these eager "evangelists" with a way we could help equip them for storytelling—their mission of teaching others about Jesus.

That idea? *Flannelgraphs.*

If you're old enough to remember how Flannelgraphs work, you also probably think that in this high-tech age, Flannelgraphs should've been tossed onto the trash heap of history now that they've outlived their usefulness by forty or fifty years. People who recall Flannelgraphs also seem to remember them as an archaic method to communicate with people. That's especially true with a generation that has access to every conceivable audio-video device known to mankind—ranging from DVDs, CDs, iPods, MP3s, YouTube, and other electronic platforms. But in an overseas setting, these devices are not even on the radar of a New Guinea tribal culture—or one in Indonesia's jungles, or in the Amazon rain forest. Modern electronic communicating conveniences don't always work overseas.

When we talk to people about using Flannelgraphs in evangelism, the results are mixed—those who are too polite to pooh-pooh our idea of using an old-fashioned storytelling device simply change the subject. Those who still think using Flannelgraphs is a dumb idea remind us that something as antiquated as Flannelgraphs is certainly not as cool as modern methods we described above—like high-tech video, projection equipment, and other devices including iPods, iPhones, and iPads.

It was almost like the movie *Back to the Future,* which featured a DeLorean automobile as a time machine to travel back and forth in time. Michael Fox starred as the protagonist in the movie who first went back in time to his parents' high school days—when, of course, he hadn't yet been born.

The audience laughed when Fox ran into "old fashioned" implements and devices, and at how he overcame the lack of his trusty modern conveniences by cobbling together implements of the 1950s to help him "invent" a modern skateboard and get out of a jam and somehow get "back to the future."

Well, let me take you *back to the past*—in the 1940s and 1950s—when Flannelgraphs were used in almost every church and Sunday school. Flannelgraphs also got notoriety, of all places, in the comic strip panel of Charles Schulz and his *Peanuts* gang. You might recall that ongoing story line about Linus and his blanket. Several of the *Peanuts* characters try to think of ways to "wean" Linus from his dependency on it. Snoopy even snags it right out of Linus' hands at times. In one famous strip, Lucy sneaks Linus' blanket away from him and buries it in the backyard. Another time, to Linus' horror, she makes "Flannelgraph" cutouts from his blanket.

If you were born after 1960—after Sunday school and elementary teachers stopped using Flannelgraphs—you probably don't even know what they are. Think of it as an illustrated PowerPoint presentation, but without a computer and software.

Flannelgraph was a popular medium for telling Bible stories to young kids in Sunday school classes or churches because it was relatively inexpensive and easy to use. (Radio stations dramatized daily children's stories—something like television cartoons without pictures, just audio.)

Flannelgraph stories were the prime storytelling method used for Sunday school and elementary-level Christian education in the '40s and '50s; it provided a more vivid *alternative* to storytelling *without visual illustration.*[1] Teachers provided the narrative and used the visual pieces to tell the story. But by using a narrative story accompanied by the visual pieces, the memory level is improved by 70 percent.

The Flannelgraph background board was generally rectangular and rested on an easel. The teacher used cutouts of people, animals, and objects to draw the audience (usually kids) into a story that communicated visually and orally to these listeners.[2] Flannelgraphs were used very effectively by Child Evangelism Fellowship to share the gospel with youngsters for many years.

We weren't thinking of American audiences when the idea of Flannelgraphs came to us. For the past couple generations, Flannelgraphs hadn't even had much use in America. With the introduction of more animated visual devices—first, portable record players and tape recorders, and later, VCRs, DVDs, and computer-generated clips from YouTube—Flannelgraphs became passé.

Our thoughts were focused on the children of poverty living overseas and lacking what Americans might call "basic needs" that humans can't live without—electricity, television sets, computers, and other high-tech devices that we take for granted.

Even if a child in a remote village in India, Ghana, or rural Kenya *did* have a DVD player and a well-produced program created with high production values on a DVD disk, the overseas youngster may not know how to use it—for starters. Even if by chance the child or parent figured out a way to make it work, there'd still be the problem of a TV monitor to view it—and you'd also have the problem of no electricity to power it.

"Aha, portable DVD players with LCD screens operate on batteries," someone says, thinking that ends the discussion. It doesn't.

Batteries hardly last beyond a couple showings. So then the question is: how to recharge or replace them?

Someone who's never been to rural Africa, India, and other third-world places probably never gives a thought to these rather typical situational problems and difficulties. In Western countries the problems of electricity or batteries, and equipment, can readily be solved. Yet, as Dr. Willis and other pioneers in the Orality movement have suggested, *two-thirds of the world's people face this kind of dilemma*. So what's the answer? *How do we communicate?*

It's the same dilemma that the apostle Paul expressed in Romans 10:14 (ASV): "How then shall they call on him in whom they have not believed? and how shall they believe in him whom they have not heard? and how shall they hear without a preacher?"

That's the real problem. How can those four billion people who know nothing about Jesus believe in Him if they can't *"hear"* the gospel communicated to them by a "preacher" who speaks their language and knows their culture?

A curious thing happened as we were doing some testing of the Kids Around the World Flannelgraph programs. We discovered there were local "preachers" who had learned Bible stories from missionaries or other Christians, who were in these far-flung areas of the world where people couldn't understand anything we Americans might say to them—at least without a translator.

We saw some of those local believers—a dedicated handful—who were enthusiastic about telling their friends and neighbors about the gospel. It had changed their lives and behavior, and they eagerly wanted to share this good news with their family, friends, and neighbors. These local people, without professional training or schooling, went out among their people, a few at a time, and simply followed Jesus' plain command recorded in

Mark 16:15: "Go into all the world and preach the Good News to everyone" (NLT).

These local believers found audiences that would listen to them. As the people *heard,* many understood the gospel, and some even made decisions to be a "Jesus follower."

We began to seek out these "storytellers" and watch them at work. Then we provided them with Flannelgraph sets that helped them tell their memorized stories from the New Testament accounts of Jesus' life, death, and resurrection. The more they used the Flannelgraphs, the more effective their presentations were.

We were sincerely touched by their devotion and commitment to their calling—as "preachers" who ministered without a secondary school or college education, let alone a seminary degree. Yet everywhere we went we found these people—and we looked for ways to help and encourage them, and to train them and multiply their effectiveness.

Someone told me recently, "Kids Around the World has created a means, through simple theater, to reach kids for Christ." In chapter one of this book I mentioned that we've already trained some eighteen thousand of these teacher-preachers all around the world. Some knew English, and they learned from our puppet teams—or from Jim Rosene, Chris Marshall, Mike Young, and others from our leadership—*how to train other teachers*. Once the initial teachers are trained and given Flannelgraph sets as tools, they eagerly go out to capture the interest of kids *and adults* in the audience, who listen attentively and become new believers or grow in their faith. In this process, the storytellers of the Flannelgraph presentations are mentored and trained—and then they go out to replicate themselves through other storytellers.

Those people memorize the Bible through the stories and share the same truth as from the published, literate Bibles. I'm constantly impressed by their memorization skills. Most in the West learn by literate means—while most of the world learns from visual-oral traditions and history.

Our Flannelgraph stories—ignored or ridiculed as "low-tech dinosaur methods" by most contemporary churches—are being reconsidered. Kids Around the World uses them dramatically—as was also pointed out earlier in our book. Each of the more than eighteen thousand teachers who have been trained are now making Flannelgraph presentations to audiences averaging thirty to fifty kids and/or adults—*every week!* That means more than *three million* children a year have been reached so far! That number is growing week by week as we train new teachers and preachers and supply them with Flannelgraphs, and as those that we train begin to train others—and share the Flannelgraph sets. Reaching a million kids a week can quickly double, or triple, as this happens.

Something occurred in 1993 that opened the door for greater effectiveness. Evie and I had taken a portable film projector and a 16mm print of the JESUS motion picture to Ukraine and showed it there to audiences who watched it—listening to the story with their own language dubbed onto the sound track. Then we did the same thing in Lira, Uganda, with Doug Hansen, my nephew, who as a civil engineer helps Food for the Poor get clean water.

Those people were open to its message, and the local pastors and evangelical leaders used the film as a means of communicating the gospel story, building on the framework of the JESUS film—which is a "super" storytelling method. We'd used that film in other countries, with the same response.

Yet in every one of those places, Christian leaders were looking for a means of follow-up with those who responded to the JESUS film and needed to grow in their newfound faith. Then I recalled the success of teachers we had trained overseas, using our Flannelgraph Bible stories.

One day, Dan Arnold, who was active with Campus Crusade's program History's Handful, met us for lunch. He talked about the fantastic effectiveness of the JESUS film, and I reported on our success with Flannelgraphs. A strategic idea came out of that luncheon: Why not *combine* the two ideas?

However, exploring the concept was like inventing the Flannelgraph process from scratch since its introduction more than a half-century earlier.

To make the Flannelgraph set colorful, with the characters and scenery permanently affixed to flannel, we'd need to find the best equipment to make them. I flew to England to check out quite a few machines to manufacture the Flannelgraph materials and make the artwork. My trip also took me to Italy, where I found exactly what we needed.

Jim and I set up a meeting with a longtime friend, Steve Douglass, president of Campus Crusade for Christ, and pitched him an idea for a ministry partnership. We learned that Campus Crusade had bought the rights to the JESUS film and that the final details of the contract were being worked out.

I said, "Steve, we've developed some Bible stories for our Flannelgraph programs, and we've had a great response to them. We'd like to create a series of Bible stories using the characters and stories that are portrayed in the JESUS film. That way, we can follow up the film showings with Flannelgraph stories told by teachers who are experienced, and they'll teach the Bible to the people who've seen the JESUS film, and they can reinforce the powerful impact of the JESUS film by telling audiences more stories about Jesus. I believe it can be a whole new method of evangelism."

Steve was enthusiastic, and after Campus Crusade had the necessary rights to the JESUS film, we commissioned an artist to create characters based on those in the film. We created forty-six Flannelgraph episodes from the JESUS film and put them into use right away. They turned out to be very effective—not only as follow-up to the JESUS film, but in places where the film *hasn't* been shown, as a stand-alone product that's visibly and effectively changing lives. Paul Eshelman and Jim Green gave their support to the partnership, and now it was time to get to work. The machine from Italy was delivered, along with huge rolls of clean white felt, and a work space was set up at the Kids Around the World facilities for volunteers to come and do the manufacturing work.

Our basic concern is how to produce enough Flannelgraph sets for the JESUS film stories and get them to the continuing list of trained teachers that we're recruiting. Sometimes the teachers in the same area have to double up in using the Flannelgraph sets—and sometimes even have to share with three or four other teachers vying for their use.

With the best equipment and materials, and the volunteer workers to make the components for each of the Flannelgraph sets, the Flannelgraphs were manufactured. Other local volunteers come in to affix the printed backgrounds—using dye sublimation inks that are used in printing patterns on shirts, blouses, and other material—on the felt background sheets, a process that makes use of pressure and heat. Then the volunteers prepare the cutout pieces, fold the sheets and assemble the sets and easels, add scissors and an instruction booklet showing what pictures go with what story, and finally package everything into a carrying case—after which they're shipped overseas. Unfortunately, demand has exceeded our budget, and we're not able to keep up with the requests for the Flannelgraphs featuring JESUS film story kits.

It's truly a good feeling when we return to various overseas sites where we've been before and see our Flannelgraph sets being used by local teachers who are also skilled storytellers, communicating the Bible stories that are changing lives all around the world.

Of course, not everyone is a natural storyteller, and that's where new organizations like the International Orality Network (ION) can help. The ION group offers training and seminars for ministry leaders and new church planners to help them learn how to tell a story effectively and in an engaging manner. Jim Rosene, president of Kids Around the World, is a member of ION, and Jim and I, along with Jim Hessenthaler, Chris Marshall, and Paul Bierhaus, participated in the Lausanne Congress forum that took place in October 2010 in Cape Town, South Africa.

The idea of storytelling as evangelism is no longer a novel idea. Storytelling is a natural and powerful method for reaching kids. It has been proven effective everywhere it's been tried.

Chapter Eleven

STORYTELLING AS EVANGELISM

One of my friends gave me an article written by Michael Cassidy that takes off on the chapter title above and gives an added dimension to the idea of storytelling as a means of evangelism.

Dr. Michael Cassidy is from Johannesburg, South Africa, and he founded a mission work there in 1962, when South Africa was still troubled by apartheid. His work, Africa Enterprise, gave Michael recognition in the United States, when he came to Fuller Seminary in Pasadena, California, for a divinity degree.

He's been active in helping end apartheid and in bringing peace in South Africa. He worked with then-president Nelson Mandela, who asked him to spearhead Project Ukuthula, an extensive and successful peace initiative in KwaZulu-Natal leading up to the province's local government elections.

Michael is also a radio broadcaster in South Africa and a prolific author. He's an accomplished communicator and has written an article on how to use a personal testimony and storytelling as a highly relevant method to communicate the gospel of Jesus Christ, and his ideas are pertinent to what I've discovered as well. One of the ideas he shared was based on a story told by the apostle Paul: "Paul used his own personal story … in Acts 24 when he was before Felix and then in Acts 25 and 26 when he was before Festus and Agrippa."

Dr. Cassidy believes in storytelling as a means of effective communication to people who are among those to whom we direct our efforts of evangelism. He says, "It is simply reintroducing the notion of story, a testimony and biography into your preaching, teaching, writing and personal witness."[1]

He also suggests that in these postmodern times, when people are more interested in demonstration than debate, and when they resist the dogmatic, one-sided arguments but are open to the personal expressions of what God has done for us, that, "We must reinvestigate the place of story in our ministries generally and in our evangelism specifically."[2]

His comments remind me of a friend I met a number of years ago when he came to our city to hold a series of evangelism meetings. Dr. Ford, a prominent speaker, author, and evangelist (and brother-in-law to Billy Graham), is another practitioner of these ideas. We also met Leighton Ford in Albania. In his book *The Power of Story,* Leighton Ford adds to Michael Cassidy's thoughts:

> Conversion, in a true sense, is a collision of narratives. God's Story touches my story and your story, and a collision takes place. People encounter the stories that call their own [personal] stories into question, and they are forced to consider: *What if my story isn't the whole story?* …
>
> In the process of reconsidering their own lives, they become caught up in the Story of Jesus, and they are *changed*.…
>
> This is a book with a very simple theme, a very basic strategy. It is written to encourage the average layperson to tell his or her story, and in the process, to help spread the Story of God. This is a book for the person who says, "I want to be a more effective witness.…"
>
> If you have become a part of the Story of God, then you have a story to share with the people around you. They are eager to hear it. They are *dying* to hear it.[3]

Dr. Cassidy seems to add to that review by Leighton Ford. He says, "People love stories, whether they are seeing them in movies, TV or the theatre. Everyone loves a story. Even little children say endlessly: 'Tell me a story.' … One finds the Scriptures endlessly laced and jam-packed with stories.… Embedded in them are profound theological truths and lessons, and very often directly the evangelistic content of the Gospel."[4]

Michael Cassidy and Leighton Ford have both eloquently defined how communication skills and strategies can make us more effective in reaching other people, and they both separately point to Jesus as the Master Storyteller.

I'm constantly reminded of this. I think of instances where Jesus presented someone with a story or parable. He was at home in any situation. Jesus used His mind and personality to bring to an audience the very thing that would have the greatest impact upon each listener. He customized His presentation for His audience. To the woman He met at the well, He spoke directly—even bluntly, without sugarcoating facts as He knew them—a surprising tactic that startled the woman … but suddenly Jesus had her attention. That direct approach got past her defenses.

To the learned leaders at the synagogue Jesus not only read the Scriptures from the Torah, He interpreted them in their presence. That unexpected approach may have felt unseemly to the highly educated biblical scholars and other teachers—but again, certainly Jesus must have had their attention.

When the woman caught in the act of adultery was brought before Jesus, He said to those in the crowd, "If any one of you is without sin, let him be the first to throw a stone at her" (John 8:7). The Bible says that they all left the scene without acting on their previous impulse, perhaps getting out of there before Jesus exposed them and the sin in their own lives. Don't you suppose He also truly had *their* attention?

The Gospels tell us that when Jesus spoke to the crowds on the hillside, there were many instances when great crowds sat before Him, listening. The Scriptures also tell us that they were so attentive that they stayed—even though they hadn't eaten. (Good thing Jesus and a little boy with some buns and fish were there to create a miracle—so the crowd could stay and listen to more of what Jesus had for them to hear.)

The story of the miracle of feeding the huge crowd with meager food is still repeated today—over and over—because miracles are stories to be told for generations. Jesus as the Master Storyteller crosses the bridge from the written to the spoken word effortlessly. You can count on the written Scriptures to have an impact on its readers. But for people who couldn't read, Jesus could tell His listeners, "The Scriptures say …"—and He'd recite from the Torah, and then He'd add, "But *I* say unto you …"

Can't you visualize the people sitting there on the hillside, attentively hearing Him recite the Word—and then He pauses, looks at them, making eye contact with many gazing in His direction—and the crowd hears Him say, "Listen … let me tell you a parable. A man had two sons.…"

By telling a brief, emotional story with drama and elements with which every listener could identify, Jesus had their attention from the start. What person, what family—in that first century as well as our present-day time—hasn't known of a "prodigal son" who went the wrong way in life? I think most of them probably identified with the older brother and were shocked when Jesus got to the part of the story about the father who—instead of turning his wayward son away—forgives the youth and showers him with blessings because the young man had repented, come home, and asked for his father's forgiveness.

For many of us who have identified with that elder brother in that parable, the father's preference for the wayward brother had to sting. There was a message for everyone who heard Jesus tell the story of the prodigal son—a story that still resonates today. In fact it's a story that has been retold by writers, speakers, and filmmakers in countless dramatic styles—from Charles Dickens, Oscar Wilde, and T. S. Eliot to modern storytelling venues such as motion pictures, novels, and YouTube clips.

The four Gospels in the New Testament are usually thought of as a biography of Jesus, since within each of the Gospels, we see His life story portrayed. However I like to think of it more as an *autobiography*—for in the narratives we can "hear" firsthand the stories and parables that Jesus shared with His first-century contemporaries. There are allegories and metaphors in Jesus' stories and parables that help us to identify with those whom He described.

Those stories, even today when we read about His encounters in the New Testament, stop us and hold our attention—two thousand years after Jesus told them. His stories *still* have great power, resonance, and persuasion.

"Talking about having the right spiritual foundations in life, Jesus tells a story of two men, one who built his house on sand, and the other on rock. Neither the story nor the point of the story can ever be forgotten," says Michael Cassidy, who offers another example: "Showing how people have different responses to the preaching of the Word, He tells the story of 'a sower who went forth to sow …' and whose seed fell on four different types of soil. This story is really more about the seeds and the soils than the sower, but the import of the parable, only a few words in length, has ricocheted profoundly down the corridors of time."[5]

I believe that these examples are there to let us know that we can share Jesus' stories with those in our contemporary society and watch, as the power of this timeless storytelling is applicable to anyone and everyone living in our modern times. We can also paraphrase them, personalize them, add other examples from our lives or from Scripture. These "customized" *real* stories, borne out of our own lives and experiences, can change the lives of others.

"If communicating with children," Samuel Chiang noted in an email to me, "it's important to include what kids love: the themes of music and songs in the heart language of the culture."

That's good advice for so-called "postmodern" times. People shy away from conversations that turn into arguments. Yet they'll listen attentively and politely to personal stories that demonstrate a changed life. They don't want preaching or dogma, but they hunger for stories that resonate with truth—stories that are personal and that convince them that what you have is what they're seeking.

Chapter Twelve

START AT THE BEGINNING— WITH CHILDREN

A train came barreling down the tracks, and my wife, Evie, and I were in our car, just behind a few other autos waiting for the train to pass. About 120 railroad cars passed through the crossing, and something seemed wrong. I told Evie, "That train seems to be going too fast."

The train finally passed, and the crossing arms were raised and we crossed the tracks. The Dixie Highway ran parallel to the tracks, and I had a sudden impulse to take the highway and follow the train. I caught up to it, and we proceeded north, parallel to the train.

Not long afterward, I was driving opposite the engine pulling the long train, and I said to Evie, "It looks like he's slowing down." Sure enough, the engineer had not only slowed—the train was coming to a stop.

After what seemed to me that the train was going too fast—it was *slowing,* and it came to a dead stop. I told Evie, "The train must have hit something or someone near that crossing."

We drove up next to the engine and turned into a nearby parking lot. I found myself looking at a vacant engine cab. No engineer or conductor in sight. However, a fire truck arrived quickly, then an ambulance and police squad cars.

To me it looked as though the train had certainly struck something at the crossing.

Nothing appeared to be hit on this side of the track. So I turned around and drove back toward that intersection to see if someone or something had been struck. Now I was really curious—but saw nothing.

I had a police scanner in the car and turned it on to listen for what was happening. As I tuned the radio scanner, I was drawn to a conversation that must have been taking place. I heard what appeared to be the voices of the train engineer and the conductor—apparently talking to each other and a police dispatcher.

"One of the bearings on a wheel must have seized. We found out which wheel it was, 'cause it was red hot and glowing …" one of the railroad men reported on the radio. "It was so hot that it spewed molten steel from the wheel box."

We listened to the police scanner as the other railroad man's voice explained their dilemma. "The railroad has a special detection device, located about every twenty miles alongside the rails. That monitor had picked up the fact that a wheel was giving off heat and potentially would freeze the rotation of the heavy wheel and cause the train to derail. A signal was sent to the engineer, and soon he saw the warning on his instrument panel."

Another voice came on the line. "Yeah, I'm the engineer. When I saw that warning light, I immediately hit the brakes, but this is a very long train. It took me a long time to slow it down."

"Good work," said a third voice, whom I guessed was the police dispatcher. He added, "It's a good thing you acted quickly. If you'd *waited* to take action—it'd be a disaster."

The conversation continued between the train engineer, conductor, and police. The conductor spoke up with some urgency in his voice. "There's only one track, and we're stalled on it. If we tried to remove and change the wheel here, it'd cause many other trains scheduled to pass this way to be delayed—and that includes both passenger trains and mail and freight cars. The next siding is up ahead, about three and a half miles. We were wondering if the wheel would stay on the car if we kept moving—but very slowly."

The men discussed the options—stay on the tracks and block the other trains and create a real mess, or limp along for several more miles to the siding.

The conductor—who usually rode in the rear car or engine of the train—decided that he'd walk alongside the train and watch the broken wheel. He could alert the engineer by radio if anything was about to happen. "We'll have to go slow, and baby that wheel. We don't want it to fall off or seize up. It'd cause that heavy load of limestone the car is carrying to get dumped on the spot—perhaps getting people hurt."

The conductor added his own concern: "We don't want that to happen, but I certainly don't want the conductor to put his own life at risk."

By now it was pitch dark, but within minutes, the train started up and moved ever so slowly down the tracks. Red hot metal was still flowing from the bearing box as the railroad car with the wheel problem passed by our vantage point in our car. We saw the conductor walking alongside and talking to the engineer on a small radio.

Evie and I watched and followed the train for nearly four miles as the conductor walked beside the damaged train, making sure things wouldn't get worse and derail the train.

We watched the train slowly edge itself onto the siding and shift from the main track to the one where they could safely make a wheel change. Evie and I talked about the incident as we continued our drive back home. We thought, *Our lives are like that—and so are the lives of our kids. There are times when we have to slow down and get onto a siding to care for the problems.*

We thought about our kids, racing down the track at one minute, full of life, full steam ahead—and along their way, God has placed a mom and a dad as engineers to steer them down the right tracks and see that they get to their intended destination. God also places grandparents—just like the warning posts every twenty miles along the track. The warnings alert the engineer and conductor: "Stop! Something's wrong. You're in danger of going off the track."

Faithful friends, Sunday school teachers, or Dad/Mom then walk alongside the youngster—until he or she can reach a siding, get their bearings, repair the damage, and make things right again—to get them back on the right track spiritually.

There's another story about a train, much like the one I just described.

A terrific rain had drenched our city. The creeks were fast filling up, the streets were already flooded, and many were too deep to permit cars to go through.

Evie and I were driving near Stockholm Inn on Charles Street when we heard the police scanner send out a message, saying that a call had just come in that there was debris and floodwater on a major railroad track.

We suddenly heard a train whistle in the distance. I told Evie, "That train's gonna run into the stuff on the track. If it does, it could cause a terrible wreck." We wondered if anyone had tried to contact the engineer.

We drove under the viaduct and approached the railroad crossing. The gates were down, and we were the third car back from the crossing. I watched the train rush down the track, as the *clickity-clack* of the steel wheels on iron tracks supported the railroad cars.

Then I saw the kind of railroad cars they were, and the hair on the back of my neck stood up—it was an endless train of tank cars with long, round black cylinders with the word *ethanol* stenciled on the sides. I thought to myself, *If this train gets derailed by debris on the tracks, who knows what kind of disaster that could cause!*

After the train passed, we headed for the nearest street that paralleled the tracks, attempting to follow the train. Within a few minutes we heard a message come over the police scanner: "Check out a report of a large explosion at Mulford Road near the railroad tracks south of Harrison. Could be a train ran into debris and the floodwaters on the tracks and derailed."

It turns out that that was exactly what happened.

A moment later we saw a huge explosion. Intense flames towered into the sky. Thick, black smoke boiled up through the pouring rain. Cars, filled with people waiting for the train to pass, emptied as the passengers poured out of their vehicles to run in the opposite direction of the explosion.

As we approached we could see people were running, crying, screaming, and struggling to get away from the fiery inferno. The flames were so hot that they melted the front of a nearby fire truck. By now the column of fire reached a mile high, and a fireball roared out half a mile in all directions.

This tragedy could have been averted. All it would've taken is for someone to radio the train's engineer. Yet no signal ever came through to the train's console. The engineer got no warning of debris and rising floodwaters alongside and on the track.

So as the train passed through the three feet of water, the bottoms of the volatile ethanol tanks were lifted on top of the water and began to float inches above where the wheels kept them on the tracks.

The deadly tank cars, flying and bouncing like torpedoes in the surf, began to lift off the tracks and strike one another. Sparks flew and set off the monstrous explosion, right at the crossing where cars had waited to pass. Some made it out of their cars and ran toward higher ground. Some were frozen in fear and could not run away. They were caught by the flames and were burned.

In the story of the first train, the company had placed devices to warn the engineer of danger ahead, and the train stopped. The conductor personally took the time to walk alongside the train until it reached the siding where the damage could be safely fixed, and no one was hurt.

The second train never got a warning. There was no way it could stop and avert the disaster that occurred—and things turned into a disaster in which people died.

There's a strong analogy there. Without a warning a young person can go off the track of life and crash. Without a warning of an impending "train wreck," we can't help them.

Sometimes it's a faithful Sunday school teacher who teaches a lesson, who tells a story, who encourages the child—like the conductor of the train that's in trouble (or the child). The warning detectors might be Mom, Dad, or a friend. They generally provide the warnings—like conductors who are willing to walk for miles to prevent disaster—to keep their charge from going off the track and crashing.

The Bible is full of admonitions and stories about life and warnings to avert danger. One thing that my wife, Evie, and I have noticed with our grandkids is that they're always willing and eager to listen to such stories (and we're just as willing and eager to *provide* the stories being told).

Interestingly, kids don't all listen in the same way. Perceptions of the story come to boys and girls differently, perhaps because of the right-brain, left-brain distinctions between boys and girls. Generally, people who rely more heavily on the right half of their brain tend to be more imaginative. They often have creative or artistic ability—like singing, painting, and writing.

I recall reading somewhere that left-brain–dominated people are quite opposite in the way they think from right-brain–dominated people. Left-brain–dominated people tend to be more logical and analytical, and they usually excel at math and word skills.

Yet this doesn't mean that a person who is left- or right-brain–dominated doesn't use the *other* part of their brain. For most of us, *both parts* of the brain work nicely together and enable us to function as well-rounded personalities.

Teachers learn to recognize these differences in smaller children. Generally, they notice that girls listen quietly to a story, while boys are more animated and might want to help the storyteller with physical actions or sound effects that are connected with the story—like arm and hand motions or vocal responses that accent points of the story.

There seems to be better retention in a storytelling than in a setting where a teacher or leader simply reads passively to their audience to get a point across. In storytelling, retention rises above that of reading from a book or outline, and it rises even more when visual pictures or other colorful objects are a part of the storytelling. As with Jesus' storytelling—He always got their attention.

Training of teachers is very important. When Kids Around the World conducts teacher training, our people take the time to let each teacher make a presentation while others watch. Then, others give the same lesson while the previous presenter watches. Everyone gets a chance to both see and hear—and that helps them judge for themselves what elements make a story come alive. Practicing them over and over helps the teachers become more confident and better communicators.

I think that these are important points. What we learned overseas in the training of teachers can be imported back here to churches within the United States: The key to making Sunday schools *interesting* for those *age ten and under* is a well-trained, well-equipped teacher who has an ability to be a visual-oral teacher—a storyteller.

Samuel Chiang observed, "In the overarching theme of storytelling, telling and retelling the story is something the kids already do! This subtle theme goes beyond just teachers; it goes into the next generation and the next generation, and the multiplicative effect is enormous."[1]

On the other side of the equation, I've seen dozens of statistics that indicate that if a child is bored at age ten in church or Sunday school, then by age thirteen, he or she will choose to drop out and leave the church. That means there's an urgency to reach kids *before boredom sets in* and causes them to veer off in another direction.

Scientists explain that beginning at age two, a child's brain begins to develop greater numbers of brain cells, a process that continues until the child is about ten years old. That also means there's a capacity for more brain activity and that young children are eager for an *expansion* of learning—new languages, math, art, music, experimentation, and even physical challenges of sports, outdoor life, or other kinds of learning that, to youngsters, sound more like play than learning. They also *remember* those stories being told!

Someone sent me an email clipping reporting that researchers at a school of medicine discovered that when children are deprived of a stimulating environment, the child's brain suffers. Kids who don't play much or are rarely touched develop brains 20 to 30 percent smaller than normal. Rich experiences, on the other hand, produce rich brains.[2]

The new insights into brain development are more than just interesting science. They have profound implications for parents and policy makers. In an age when mothers and fathers are increasingly pressed for time—and may already be feeling guilty about how many hours they spend away from their children—the results coming out of the labs are likely to increase concerns about leaving very young children in the care of others.

What lessons can be drawn from the new findings? Among other things, it's clear that foreign languages should be taught in elementary school, if not before. Remedial education may be more effective at the age of three or four than nine or ten. Each week in the US alone, some seventy-seven thousand newborns begin the miraculous process of wiring their brains for a lifetime of learning.[3] If parents and policy makers don't pay attention to the conditions under which this delicate process takes place, we will all suffer the consequences. The studies also say that physical exercise is important during this brain growth during early childhood.

Curiously, even the brains of such little children are mature enough to grasp basic philosophical and theological truths that guide conscious behavior, fidelity, and even faith in God and Jesus. When a little child sings, *Jesus loves me, this I know, for the Bible tells me so,* I'm genuinely touched. I'm amazed at the power of the gospel that's already in the life of that little one. Planted in his or her brain are timeless truths that—I hope for the rest of that child's life—will always remind him or her of that powerful statement of simple biblical truth: *Jesus loves me.*

All this has spiritual implications. Scientists and researchers discovered that a child's play time was critical in bringing happiness and perpetuating enjoyment of life when all these criteria are nurtured in the child's early years. There's a catch, however. The opposite was found in the lives of those who were raised in a *depressed* environment.

Parents and teachers can create the settings to nurture good child development—including child care in church and Sunday schools, by using the tools of learning, singing, repetition of words and phrases, and teaching melody—because all this research confirms that even young kids can learn a great deal. But of course, the flip side occurs when uncaring or thoughtless parents and teachers—instead of being cautious and protective "engineers" and "conductors" that are always seeking to avoid a "train wreck"—are in reality causing one instead. It doesn't take much to do the right thing to bring about future dividends for the kids.

A child under a year old and up to age two can learn by the repetition of melody lines—short, simple verses sung by parents or teachers. Researchers say that the potential for greatness may be encoded in the genes, but whether that potential is ever realized in later life—as a gift for mathematics, say, or a deviant criminal mind—depends on patterns etched by experiences in those critical early years by those who have the care of teaching them.[4]

This biblical pattern of "training up our children in the way of the Lord" is not new—it's been a part of humanity's history since Adam and Eve. It seems to me that what makes parental teaching of scriptural precepts unique today is the fact that it's still the most effective way of training children despite the universality of other systems and ideologies across the world.

Other systems—ranging from teaching by modern secularist/atheist educators to brainwashing by Communists, despotic dictators, or militant Islamists (many of whom kidnap boys and train them to be children soldiers and suicide bombers)—have their own "moral" imperatives for teaching their youthful charges. As a result, people must carefully evaluate these other "systems" and choose whether these other systems or the biblical pattern of the Golden Rule is the right one. Most people—even nonreligious ones—would likely agree that the precepts that Jesus taught were the right ones.

Parents, teachers, and grandparents are in positions to keep kids on the right track and protect them from life's train wrecks. I for one want to make sure that I'm giving priority to that directive.

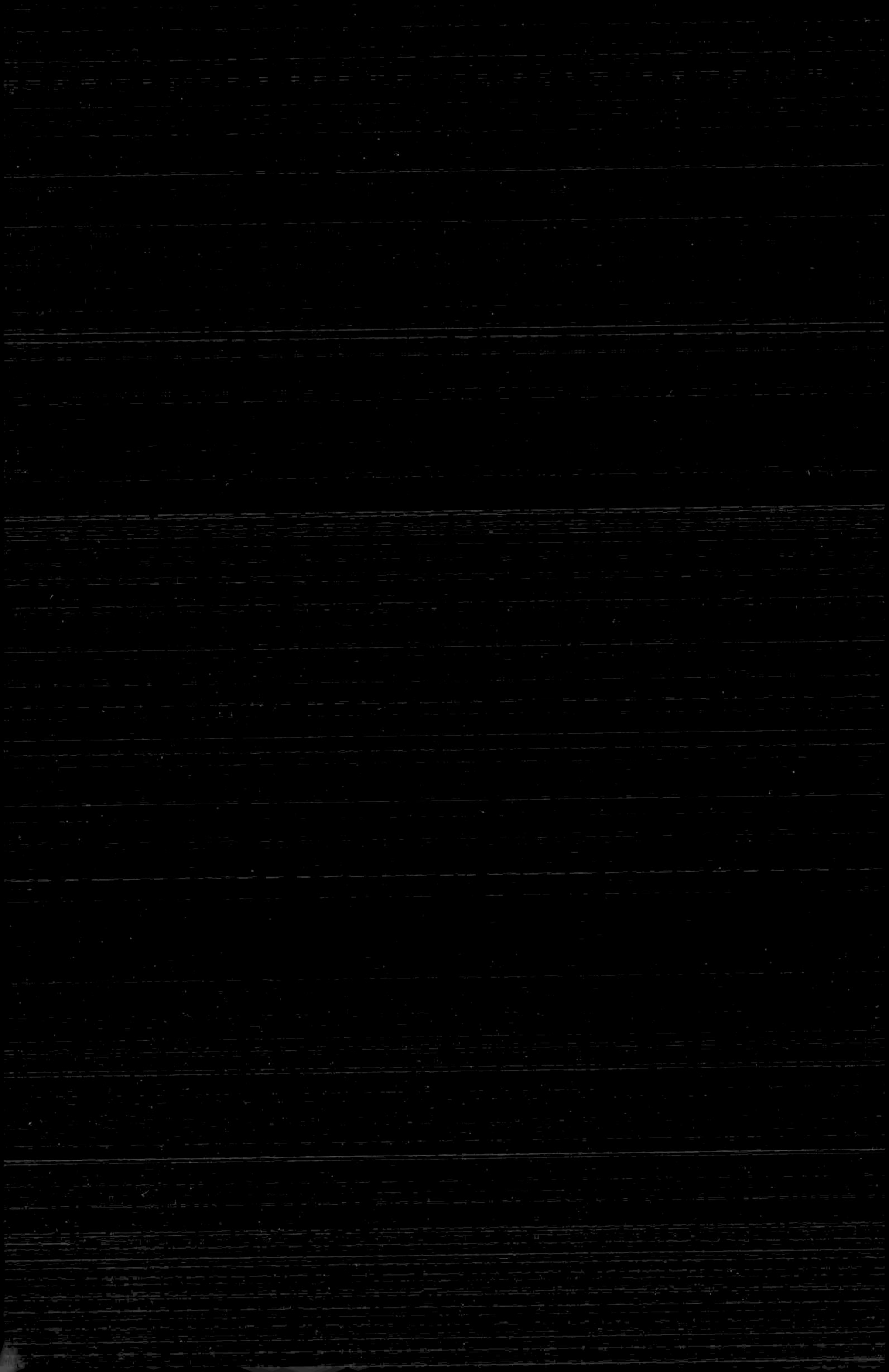

2/3

of the

WORLD

can't read

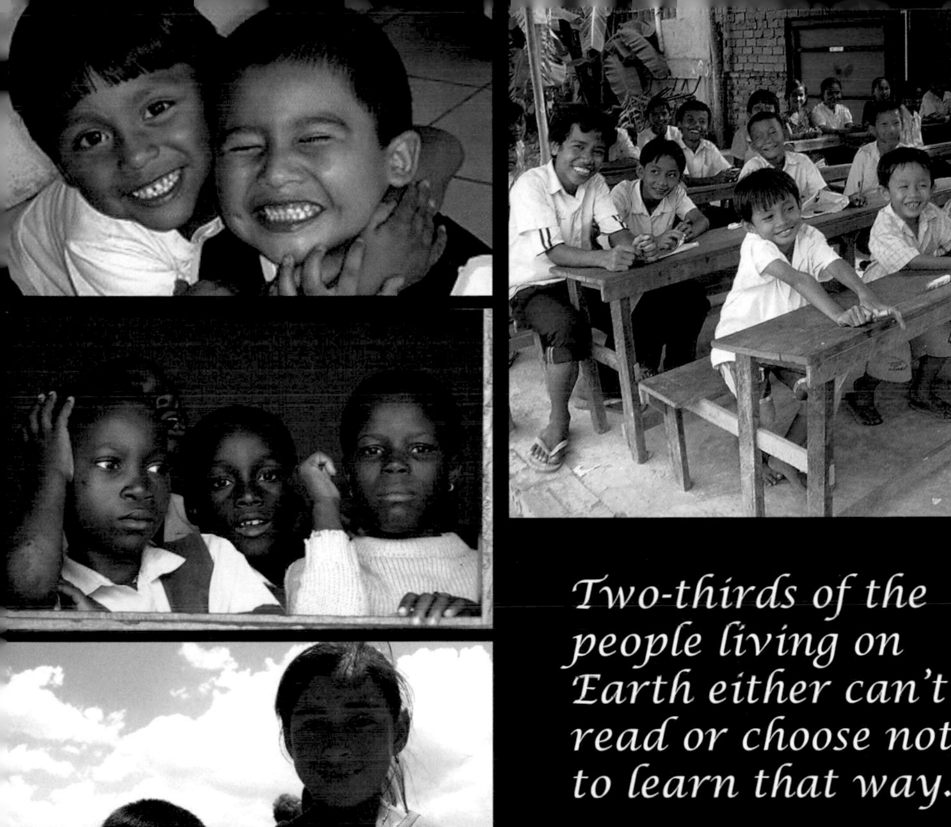

Two-thirds of the people living on Earth either can't read or choose not to learn that way.

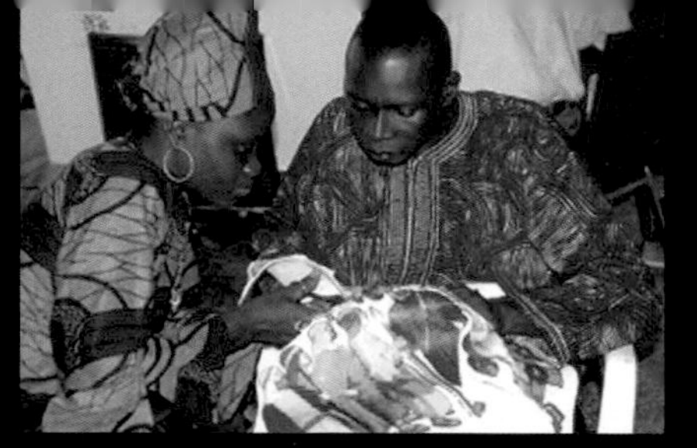

equals

Orality, or storytelling, is the best way to reach kids.

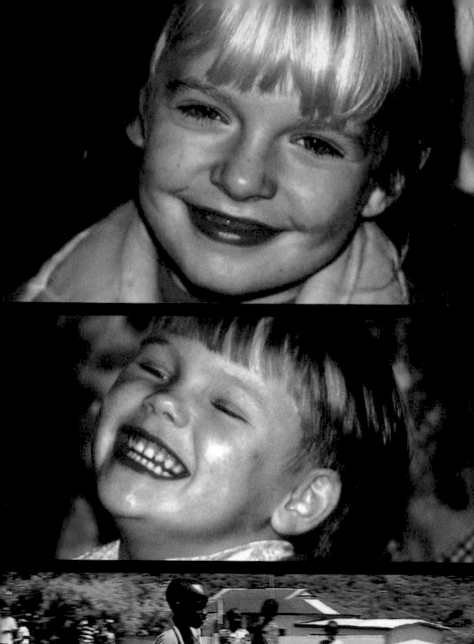

Storytelling is the way that most of the world learns.

STORIES

and songs

WHY?

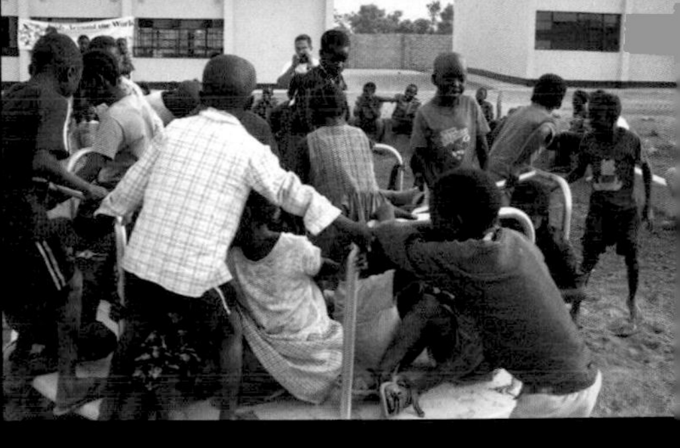

Why is it so important that we understand Orality and use it more?

WHO?

Who is doing the job of reaching kids?

Kids Around
The World uses
orality to reach
and disciple
children.

ORALITY

is a

STRATEGY

Churches seldom invest enough resources into children's ministry whether in the U.S. or abroad.

churches must

INVEST

in children

if you

BUILD IT

they will

COME

Building playgrounds is a non-threatening way to break the ice in other cultures and open doors of opportunity.

KIDS

need to

FEEL

they belong

Many churches do not understand the importance and value of belonging.

WHAT *is heaven* LIKE?

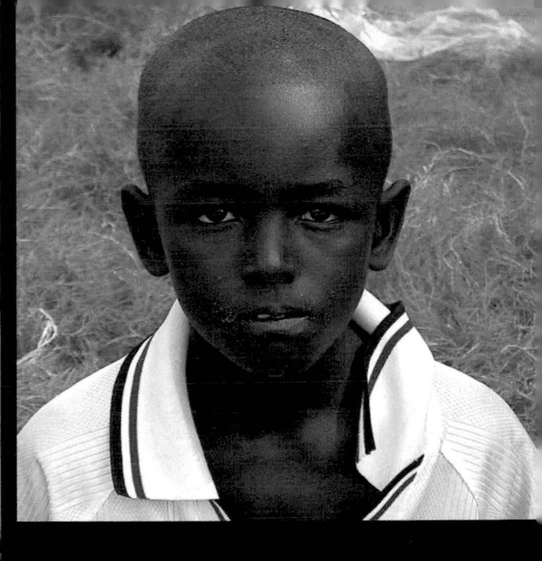

Not enough churches and Christian leaders are telling kids about heaven.

the ART *of* SIMPLE *theater*

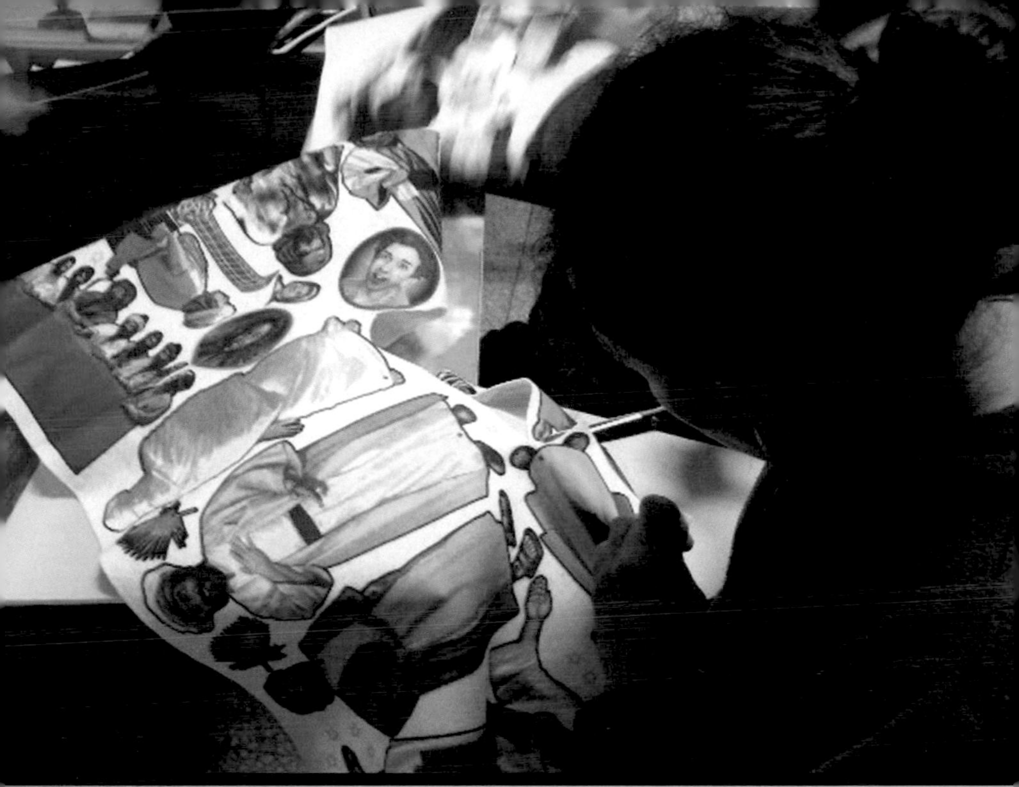

Chapter Thirteen

THE NEED TO HELP CHILDREN GET TO KNOW GOD

When I was in Brovary, Ukraine, we visited a public elementary school. We had heard about a boy with a crippling injury that made it all but impossible for him to go to school. It was this kind of tragic situation that weighed heavily on my heart. When we returned to the US, we made inquiries on how we could purchase wheelchairs and be able to bring them to that little boy in Brovary and others like him.

When we next arrived in Ukraine, we told the school administrators that we'd brought a wheelchair from America for the boy.

Someone wheeled it into the classroom while I documented the event with my video camera. The boy joyfully received the gift of the wheelchair. I was still taking video footage and continued my interview with the teacher.

This was the time I wrote about earlier in chapter four, when I asked that teacher, "What are you teaching the children today?" and she told me that the Ukrainian public school was studying about Jesus Christ.

I'd been surprised to hear her answer to my question about how the government permitted her to teach about Jesus. She said, "Why not? Jesus Christ is a famous figure in history. His was great moral teaching. He is a great example I want my children to know."

I thought, *Wow—because of adverse court rulings over the past forty to fifty years, American public schoolteachers can't do that!*

Later, as I thought about our exchange in that classroom, I also said to myself, "That teacher makes great sense—she's teaching *history* and examples and principles of great historical figures. Why *not* Jesus? *Who better to model their lives after?*"

As I reflected on that day, it seemed ironic that the formerly atheist government would see the logic of letting the teachers instruct their students about role models for positive values and principles—including the ones that Jesus taught.

Everything Jesus taught in the Bible was in some way demonstrating valid morals, principles, and ethics that would make His followers—or anyone for that matter—better human beings. It was amazing to me that the Russian authorities could see the value of that and American school administrators can't.

I wish that American public schools could be as open-minded. Can you think of *any* history classes or social studies that present Jesus as a positive role model for our children that include His values and principles that you and I give prominence?

Being on the board of Rockford College and having served on the board of Judson University, I've had the opportunity to see the value of education. However, as a parent and grandparent I'm concerned about the *quality* and *quantity* of *the kind of education* that our kids actually receive.

I've often thought, *What should be the goal of life's priorities?* Essentially we want to know by the end of our life:

- That we're going to heaven in an afterlife (most other religions have that tenet).
- That we have accomplished what was expected of us.
- That our family relationships were good.
- That we did our best to rear our children.
- That we want to be known as a loving person.

And during our productive years:

- We want to enjoy our profession and our role in the home.
- We want to have a family that loves and respects one another.
- We want peace in our lives and workplace.
- We want a feeling that we are making a difference in our family, work, and community.
- We want the satisfaction of creating our social networks (church, clubs, organizations).

- We want to establish networks we need for a worthwhile life and for making friends or choosing a spouse or business partner.
- We want to make the best of our education and career skills.
- We want to acquire the best moral and ethical knowledge (that includes finding a church that will meet our needs).
- We want to maintain our relationship links to family and friends.

Ironically, most of Western civilization's laws and moral principles were derived from the Bible and Judeo-Christian ethics. Yet this truth is totally ignored in modern textbooks. If we can't cover morality, ethics, values, and principles in the public schools and integrate these qualities into our kids' educational processes, we're left with the prospect that we have to do that job ourselves, or we'll see it delegated to those who may not have our confidence.

I think it's so very important that we find ways to teach kids about Jesus, so that they can develop the standards, values, and ethics that most Americans—even those who are not Christians—have always given high regard and prominence. That concern is paramount in my desire to help kids learn and understand the gospel. If we don't do it when they are young and while we have the freedom to do so, the opportunity may pass us by.

According to an online blog I read recently that quoted information attributed to the Barna Research Group, 80 percent of our children who make the decision to follow Jesus do so before age fourteen. I've seen the way these statistics play out in countless families, when kids turn their backs on church or God, but an early interest in living by godly standards might keep kids from giving in to peer pressure or outside vices as they approach adulthood—and that's why we may only have the time until they reach age fourteen to do something about it.

Our work overseas also bears out that fact. Moving away from their moral compass is all too often a universal temptation. People of my generation can even see the reality that we never know what our children and our grandchildren—who right now are so open, trusting, and unquestioning—will be like in ten, fifteen, or twenty years as they mature.

There's another problem though, and I touched on it in the previous chapter. At best, kids are being taught the truths that Jesus presents in the Gospels. The kids receive this teaching in various youth programs in churches for one to three hours a week. That opens them to a chance that some of Jesus' values and principles will be taught during the 50 to 150 hours they attend church and/or Sunday school each year.

When that's compared to the classroom time kids get in public schools—about 585 hours (day care and kindergarten) or 1,000–1,500 hours (first through fifth grade) for a nine-month school year—it doesn't seem like much. Public schools give *ten times the teaching on non-Christian teaching than churches do with Christian teaching.* That's quite a disparity.

George Barna, who heads Barna Research Group, Ltd., adds some other statistics. He writes, "Half of three- and four-year-olds enroll in [a day care] school and nearly two-thirds of five-year-olds enroll in all-day kindergarten programs. But neither school spending nor student attendance is a viable indicator of educational achievement or quality."[1] Barna suggests that those programs for kids may be little more than babysitting services and the preschools and kindergartens aren't living up to their responsibility to *teach* our children.

Two major studies cite *poor reading skills* as a forecast that kids are likely to be drawn toward teen pregnancy, criminal activity, poor academic achievement, and dropping out of school before graduation.[2]

To compound that gloomy forecast, *more than a million kids* missed at least one day of school because of fear of bullying or physical violence.

It makes me a little fearful about what happens when teachers with a non-Christian worldview influence our kids for so many hours a day. It points out the need for grandparents and parents to be vigilant and be ready to offer godly responses to the questions/answers that their kids and grandkids are getting in school. Many times, a great story by Grandpa *is the one they remember.*

As pointed out earlier, children have more brain cells functioning by the age of eight to ten than at any other time in their lives. During this explosion of brainpower they learn to memorize facts, remember words to songs, and can readily memorize fairy tales and stories. The very best time to reach them is before the age of ten.

I found it interesting that, a few pages earlier in this chapter, Barna concludes that *most children* make a faith commitment between the ages four to fourteen. He also added a scary comment to his statement of "most children" (in the US)—it means up to 80–85 percent of kids will make that decision before age fourteen. However, the flip side of those stats infers that *after age fourteen, not many will make that decision.*

I would think that Barna's research also applies to kids growing up in overseas countries. There, too, the fact is that most kids will make a decision regarding their faith commitment before age fourteen. That's precisely why I'm so eager to see us do a better job at reaching kids.

If we wait until they're beyond age fourteen or older, *we may never reach them at all.* It'll be too late. Recently Jim Rosene, Chris Marshall, and I had breakfast with Dr. Wes Stafford, president and CEO of Compassion International. He understands our commitment to kids before it's too late to reach them. His organization has a similar concern, as Compassion seeks to reach and help orphaned or needy children by finding sponsors to feed, house, and support them and provide schooling for them. Compassion is working with local churches worldwide to not just meet their physical and educational needs but to bring these orphaned kids to a working knowledge of Jesus Christ and what it means to be His disciple and receive eternal life that He offers them.

Children begin to understand the difference between good and bad behavior as early as two or three, and they'll have a definite code of behavior established by eight to ten years. Parents, grandparents, and teachers are trusted confidants, and they help youngsters form these rules of *following good* and *avoiding bad* behaviors. It isn't until sometime later that kids begin to be influenced by other kids and peer pressure starts to erode their behavior codes.

Even at a very young age kids are able to put those things together—*when they are led and stimulated in the right direction.* The trouble is, *it's more than likely that they won't learn facts about good behavior and solid role models—or about God and Jesus—in public schools.*

So how are young kids going to put it together that Jesus is God's Son and what it means to be His follower? The obvious answer is, *we have to help them.*

These are smart kids. They've already been taught how to think clearly and exercise their brain cells. Their brain cells begin to trigger the explosions of connected neurons that create the brain networks that will last them a lifetime. But at the same time—they're still kids, and they still need direction and guidance.

The problem, stated earlier, is that our kids spend ten times as many hours a week in school than in church or Sunday school. So it's important to focus mission dollars on children. That means not just the mission projects overseas but the ones in our own cities.

Every "community" has needs—what's more important than the neighborhood small church that has traditionally had a part in this process of teaching morals and Christian values? The community church, traditionally, is a place where kids get a feeling of belonging, meet quality friends, and learn about the most important factors of life—how do we get to heaven, where is heaven, how long is "forever," and how can we live a godly life here on earth by following the principles, moral values, and guidelines of Jesus?

I contend that parachurch "support agencies"—and even the churches—are located in the wrong parts of a city. If you were to take a map of your city and place colored pins in locations where all the churches are in your city, you'll probably be surprised to learn that *most are not in the areas of the greatest need.*

Many, if not most, churches are in different parts of town, usually in the suburbs, and demographically skewed toward families and people who can contribute toward the work of the church. Sadly, that's also the part of town where much of the contributions of those families goes for the upkeep of the *church facilities* and *its* programs.

Not many churches have programs specifically sited in needy areas, as those are usually across town, where there are fewer churches. I wonder what fantastic results might happen if the churches either relocated or planted a satellite church that received the same quality of ministry and Christian education as in the "mother" church that's across town.

What if you were to take different colored pins and put them, say, where the gas stations, drugstores, or 7-Eleven mini-marts are located? I think you'll find that the parts of the city that have the greatest need for churches are already being reached by those businesses. Those stores are where they're most needed. Why aren't churches? Do you think that it'd be more or less likely that we'll ever see a more even distribution of church ministry in those locations?

Think about it. What's the same for gas stations and food stores and—even more tellingly—elementary schools is that each of these categories that serve people are spread evenly across every demographic section of the city. Yet churches seem to cluster *away from* the poor neighborhoods, high-crime or gang-dominated communities, and blighted areas.

If churches were located *where the needs are,* and with more funding for children's work in their budgets, our churches could make a greater and more dramatic impact in the lives of people who most need that help. It doesn't take an inordinate amount of money for staff—most of it can be handled by volunteers rather than full-time paid staff—as in my illustration of the Blackhawk Court projects where my mom and dad volunteered to hold a Sunday school service.

By *not* locating near where the needs (and the kids) are, there's a danger that within a generation or so, the church will be irrelevant and lose its way in fulfilling its mission. Who's going to help the kids in need? Many church families somehow manage to find the time and money to care for the moral training of their own kids but can't seem to find the time or money to help kids in other neighborhoods—kids from dysfunctional families or single-parent homes, or kids who maybe have a parent in trouble with the law or gangs or even in prison? Who's teaching these kids the moral and spiritual lessons they'll need to live a positive and productive life when they grow up?

Local churches must take a serious look at their mission statements and begin to ask tough questions about their responsibilities to the communities outside of their neighborhoods.

And you know what? Those of us who have a role in mission work overseas need to pose the same questions to our churches about their participation (or lack thereof) in overseas mission work—and in particular, the two most important questions: *How much does our church contribute to overseas evangelism* ***for kids?*** *And how much does our church spend on child evangelism in other parts of our city?*

I'm always pleased to see children being taught about Jesus. They hear the stories from the Bible, and their growing brains readily soak it all up. They listen—and then they *believe!*

Something happens after kids get to be eleven, twelve, or older. Other factors come into play. Kids over fourteen become conditioned—to be less trusting and to question almost everything they hear—especially from grown-ups. They put up walls and other barriers to avoid accepting spiritual truth and the rationales and reasons for what they *should* be and should *not* be doing, and to avoid behaving as they're told. However, there's usually very little resistance to teaching these precepts to five- to ten-year-olds.

Younger kids seem to have an intuitive acceptance of the things they learn, especially when it relates to forming a worldview or principles to live by. Even at age five, seven, or ten, these youngsters can relate to a God who accepts them without conditions, who makes it easy for them to understand His laws and precepts, and who helps them differentiate between right and wrong, good and evil.

Because of the pervasive presence of television and media news reports, I think even the smallest of innocent American boys and girls knows that there is evil in the world. These children usually know from firsthand experience that there is a Devil called Satan, though they may not be intellectually sophisticated enough to describe it that accurately. Still, I think they can intuitively understand the concept of evil.

Our children perceive evil as a reality but may not be able to fully articulate it at a very young age. The concept of understanding the reality of evil isn't always universally true across the globe.

Chapter Fourteen

WHEN GOOD MEETS EVIL

My first experience with *obvious* evil was in Rwanda in 1994—at a refugee camp, following the Tutsi-Hutu genocide, where about *eight hundred thousand Rwandans were killed in the space of a hundred days.*

Now I recall the newspaper headlines announcing that so many Rwandans were part of the genocide of that African civil war. But none of the Western nations were doing much to help stop the killing and to tend to the critical needs of food, water, sanitation, and refugee camps. The UN responded, as did some of the cutting-edge Christian relief agencies.

It wasn't until the footage from TV cameras and the photos taken by missionaries and refugees came to light that the world took notice. This event was, to me, a dramatic example of how visual-oral methods work, even in a literate society. In effect, this chapter is presented in a literate (printed) format, but my first-person account of my experiences is a real example of what we mean about visual-oral *storytelling*.

When it became apparent that the Tutsi rebel group was going to be victorious, two million Hutus fled to Zaire (now the Democratic Republic of Congo) to escape the genocide. The mass killing of *eight hundred thousand Rwandans* over the first hundred days of the conflict *ultimately reached one million*—equal to 20 percent of the entire Rwandan population.

Most of the dead were Tutsis—and almost all females who survived the genocide were direct victims of rape or other sexual violence. *Horrific* was the only adjective that came to mind when I saw what was happening.

The US government tried to avoid involvement in Rwanda and refused to label the killings as "genocide," a political decision that President Bill Clinton later came to regret. In a PBS television interview, the president lamented the events in Rwanda and said that in hindsight, he believes if he'd sent five thousand US peacekeepers to Africa, maybe half a million lives might have been saved.

The two million refugees who fled from Rwanda to neighboring African nations fared only a little better than the one million Rwandans who were killed. Thousands of refugees also died—primarily in uncontrolled epidemics of diseases that ravaged overcrowded refugee camps. Deaths skyrocketed exponentially as men, women, and children by the tens of thousands were decimated by cholera, dysentery, and hunger.

After the war I went to Rwanda with International Aid, a Christian relief agency, to document the return of refugees who wanted to reclaim their former homes in Rwanda. I took a video camera to interview aid workers and missionaries who were trying to help. The crowds of refugees coming back into Rwanda seemed like a continuous stream of people, stumbling along the highways like zombies. A few managed to hitch a ride in large trucks, but most, emaciated and thirsty, just stumbled along toward "home."

The Office of the United Nations High Commissioner for Refugees (UNHCR) controls and supports over four hundred refugee camps around the world. I met with Claude Marshall, of the UNHCR, in Geneva, Switzerland, in the fall of 2001. In 2002 I learned that UNHCR was working with over twenty-one million persons worldwide in need or suffering specific concerns—such as war, AIDS, disease, and hunger.

Among these twenty-one million people in need were *twelve million refugees!* I had trouble trying to grasp the enormity of what he was saying: Twelve million people had fled their homes, often at the threat of their lives, and were living hand to mouth—homeless, sick, dying, at the mercy of bandits, rapists, murderers, and roaming gangs. *Twelve million people* with nowhere to go and with nothing at all in the way of food, clothing, bedding, and shelter. Nowhere they could call home and feel a sense of *belonging.*

Twelve million refugees is more people than the entire combined *population of Chicago, Philadelphia, Dallas, Indianapolis, Los Angeles, San Francisco, and San Jose, California!*

These twelve million people were simply trying to escape genocide, civil war, major catastrophes—and cyclical threats like floods, earthquakes, typhoons, and other disasters.

I was told by UNHCR leaders that most potential terrorists come from these *more than four hundred* nightmarish refugee camps; other terrorists are recruited from prisons.

However the majority of the population of these refugee camps consists of mothers and their children. More often than not, husbands and fathers are forced into involuntary service to fight for one side or the other, or are likely to die as slave laborers long before (or if ever) getting to a refugee camp.

Mothers and children also struggle to get to the refugee camps, where they hope to find food and shelter. Sometimes they make it; other times they don't. They come with whatever they manage to carry on their backs—along with their babies and little children. Often a five- or six-year-old child will carry a baby or toddler on his or her back for the many difficult miles it takes to reach a refugee camp.

I've been to many of these refugee camps—and they break my heart every time I visit them, even the ones that are well run. The people inside them seem dazed, listless, and hopelessly depressed. Another unspeakable reality of the refugee camps is that they sometimes become *permanent* places to imprison the hapless refugees of war, terror, disease, and starvation.

To get to a refugee camp is physically and mentally arduous for them. They can hardly place one foot in front of the other as they stumble toward what they hope is refuge. The highways are strewn with cooking utensils, clothing, cardboard mattresses, and other litter left behind—anything to lessen the weight of what they carry.

There always seemed to be several children with each parent. None of the kids appeared to be older than eleven or twelve. Long before they got to the relative safety of a refugee camp, kids who were older than twelve were often rounded up. These adolescent boys were forced into military units—called "children's armies" by the ones who controlled them. The adolescent girls were often viciously raped—sometimes violently killed—or taken away into a horrible life as sex slaves.

Can you see why refugee camps—and their reason for existing—always break my heart?

I watched as mothers and their small children and babies came to the camps and were pointed to a place they could stay, told to put up a tent (if they had one) or a blanket lean-to, spread out their meager clothing and utensils, and wait for the tragic event that brought them there to end.

Another thing that broke my heart was the growing number of little kids who were lost or abandoned by a mother or father who could no longer care for them. Standing beside the road or outside the gates of the refugee camp, they were often crying and looking desperately for a familiar face of a parent.

Rwanda was the greatest evil I had ever personally encountered. I felt absolutely helpless to do anything to help such an overwhelming need. Still, I thought of some small thing that I could do.

I bought several Polaroid cameras and a thousand Polaroid film packets for the missionaries to use. They took Polaroid photographs of lost children and posted them in a conspicuous place, to help frantic mothers locate and reunite with their kids.

These kinds of things happen continually in such a chaotic environment, with crying babies wanting milk and the other children underfoot as the mothers try to set up a campsite or prepare a meal.

That's when another idea came to us: *What if there were a playground here?* At first it seemed an incongruous idea. How could we imagine such a thing as a child's playground in such a terrible environment? But that's the very reason that convinced me it was a good idea—there was a genuine *need* for one.

I thought, *What if the mothers had a safe place to send their children to play while their assigned spot in the refugee camp was arranged?*

When a family finally makes it to the refugee camp, the mother is worn out. Yet she still needs to fix her children something to eat and make a place for them to rest. I thought, *If there was a place the kids could go to while she did those chores, it could be a great help.* Her kids could find a few moments of happiness in that community of otherwise hopelessness.

I knew that a playground might be part of the answer.

Those dire conditions were what brought me to Switzerland to meet with Claude Marshall of the Office of the United Nations High Commissioner for Refugees, which is based in Geneva.

Marshall told me that the UNHCR had money and resources to provide only basic humanitarian care, and they had no funds for playground equipment. They had their hands full coordinating with other agencies—such as the International Red Cross, International Aid, World Vision, and similar organizations—to help with food, health care, and other similar relief needs.

I asked if the UNHCR had ever provided or helped to build playgrounds for refugee camps. Claude Marshall told me that very few refugee camps in the entire world had playground equipment—I guessed that even those were available only because a particular refugee camp was sited on or near a school that already had a playground.

In other words, the UN couldn't pay for the equipment, even if we had volunteers to construct the parts into a finished playground. Marshall said that he wanted us (Kids Around the World) to work with UNHCR to build playgrounds in some of the neediest refugee camps. Specifically UNHCR asked us to build a playground in Bosnia; three in the Democratic Republic of Congo; and one each in Yemen, Georgia, Azerbaijan, Armenia, East Timor, South Algeria, and Pakistan/Afghanistan.

There have been other places closer to home that drew us to needy children.

In 2009 we partnered with Food for the Poor to ship 85,536 meals to their distribution center in Port Au Prince, Haiti. Along with the shipment of food, they were willing to take playground equipment into the country for a beautiful new playground in Sarthe, Haiti.

Later, a magnitude 7.0 earthquake shook Haiti's capital in Port Au Prince on January 12, 2010, killing up to two hundred thousand people—leaving *a million people* homeless in that nation of nine million people. Authorities and aid workers cleared tens of thousands of bodies from the rubble and provided water and food supplies for makeshift refugee camps.

Kids Around the World partnered with Heartland Community Church in Rockford in packing two hundred and fifty thousand meals destined for Haiti.

It was an incredible event with over fourteen hundred volunteers all united in that purpose. Then volunteers from Village Bible Church in Sugar Grove, Illinois, packed another fifty thousand meals. These events were only a few of many packing events we conducted. Before long half a million meals went to Haiti with the help of more than three thousand Midwest volunteers!

Kids Around the World reached its original goal of five hundred thousand meals, but the largest event was yet to come. The city of Rockford, Heartland Community Church, and many area schools packed more than seven hundred and fifty thousand meals for Haiti.

Our team traveled to Haiti in April 2010 to work with Love a Child, the first of two partners we have in Haiti, to construct playgrounds and be part of the food distribution.

We also previously partnered with Central Texas Orphan Mission Alliance (CTOMA) to help fulfill their dream of providing another playground for Haitian children. We hope that's only the beginning of many more wonderful things God will do in Haiti and other disaster areas.

Sadly, it seems that we never run out of needy children. We get requests all the time to help, and then "all" we have to do is find the money to buy, ship, and bring work crews over to build the playgrounds and provide for basic needs. It's always a daunting task, and the money we need is usually more than my friends and I can contribute on our own—as we'd done for our first such efforts at building playgrounds.

But miraculously, and supernaturally, the money comes to us—from churches, of course, but also from Rotary Clubs, Lions Clubs, Million Dollar Round Table Foundation, Samaritan's Purse, Compassion International, and similar groups who catch our vision. Over a period of thirteen years, we've built more than two hundred playgrounds—many of them in the areas assigned us by the Office of the United Nations High Commissioner for Refugees and from requests that come to us from other sources—such as the playground we built in a Thai refugee camp.

Kids Around the World completed Playground Number 122 (of their total of 208) in Indianapolis with our partners from the Million Dollar Round Table Foundation (MDRT). Other MDRT members also worked on three Habitat for Humanity homes and a nearby retreat center for children with special needs. There were more than seventy-five volunteers from places around the world helping out. These international "angels" provided a sense of hope for the needy children of Indianapolis.

In 2008 we made our first trip to Indianapolis to visit potential sites for the MDRT Foundation projects, including the Kids Around the World playground. A site was chosen, and planning began. Three months later we were told the site was suddenly not available.

We made a second trip to Indianapolis to meet with local organizers to look at other possible sites. Then we heard of an inner-city church with an empty lot next to it. It turned out that this was a perfect site for a playground.

We spoke with the pastor and shared with him what we wanted to do. Then he told us about his church's desire to make an impact in their community. Two years earlier *they* had begun to pray for a playground—and persisted in prayer during those two years—but they weren't able to find the funds.

The pastor's eyes lit up when we offered to build a playground on the land owned by his church, and he got very emotional to see how God had answered their prayers. Incredible! God had a greater plan, and when He revealed it to each party, we were all thrilled to be a part of it. I was amazed that two different groups were praying to be able to construct a playground in Indianapolis—and God led us to find each other and answered both prayers in a miraculous way.

I was reminded of Jesus' words in Matthew 18:14: "In the same way your Father in heaven is not willing that any of these little ones should be lost."

Swaziland missionaries Stan and Sue Drew are serving in a horribly impoverished African nation of just over a million people, more than half of which are under the age of fifteen.

In Swaziland it's reported that there are one hundred and twenty thousand HIV/AIDS orphans. That's nearly 12 percent of the population—and every fourteen seconds, a child there is orphaned because of AIDS. *Nearly half* of the adult population (43 percent) is HIV/AIDS positive—and 90 percent of them will die early.

Only a tenth of kids under fifteen will live to be thirty-five years of age. Nevertheless, Stan and Sue are leading a dynamic church and training national workers as pastors and leaders. We've got to be proud of those who are serving the Lord and making a difference in places like this.

I have also visited several African nations that sadly have equally disturbing and devastating statistics about HIV/AIDS deaths and orphans—and it plays havoc with my thoughts and emotions to be there and see that there's often so little we can do to save them. Dedicated missionaries, doctors, nurses, and pastors are already working day and night—even though they know that they won't be able to save many from an inevitable death from AIDS. Still, that doesn't mean they'll give up, look the other way, and not do what they can. We determined to find a way to help them do battle with such obvious examples of evil in our world.

I'm convinced that Satan is real and that he wants to kill all the men—the designated leaders of our homes—where we first get a feeling that, "We belong." I'm convinced that Satan seeks to kill men by HIV/AIDS, or through wars, and other horrors.[1] I'm reminded by that verse in 1 Peter 5:8–9: "Be self-controlled and alert. Your enemy the devil prowls around like a roaring lion looking for someone to devour. Resist him, standing firm in the faith, because you know that your brothers throughout the world are undergoing the same kind of sufferings."

There's another contributing factor that points to the terrible suffering that we see in places like Rwanda and other countries that have so many dying of starvation and disease. It's a fact that in our era, and even in places where we live, more people than ever before are living in slums—which fosters the evils of starvation, slavery, wars, disease, and massive immigration to escape the horrors.

An AP/*Washington Post* story tells of an alarming trend highlighted in a United Nations report that most of the expansion of slums and so-called refugee cities—mostly the result of war and violent conflict—has nevertheless turned upside down the statistics on the number of people who live in slums around the world.[2]

Statistics indicate that both China and India have shown great strides in trying to eliminate slums. Together the two most populous countries in the world helped pull some 125 million people—about half the world's slum dwellers—out of slums through great development works.

An article on a United Nations report notes, "Almost a quarter of a billion people moved out of slum conditions in the past decade," which sounds like good news, but the number of people still living in shantytowns around the world actually *increased by 55 million to almost 828 million* due to population growth and migration, according to a United Nations Habitat report that was released in Rio de Janeiro.[3]

Forecasts project that the number of slum dwellers in the world's major cities will continue to grow by six million people a year over the next decade—despite the good efforts of China, India, and Egypt to improve the conditions that contribute to slums—and could approach 889 million, or *nearly a billion people living in slums by 2020,* the reports said.[4]

It's in these slums—where the poorest of the poor try to eke out enough to stay alive—that we need to take the gospel. Of those 889 million, at least half are children. For most of them, life is bleak and horrific with a lack of clean drinking water, enough food to subsist, and protection from monsoons, winter snows, and summer heat waves. It's almost like we're describing hell. Just this past year Kids Around the World built a playground in such a slum—right next to the city dump in a city in Guatemala. Our team included our daughter Tonya and her family—her husband, Bill, and their kids, Kevin, Jaxson, and Andrew.

These slum areas are crowded with tar-paper shacks or corrugated-sheet shanty houses connected to another hopeless cubical—no room for anything. Where could they put a playground, park, school, church, or police station in such a situation? Who could provide them with clean water or enough food and medical attention? What Christian agency is large enough, funded enough, or staffed enough to focus on an ever-growing slum population—all of them together growing at six million a year?

Jesus was very interested in this group. But how can it be done? Who will identify with the slum areas and can make sure that there will be ministries for each one? It sounds impossible, but think of the potential—finding a way to minister to hundreds of millions of people who are imprisoned inside the slums … and half of them or more are children.

Charis Gresser described a study of Guatemala children that found "the impact of being stunted at age six is equivalent [in the child's test score effect] to losing four grades of schooling."[5]

The Financial Times also reported that in another study of children in South Asia, nearly half of all children under the age five (46 percent) were underweight, or "stunted."[6] Statistics like these make us even more committed to help these children all around the world.

Jesus set an example in the New Testament of how we ought to value little children. He told His disciples not to keep them away but to "let the little children come to me" (Matt. 19:14).

If God places such a high value on children, *then shouldn't we?* Let's find a way to get it done.

Chapter Fifteen

CHURCHES IN THE TWENTY-FIRST CENTURY

Let's make no mistake about it—Jesus Christ is the only way to heaven. He said so Himself (John 14:6). He works through those who believe in Him and follow Him. This was so unique to the secular observers of Jesus' day, according to the New Testament, that they even nicknamed Christians "followers of the Way."

When we come to Christ and are drawn into His Way, others are attracted and follow. And, because we have that effect on others, family, friends, coworkers, and our neighbors are also likely to follow us—even if we go the *wrong way*. If we fail to follow Christ and miss

the mark, they could as well. The apostle Paul said in his epistles that people think that they're the ones pursuing God, but author A. W. Tozer said it is really the other way around:

> Before a sinful man can think a right thought of God, there must have been a work of enlightenment done within him. Imperfect it may be, but a true work nonetheless, and the secret cause of all desiring and seeking and praying which may follow.
>
> We pursue God because, and only because, He has first put an urge within us that spurs us to the pursuit. "No man can come to me," said our Lord, "except the Father which hath sent me draw him," and [this] … impulse to pursue God originates with God, but the outworking of that impulse is our following hard after Him.[1]

Evangelicals question a person who really hasn't experienced repentance and conversion. Dr. Tozer talked about something called "easy believe-ism," and he thought it was a reason to doubt a person's salvation if there's no real conversion or change in his or her behavior. Jesus warned about careless or casual belief—being a "Christian" without repentance and a change in a person's life and heart.

Yet it's possible that we misunderstand Christ's calling. He calls people to follow Him on a path of righteousness—a path that will take us ultimately to His kingdom. *The Way* was a colloquial term in the New Testament that referred to the moral path that the early believers took in response to Jesus' call. Their nickname—"Christ-ones"

or Christians—was used interchangeably with another nickname, "followers of the Way." Jesus referred to "the Way" and said, "The way is narrow and difficult"—nevertheless, He urges us to follow it.

Christ's calling is intended to excite the person to *dual* action. If you come *into* the place where Jesus calls—which Jesus called the kingdom—you have to move *out of* the place you were. When Jesus gives His invitation (calling), the expected response is a dual, simultaneous movement—*out of* and *into.* We *turn our back on the world's realm and leave* that kingdom (with its temptations and other influences) to *come into* His presence and kingdom.

Perhaps this word picture will help illustrate the dynamics of the action: There's a *change of direction* (repentance) as well as a *change in dimension* (conversion) when we leave the realm of this world and move into the kingdom of God.

Christ's call or invitation usually doesn't come through the church to bring people to the Lord *en masse*. His invitation ordinarily comes to us *individually,* as the Holy Spirit touches us and excites us to "come out of the world" *and* "into the kingdom" of the Lord Jesus Christ. When we begin our new adventure in Christ by entering into the kingdom here on earth, we then "belong" to a citizenry of other believers.

Those of us who work with children find that this is a wonderful analogy for children. There is also a "kid's kingdom of God" here on earth. Kids understand the word picture. They have heard stories about kings and queens and those who are subjects of a king or queen. "Good" subjects of the king understand that we have a responsibility to work and play well together—helping each other, loving our neighbors, and being subject to the laws of the king.

These are concepts even a four-year-old can understand. Older kids grasp the reality that these are stories that teach us what it is like to follow Christ in our "kingdom." In fact, Jesus (in the New Testament Gospels) mentions more about the kingdom of God (on earth) than He does about heaven.

A study of adults who had previously spent at least six years in Awana youth programs when they were growing up reveals that a surprising 90 percent of them had remained faithful to the things of God and their church, and they are still active in their faith, including personal evangelism with others.[2]

High among the reasons why people leave a church are things such as not feeling connected in the church, ineffective teaching, or a lack of pastoral care—perhaps a feeling that they *don't belong.*

There's another reason that I think is more important—and it's the neglect or absence of a youth and children's ministry. I believe that having an effective children's ministry is critical for a healthy church—but that belief is also critical for many Christian leaders, according to the Francis Schaeffer Institute of Church Leadership Development.

In a more practical example, Dr. Rochunga Pudaite and his wife, Mawii, started many schools in India, with the primary goal to reach the children. Interestingly, these schools then become magnets for the parents who see the positive changes in their kids—intellectually and spiritually—and so they are more receptive to attend church services. From this small nucleus, first children and then their parents become seekers. Churches are then planted, sometimes in the same buildings where their kids go to school, and a body of Christian believers is created.

In similar fashion Dr. Wes Stafford of Compassion International points out that five of Compassion's sponsored orphans and needy children became followers of Jesus Christ and are now attending Moody Bible Institute with full scholarships. He has no doubt that they will be among the leaders of tomorrow's church.

These examples point to concepts that I presented in earlier chapters concerning my convictions of *belonging, believing,* and *behaving* as the foundation of Christian evangelism.

A playground like those built by Kids Around the World—especially those that were built next to a church—can be a place where kids can come to *belong,* not just to enjoy the playground, but also to hear the good news and *believe,* and parents see in the lives of their kids the attraction and benefits of following Jesus Christ, and they, too, come to seek God. Their incentive to want to believe is reflected by their kids' *improved behavior.*

In the case of local teachers (with whom Kids Around the World often partners for Bible teaching and discipleship), Kids Around the World proved that they can broaden their lessons and storytelling by including parents and other adults as well as the kids—thereby involving *two generations* who want to become Christ followers.

Most modern churches have home and foreign missions strategies that focus exclusively on adults and church planting—but the work among the kids is neglected. However, what if a group of street kids hangs out at a playground in a park or neighborhood? As in the case of many countries—including our own—hanging out makes it easy for those kids to get into trouble. What if these kids are child prostitutes, orphans, kids with AIDS, runaways, gang members?

Recently, some organizations, including our own, are providing an answer to that question. We hear about these areas of acute need and go to places all across the US and overseas.

We focus on the needs of kids.

We let the people know that we will come—help these kids learn how to pray, sing, and listen to stories from God's Word and help them to understand and respond to Christ's call upon their lives. Once they become Christ followers, they want to learn more about the Christian life.

That's a church, isn't it? If it isn't, maybe we need to redefine our idea of church.

I believe it was Don Miller of Compassion International who told me why ministering to the "smaller half of the world" is so important. As I recall, he said something like, "It's important to minister to children because children make up a great part of the worldwide population. Children play different important roles in society—positive ones, but also negative ones."

I've heard Don Miller point to hundreds of millions of street children in cities all around the world who *aren't* being reached, which results in an explosion of gangs and inner-city violence that's become a pandemic-like plague on almost every society. In some countries, such as Myanmar (Burma) and numerous African nations, there are even "child soldiers" as young as ten who are forced into fighting grown-up wars. And these kids need to be reached with the gospel.

Another recent "hot spot" of need is Haiti, with the majority of the population of its capital still living in thatched huts and tents or on the grounds of a golf course; they still lack the basic needs of toilets, food, shelter, and ordinary municipal features such as running water, electricity, and transportation—despite the fact that as of this writing, it's been almost a year since the devastating earthquake that struck the island nation in 2010. To help with this need, Kids Around the World is partnering to build thirty-five playgrounds in Haiti, at the request of Compassion International.

As an adjunct feature to building playgrounds in Haiti in 2011, Kids Around the World also trained hundreds of children's workers in Ecuador, Chile, Guatemala, Costa Rica—where our granddaughter Adi helped Evie and me with training—and Mexico.

Patrick Johnstone of AD2000 & Beyond also addressed this matter in 2004. He stated, "[That ministry to children is often ignored and underfunded] is tragic. Our clear experience from places like South Korea … is that if children's work is neglected you lose the next generation."[3]

That's a tragic forecast. In South Korea, parts of Latin America, and even in the United States, children who don't ever hear a storyteller share the gospel will likely grow up estranged from the church and disillusioned about Christianity.

When churches and mission outreach programs ignore or neglect the children, we sacrifice the future—and at a terrible cost. My greatest passion is that church and mission leaders will see that threat and *start initiatives immediately to win and disciple the children.*

Orality is the key. Storytelling. Just as Jesus changed the lives of those who listened to Him on Judean hillsides and city streets—we, too, can also have success in reaching others, especially kids, by using storytelling.

Telling kids stories is a simple strategy—and maybe it's why Jesus used that method to win people and why He said, "Let the little children come to me." Discipleship is key to this strategy, but there's a big stumbling block when it comes to children. The problem is, most adults don't take kids' decisions seriously—when it comes to becoming a follower of the Lord Jesus Christ.

In the New Testament, Jesus went about telling parables and telling stories within a broader presentation of His teaching; He scolded His disciples and other adults to not prevent the children to come to Him. Jesus had, and still has, a great compassion for helping kids come to Him, even some two thousand years later. *Jesus took kids' decisions seriously.* We should too.

Chapter Sixteen

VIETNAM 1993—HO CHI MIN CITY

In April 1993 I flew from the Midwest to Hong Kong by way of London, rather than the usual flight via the West Coast. It saved me an extra day of travel, which I used to spend time in Hong Kong, where I visited the United Bible Society (UBS) offices.

I had learned that the Bible society had received permission the previous year to ship fifteen thousand Bibles to the "recognized church" in Vietnam—that is, the Evangelical Church of North Vietnam. That Protestant denomination received its recognition from the Communist government in 1975, and I knew the ECNV had its beginnings with the Christian and Missionary Alliance churches and thus was a biblically sound organization. I asked if our group could take some Bibles allocated to that original official permission and import them into Vietnam with our luggage. The man at UBS referred me to the Hong Kong Bible Society, so I thanked him and got directions to their office.

It was well known among evangelical churches and Vietnamese Christians that there was an extreme Bible shortage in Vietnam. Black marketeers were clandestinely selling them for the equivalent of ten US dollars—a modest cost for Americans but one that was still far too expensive for a poor Vietnamese: It was a matter of having to come up with two weeks' worth of salary to pay for a Bible in his or her own language.

The Hong Kong Bible Society arranged for me to buy thirty-two Bibles, seven sets of Bible Story books, and one hundred pieces consisting of three sets of illustrated tracts in the Vietnamese language. I paid for the materials and brought them back to my hotel so I could better pack them among my clothes and other belongings, knowing that I'd probably get nicked for a hefty excess baggage surcharge for that extra weight. I also didn't want it to be noticed by customs officials who might make an arbitrary decision that it was contraband and confiscate it—but sell it on the black market for their own personal gain.

All the men in my group and I met up at our Hong Kong hotel. Meeting me were Ralph Plumb, Dr. Jack Henderson, Joel Samy, J. C. Huizenga, and Bud Hoffman—all leaders from International Aid, a Christian faith-based relief and medical agency headquartered in southwest Michigan. Another separate group would meet up with us later, and I'd be involved with some of their appointments.[1]

The International Aid group flew out the next day to Hanoi and experienced no problems—except for the costs for overweight luggage of Bibles and video equipment. Although I was nervous that the Bibles and other Christian literature might be confiscated when we landed in Hanoi, it wasn't.

Airport security in Hanoi offered no problems. Getting processed was easy and remarkably quick. We had no delays or questioning—no rummaging through our luggage. We had divided up the Bibles among all the luggage of the group to make the Bibles and other materials less conspicuous, but it turned out to be unnecessary. Our Vietnamese hosts had already prepared the way for us—and only a cursory search was made. The Vietnamese Ministry of Health representatives were there to greet us. They had provided vans to take our group to the hotel, a forty-five-minute drive from the airport. The ride was very scenic as we drove toward the city of Hanoi. As we drove along, terraced, lush, green rice paddies were as far as the eye could see. I watched the farmers—men, women, and children alike—bent over, working, with only woven straw coolie hats shading them from the hot afternoon sun.

I didn't see any mechanized efforts to help the farmers plant or cultivate the rice seedlings—only oxen tilled the paddies' three rice harvests in a year. The fields were also fertilized by hand. I saw workers grab manure from a wagon; then they'd sling it into the fields, and it'd land exactly where they'd aimed every time.

Traffic on the highway was unusually busy for what was a rural region. Still, bikes, motor scooters, and even an occasional automobile dominated the lanes of the highway.

Our group had planned to stay at the Pullman Metropole Hotel—supposedly the best-rated hotel for Westerners. However, our advance man, Joel Samy, discovered the day before our arrival that the hotel had overbooked and had 25 percent more prospective guests than rooms. Joel, not willing to take on the challenge of trying to find a half-dozen rooms in an overbooked hotel, quickly moved us to the Hai Yen Hotel—which as far as I could determine, was every bit as nice as the four-star–rated Metropole; the Hai Yen Hotel only had a "no star" rating because it wasn't listed in our guide book.

The Hai Yen Hotel was three stories tall and had just forty-one rooms, which were clean and air-conditioned. The hotel hostess was friendly and even took the time to show me how to switch on the hot-water heater for the handheld shower hose hanging on the wall in the bathroom. However, we did have a television set in the room—and it carried the English language broadcasts of CNN.

After getting settled in our hotel rooms, the group met in the lobby to go to dinner—even though, after crossing so many time zones, our systems were out of synch regarding meals.

We decided on a restaurant and were met outside by half a dozen enthusiastic "rickshaws"—a name left over from colonial days when a tourist was transported from place to place in a cart that was pulled by a strong man. In modern times, that contraption had been updated to what was called a "pedal cart" or simply "cycle"—or "cyclo," as the locals mispronounced it.

The "modern" rickshaws combined a bicycle with the driver—instead of a man racing down the street, pulling a cart, he simply made do with pedal power to get us to our destination. Some contraptions were upgraded even more—a hybrid of the cart had a motor that powered the ride. I think these were called "minicabs" or "bike taxis."

We got into several of these cycles to take us to dinner. Getting to our destinations was something that touched every one of our senses. Every sight was an exotic snapshot. The smells of cooking in nearby stalls anticipated the tastes of our dinner and made our mouths water. The sounds of bells and horns of traffic filled our ears, and the feel of every bounce as the cycle raced down the narrow, cobbled city streets tested the resilience of our clenched muscles.

We stopped at the Piano Restaurant and went inside, where the entire group was seated at a large table. The waiters bent over backward to show us great service. Fried rice and deep-fried fish was the special of the day—although we were also encouraged to order from the menu. I skipped some of the things placed on our table—not knowing what I'd be eating—but I also turned down the prawns for reasons I can't recall.

The restaurant was filled with Westerners. I was told that at one nearby table, the ambassador to Vietnam from Belgium was eating. For entertainment, we heard a great violinist accompanied by an equally talented pianist.

After dinner, the ride back to Hai Yen Hotel took us past the infamous "Hanoi Hilton"—where American prisoners of war were held during the Vietnam War. The tall, fading yellow walls seemed to go for blocks. Someone mentioned that he heard the old POW prison was going to be razed for a new Japanese hotel. I secretly hoped it wouldn't—it's too much a part of modern history, even though the memories of it are so bitter.

Our "convoy" of powered-bike rickshaws detoured to a pond or lagoon not too far out of the way. However, by now, it was very dark outside, and it was hard to see what we'd been brought to visit. Several of us had flashlights, and we shined them across the water. Then we saw huge sections of metal—some kind of manufactured structure—and someone asked the guide what it was.

"It is an American B-52 bomber that was shot down over the city and crashed into the water," he said.

Instantly I had a lump in my throat. I could make out the aircraft wreckage in the weak light of the flashlights—focusing first on the undercarriage of the wheel-well of the plane, resting upside down in the lagoon. My eyes began to mist. American airmen died here. Someone's dad, brother, husband, or someone else's son. Likely an entire bomber crew lost their lives in the horrific, fiery explosion of the crash that claimed them before they could parachute safely away.

I recall thinking, *What a lousy way to end our first day.*

Joy My Lien met us in the lobby the next morning. Joy had been born in Vietnam but spent four years in a Hanoi orphanage—until after the war, when she was adopted by an American couple from Wheaton, Illinois. Joy spent the next twenty years in America, but then, with the new openness in Vietnam, returned to give the next year of her life to the promising new life of her native country. Her area of expertise was helping to place orphaned children into good Christian homes, reflecting the cycle of hope, mercy, and life that *she'd* experienced, because she wanted to pass on that legacy.

She told us that she, along with Michael Hon Veola-Vu—program director for an adoption agency, Bethany Christian Services—would be taking part of our group to visit the orphanage where the two of them were reared as children.

However, as the others visited the orphanage, three of our group planned to meet with the director of the Institute of Medical Equipment for Vietnam. After that, the entire group ended up at the orphanage, where we were welcomed by fifty happy, beautiful children. The three of us who were planning to meet with the director of the Institute left the orphanage and climbed into a four-wheel–drive vehicle and were told to sit back for the two-hour ride from the orphanage, back to Hanoi.

Back in Hanoi, we found out that our meeting was not far from our hotel. Once we arrived at the ornate old building, we were ushered through a huge iron gate in front and led to a second-floor office. Professor Pham Gia Khoi greeted us. He was a distinguished man in his sixties, and director of the Institute of Medical Equipment for Vietnam. He offered us tea, grapes, and fresh tangelos as we sat and got acquainted. Dr. Khoi told us some of his background and about some of the things he'd been doing for the Vietnamese people.

Tears filled his eyes as he finished, and his sincere, deep-felt emotion underscored his words. "I just want to help my people," he said with great feeling.

Dr. Khoi shared how after he'd left his teaching position at the university, he was appointed head of the Institute. He now continued to work on his own because the government had no funding for his work. He told us about several of his projects that were now in limbo for lack of funding. "I have a dream," he said, "to furnish a medical kit for each doctor in the ten thousand clinics in the North."[2]

"How much would it cost to fund this project?" I asked Dr. Khoi.

"I could assemble them for just two hundred US dollars each. We do not have access to *dong.*"

Dong was the Vietnamese currency that the government had paid his Institute previously, but they didn't have those funds now. When the USSR fell after the collapse of Communism, Russian foreign aid dried up, so the Vietnamese government had no currency to support their own currency, and budgets were slashed at all levels of the government.

After a while, there was a somber pause in the conversation, and I broke the silence with a question. "What else do you want to do for your country?" I asked.

"I am trying to locate and assemble used medical equipment to repair and rebuild. It is a way to bring needed equipment for our clinics, since we cannot afford to buy new equipment."

Dr. Khoi next laid out a "shopping list" of the kind of equipment he was looking for: portable X-ray machines, PET scans, CAT scans, blood testing equipment, surgical instruments, monitoring equipment, and similar necessities for the clinics. "We can get them fixed and send someone to train the clinic personnel on how to use the various items," he explained. "When the government gave us funding, we bought many things from hospitals that were outdated or broken. Then we brought them back here and fixed them, or refurbished them, and sent them to our clinic doctors. They saved many lives using this equipment."

Dr. Khoi took us on a tour of his facilities in Hanoi. In a nearby room, half a dozen women wearing bib aprons similar to those of a butcher were making sutures for use by the clinics.

"We cannot afford to buy the new materials for surgical sutures. We use the old methods and material, like what is called 'cat gut,' for sutures. It is really made from cow or sheep intestines," Dr. Khoi explained, as if the distinction made a difference.

As I watched, the women worked with huge basins of intestines. As two women worked on a batch, one pulled on one end while the other held the length being pulled under running water in a sink. After cleaning the intestines and squeezing much of the water out of them, the women unrolled the lengths onto a rotating drum-like container that wrung out more water and stretched them smooth and flat.

Then the women flattened them to be cut into long, three-eighths-inch strips, and the thin strips were stretched, twisted, squeezed, and dried. After drying these extra thin "threads" that were just recently part of an animal's living organ, the women polished the threads smooth. There were a few other steps in the process involving some kind of chemical solution, test tubes, and a glass blower—which I didn't understand but felt that even if I'd asked Dr. Khoi, I probably still wouldn't understand.

He summed up the demonstration in words that I did understand: "We are doing things in the old-fashioned way, but it's clean and safe. We are producing a million linear meters of sutures each year in this plant. Yet there is a need for more—we must have another *eleven million* meters. The only other plant producing sutures in the entire country is in Saigon, in the South. Like us, they have no foreign currency with which to buy sutures from abroad. We have to do this if our doctors are to be effective."

The executive director of International Aid, Ralph Plumb, said to Dr. Khoi, "Our organization ships the kind of used equipment that you need. We ship to more than a hundred countries. However, our trouble is, we don't have enough qualified people to repair and refurbish this equipment, and that's important."

"Yes," Dr. Khoi said. "If equipment does not work—it will be just a useless gift."

"Well, Doctor," Ralph replied, "we'd like to work with you more. We've already been helping you since 1988, but you and we can do more. You can help us *fix* the equipment, and in return, we can compensate you with some of the equipment for your clinics in the North."

Ralph also asked about other needs for his medical work. Dr. Khoi must have been anticipating Ralph's question. He rattled off seven goals and projects, including such urgent needs as improving malaria control, a national immunization program for kids, better care for his 824 hospitals, finding supplies for sixty-four pharmaceuticals, and several other projects. "Clean drinking water is also a problem," Dr. Khoi mentioned. "All water has to be boiled in Hanoi for the nearly two million people. The old water system, built by the French in colonial days, is fast deteriorating. In the rural areas, many communities have only one well for the entire village. Our goal is to provide one well for every three households. Now all we can do is try to educate the population to the need to boil water, and teaching them not to drink from ponds or polluted streams. That's a major problem. A lot of sickness results," he said.

Dr. Khoi has a fine reputation and is respected by even the old-guard Communists who still control the country. I thanked him for working so hard and doing so much to help the hurting people of his land. "You do such a wonderful job," I said to him, adding, "It's a shame that the funding from the USSR has stopped."

I could see from his cloudy face that this was evidently a sore point, so I changed the subject. "Are you receiving any help in the hospitals—for example, such as volunteering by church members to help in care delivery? I would expect the Christians to be generous in their help here, as they are in America."

Dr. Khoi replied obliquely, "Perhaps, but there are not enough Christian churches. Right now, there are only three Christian churches in Hanoi, a city of 1.6 million."

Despite that gloomy response regarding the scarcity of Christian churches, our meeting ended on a positive note. We received wonderful reports of how our efforts and the help from International Aid was helping the Vietnamese people, and Dr. Khoi was pleased that now he'd be able to do even more with the coming provisions, equipment, and continuing help that would be sent his way by International Aid.

Looking for a Church in Hanoi

I couldn't get the fact out of my mind that there were so few Christian churches in Hanoi. It came as no surprise, of course, under a Communist regime. I decided to venture into the city on my own, to seek out an evangelical church in the city, but I wondered, *Where should I begin?*

Looking at a map of the city of Hanoi, I saw a building with a cross designation. *That must be a Christian church or hospital,* I thought. I showed the map to my cycle driver, pointing to the place of the cross, and we headed that way.

It turned out to be a Catholic church, and I went inside the chapel. I was directed to a garden outside, where I met with Father Ky. He was trimming grape vines in the garden and put down his clippers to talk with me.

I started the conversation by repeating what Dr. Khoi had told me—that there were just three recognized Christian churches in all of Hanoi. Father Ky blinked and paused before speaking. Then he said, "I am originally from Saigon. I was sent here to recruit and teach young men to become priests. The country is opening up now, and so we must be ready. Our church has eighty-three young candidates for priesthood, and I am assigned here to train them. We may have three churches now, but soon we will have another eighty-three candidates. And with more recruits to the priesthood, even more churches when they finish their training."

We talked for a while about his ministry and what was taking place in his church, and then I asked, "Are there any Protestant churches in Hanoi? Can you tell me where I can find one?"

Father Ky told me, "I only know of two, perhaps three, unrecognized evangelical churches."

"Can you help me locate them?" I asked.

He looked at the map I handed him, and he pointed to some locations. I marked them on my map, thanked the kindly priest, and left him to tend to his vineyard while I went to search for an evangelical church in Vietnam.

It wasn't until my third attempt at seeking an evangelical church that my search was the right one. I met a man,[3] who presented me with his card, identifying him as vice president and general secretary of the dominant evangelical church of North Vietnam. He was also the director of the only Bible-based, evangelical theological school in the country. He mentioned to me he was eighty years old, and that, "Of the four pastors in the North, three are over eighty, although one young man is just a bit over fifty."

I told him, "Sir, I want to thank you on behalf of Christians worldwide, for your faithfulness to the Lord during these difficult times." He had never mentioned "difficult times," but I had heard from others that the leaders of the evangelical Christian churches had gone through hell, just by staying alive. They spent much of the past forty or fifty years in and out of prison for their faith. Despite persecution and imprisonment, they nevertheless managed to serve their congregations.

As we sat together in his modest office and talked, I learned that he was the one who got government approval to import the fifteen thousand Bibles and ten thousand hymnals from a Bible society that we'd heard about earlier. "Have you made a request to order more?" I asked him.

"No … not yet. We are waiting for time to pass before we submit another request. We are grateful for approval of what we have already asked to be shipped in." He explained, "I want to be a good steward of what I had already requested, and if these Bibles and hymnals are used effectively by my churches, it might help me justify future requests."

Despite what seemed to me to be a harsh and persecuted life and ministry, he spoke of the positive things that he and his churches had done for the kingdom. Still, he had to be cautious. He was wary. It showed on his weary, wrinkled face that, after almost half a century of practicing his Christian faith in Vietnam, he would not speak carelessly. Before I stood up to thank him for his time, I showed him one of the illustrated children's books I'd brought into Vietnam with me.

His eyes lit up, and he asked in reverent whisper, "Do you have more?"

"I only have four sets, but I'll return on Saturday afternoon. I'll give you the ones I have with me, and I'll also bring half of the thirty-two Vietnamese Bibles that I brought into the country."

His eyes again expressed his deep gratitude. Both the kids' books and Bibles were like unique treasures for him. "Thank you. God bless you," he said with tears in his eyes.

"Before I leave you, sir, I have another idea. It's about the possibility of starting a school for church planters," I said. "It's something we've already done in Kiev and Manila. I'm hoping we might be able to do something like that in Vietnam."

Again the eyes of the eighty-year-old Christian leader sparkled as he said, "I have a Bible school that I teach now. I have fifteen male students and their wives—currently they are being trained exactly for this purpose. Graduation will be in May, following a five-year course."

He paused and seemed to be thinking of all that he had poured into those students' lives and of his hopes for them. He said thoughtfully, "But even fifteen new church planters are not enough. It's obvious, isn't it? It would be impossible for three evangelical churches, in a population of almost two million, to serve the spiritual needs of the people who must be introduced to Jesus Christ. If you can help us to be able to train our people to plant even more churches, we would be *so* grateful."

On my way back to the hotel, my mind raced with ideas and notes to myself that needed to be fulfilled when I got back to the United States, but I felt that just this one meeting—apart from all the other contacts and help we brought to Vietnamese believers—was worth all that went into this trip.

Chapter Seventeen

OLIVER NORTH'S RETURN[1]

The following is a good example of visual-oral communication. It's a story within a story—and the people *in* the story experiencing it that way. Those with whom they share this story become visual-oral storytellers. While this book is intended for literate learners, the *content* can be adapted for oral learners and oral speaking societies.

In the 1980s, Oliver North became an iconic figure when he testified before Congress on his role in the Iran-Contra controversy. Most people who saw him on television sized him up as a sincere patriot—someone who had taken the heat for President Reagan, and for that, he was vilified by politicians and those who were careless about democracy. The rest, watching the highly decorated Marine officer on TV, deemed him to be a hero.

While he was assigned to the National Security Council from 1983 to 1986, Oliver North's specialty was counterterrorism operations. Among his accomplishments—other than the Iran-Contra affair—he helped plan the rescue of the medical students being held hostage on Grenada.

He also planned the bombing raid on Muammar al-Gadaffi's terrorist camps in Libya and negotiated the release of hostages held by the Iranians.

When North's autobiography, *Under Fire,* came out in 1991, I was interested in his exploits in the Vietnam War and at the Reagan White House, but I was mostly impressed with his faith. That would be even more impressive to me two years later, in 1993, when—after I met Ollie North in person—we both went to Vietnam.

I helped make some arrangements for him and his film crew to visit Vietnam—by being attached to our group, which was led by Ralph Plumb, director of International Aid, based in southwest Michigan.

Ollie was working on a book and a documentary film and wanted to visit former sites where he had fought in the Vietnam War—where he served as a platoon leader and was wounded twice during combat, and for which he was awarded the Silver Star, Bronze Star, and two Purple Heart medals.[2]

When we arrived in Vietnam we heard on the CNN broadcasts from our hotel room that a document had been released indicating that perhaps as many as twelve hundred American soldiers were still being held as POWs nearly twenty years after the end of the Vietnam

War. A government report following the 1972 Paris Peace Talks put the total at 368 POWs being held by Vietnam.

The CNN news reports while we were there in 1993 stated that General John W. Vessey, Jr., would be in Hanoi about the same time that we were scheduled there. General Vessey, at the time, was the tenth US Chairman of the Joint Chiefs of Staff at the Pentagon. However, this time he was there as an envoy for President Bill Clinton, to get information from the Vietnamese about the apparent discrepancy of about seven hundred American POWs still unaccounted for.

Oliver North's group flew into Hanoi by way of Bangkok. North and his publisher, Zondervan Publishing House, were planning to release a new book, and the film crew from GF Media was in Vietnam to shoot the companion film. Both were to be titled *One More Mission: Oliver North Returns to Vietnam.*[3]

The film crew consisted of Dave Anderson, producer-director, and Heinz Fussle, the cameraman. Peter Larson and Jack Pagano were also part of the film crew. The Zondervan group included publishing execs Scott Bolinder and Lyn Cryderman, and writer David Roth.

Our group had arrived in Hanoi without any difficulty getting through customs, although our group's baggage was 200 kilograms (441 pounds) overweight—primarily because of the camera gear and extra Bibles. Yet it still took less than fifteen minutes to clear customs and immigration and to get aboard two vehicles provided by the World Health Organization (WHO) to drive to Vietnam's National Cancer Institute, one of two cancer hospitals in the country that are available to serve some thirty-five million people.

The tour of the hospital included seeing the three operating rooms that the hospital had. But someone told us that they have no autoclaves (used to sterilize their operating equipment and instruments). To sterilize their operating tools, they had to send them to a nearby hospital.

The film crew set up to tape an interview by North, asking penetrating questions about the level of care available in Vietnam. The answers were quite dismal.

A Vietnamese doctor was frank and to the point: "Only six major cancer surgeries can be performed each day—yet there is demand for more from the more than one hundred thousand new cancer patients that turn up every year."

"The need keeps growing, and the backlog gets larger every year," one of the other Vietnamese medical personnel told us.

I recalled that the previous year International Aid had shipped a twenty-foot Sea-Land shipping container to the hospital, with nearly one hundred thousand dollars worth of medical equipment inside the container. Dr. Nguyen Ba Duc had not forgotten it either. He thanked Ralph Plumb, director of International Aid, for the gift.

As the film crew toured the hospital, they were shown a young child with a shunt coming out of the right side of his neck. It was draining a cancer that apparently hadn't been detected early enough to combat its ravages.

North commented, "Wouldn't it be wonderful to provide MRI imaging equipment and bring the operators to America to learn how to use it? I mean, you can see that something like that is sorely needed here."

Off camera we discussed how to find the two hundred and fifty thousand dollars for an MRI and the cost of bringing the Vietnamese technicians to the United States for training on how to use it.

When we came up with a plan to make it possible, we shared the idea with Dr. Nguyen Ba Duc. He was overwhelmed by the generous gift we agreed to send him.

Not far from the hospital, we found the infamous "Hanoi Hilton"—the sardonic nickname for the prison where American POWs were kept during the Vietnam War, including former presidential candidate Senator John McCain.

In October 1967, McCain's fighter-bomber was shot down. Though seriously injured, he was captured by the North Vietnamese and put into Hanoi's main Hoa Lo Prison, the official name for the Hanoi Hilton. McCain was tortured, and his injuries were not treated professionally—and as a consequence didn't heal properly. He was a prisoner of war for seven years. Some American POWs were imprisoned there as long as eight and a half years.

I went with the film crew and Oliver North to see the Hanoi Hilton from the outside. It had weatherworn fifteen-foot-high walls topped with embedded shards of broken glass and four strands of electrified wires. The prison was virtually escape proof. I could see North's emotions as his eyes looked intently at the nightmarish landmark. But the infamous Hanoi Hilton affected all of us, and not just North—it was an intensely emotional experience.

After those film interviews and other footage, it was time for North to check into his hotel. I had arrived earlier and had reserved a room in Oliver North's name at the Metropole Hotel. He had only half an hour to drop his gear, shower off the grit of the film shoot locations, and get ready for dinner.

Dinner was to be at a compound called "The Ranch." Just a week earlier Lt. Col. Jack Donovan, a Pentagon investigator in Hanoi who was looking into the issue of "missing" POWs, had entertained CBS's Dan Rather and General Norman Schwarzkopf. On a post near the front gate, there was a sign: *USA MIA OFFICE.*

An Army lieutenant colonel met us and hosted our dinner, which was a cookout. A Marine cook grilled hamburgers and hot dogs on their new gas grill and also served baked beans, salad, and condiments.

The missing in action POWs were the topic of our conversation during the three-hour dinner, led by Lt. Col. Jack Donovan. I learned that the remains of 274 US servicemen previously listed as missing in action had been identified and flown home for burial.[4] Donovan told us about the Pentagon's efforts to make every effort to locate the other Americans missing in Vietnam.

A detachment of seven men, representing all branches of the US Armed Forces, had been in Vietnam looking into every lead. Donovan said that it's a one-year tour of duty for those participating, with most searching in Vietnam, but field personnel were also looking in Laos and Cambodia, across the border from Vietnam.

On Saturday morning I set out with the film crew and Oliver North to meet with the Vietnamese deputy of foreign affairs. The location for this episode of the documentary shoot was a beautiful building not far from the mausoleum and final resting place of the Communist leader during the Vietnam War, Ho Chi Minh.

In Moscow, I had seen lines of people waiting to view the body of Vladimir Lenin; curiously, the same kind of "worship" took place here. Long lines snaked through the building all day long to get a look at the North Vietnamese leader's embalmed body on display.

In the meeting at the foreign affairs office, Oliver North presented a unique gift to the first deputy—a special commemorative artifact celebrating the life of Thomas Jefferson.

North told the first deputy, "Thomas Jefferson was one of the greatest American founding fathers. He's a founder of our democracy and an author of our founding documents. I want to present this to you in recognition of the two hundred and fiftieth anniversary of Jefferson's birth. It's my hope that we can see restoration between our two peoples."

In the next part of our tour of filming various locations, we stopped at Vietnam's military museum. The museum commemorated various "victories" by the Vietnamese forces, sometimes to the point of great hyperbole and exaggeration on the ubiquitous signs.

One of the signs, adjacent to a display of an anti-aircraft artillery piece, proclaimed:

> This is a gun operated by the Nguyen Viet Xuan Battalion that shot down 124 US aircraft.

I thought about that. Though those claims were probably highly exaggerated, a number of American airmen had still lost their lives.

For that reason alone I had a lump in my throat and was immediately overwhelmed by sadness and pity.

I asked Ollie North, "How could a single gun like this have done so much damage to the American fighter planes and bombers?"

"It's because there were so many of them shooting at our guys. As a result there were so many shells fired, and so much flak in the skies over Hanoi that our B-52s were simply enveloped by the shrapnel. When they flew overhead, it was like our aircraft literally sucked up the lead and phosphorus," he explained.

I saw a photograph on display of an American flier being taken prisoner; he had no doubt been beaten by his captors, who were carrying him away from a rice paddy in a water-buffalo–drawn wagon.

I studied the American's face in the photo. He looked dazed and disoriented and was probably in pain in the aftermath of his crash and capture. His face was lacerated and bloody. I guessed those wounds were more likely from beatings of his captors than from the crash of his aircraft.

Our tour guide, a pretty young Vietnamese woman, pointed to the photo I was looking at. Her finger directed attention to the photograph. She said, "The rice farmers had only their farm implements—rakes, shovels, and hoes—and in our glorious struggle, even these simple tools brought down some of the Americans' most technological equipment."

"Yeah, sure," I said under my breath.

Ralph Plumb, a member of our group, had visited the museum a year before. He asked the guide, "When I was here last year, you had a large picture of our former president Lyndon Johnson, pictured with his head buried in his hands, and another photograph of

Jane Fonda on display. Did you remove them because of a change in politics—that it might be better for the talks toward renormalization and improving trade with America?"

The Americans in the museum understood the irony in the question, but the young woman acted like she hadn't understood. After all, we knew that the iconic photos of President Johnson and Jane Fonda had been used as propaganda to promote the antiwar cause. The Jane Fonda photos, her silliness of posing on a barrel of an antiaircraft artillery piece, and her antics at the "Hanoi Hilton," had done incalculable harm. But the guide wasn't even born when that event took place—our Vietnamese guide probably *didn't* understand Ralph's question, but we did.

On Sunday morning we got up at four thirty in the morning for a flight from Hanoi to Danang, to visit one of the former hot spots of the Vietnam War. Even this early—well before dawn—the streets were crowded with people walking, riding bicycles, dodging minicabs, and already heading to the city market.

Slaughtered pigs were strung over the fenders of cars and trucks; live chickens made themselves heard as they fluttered inside bamboo cages and baskets. Although it was Sunday, it was still a day of labor and activity—in Vietnam, the working people are busy seven days a week, twelve hours a day. There are no two-day weekend days off.

The main reason for the long and hard days is the fact that the average Vietnamese worker earns the equivalent of fifteen dollars a month, and if that isn't struggle enough, they have to deal with rampant inflation that keeps them from ever getting ahead financially.

The flight from Hanoi to Danang was about four hundred miles, and our arrival was uneventful. We were shuttled to our hotel, which offered a gorgeous view of the Han River—very wide at this fishing port city, allowing room for all kinds of boats, even oil tankers and freighters. On shore, there were large ships in dry dock, their rusty hulls being scraped and painted. Fishing boats were everywhere in the water—their occupants hawking fresh and dried fish.

Independent entrepreneurs were positioned strategically on the river bank to confront us with all kinds of enticements: Cycle drivers offered tours of the city, and a young woman offered to rent small folding lawn chairs to rest and enjoy the view—just ten cents, and she'd even toss in a coconut-milk drink as refreshment.

Yet our team wasn't there for these things. Now that we'd checked in at the hotel, we were ready to accompany the film crew to yet another site being filmed for their documentary of Ollie North's return to Vietnam.

The plan for this film shoot was to climb "Marble Mountain"—the name given to that site, which was once five islands, but the water had retreated long ago and the site had been given a new nickname.

During the Vietnam War, the Viet Cong had used one of the deep caverns inside the mountain as a small hospital. Not far away, on China Beach, American soldiers and Marines took "R & R" for a momentary diversion from the war.

The climb to the top of Marble Mountain wasn't all that difficult, but it was steep. When we reached the pinnacle, David Roth,

Oliver North's collaborator on the book and film project, walked over to North and said, "You seem lost in your thoughts up here. What are you thinking?"

North didn't answer right away and continued his gaze across the landscape. Then, flashing his famous grin, he said, "This is one heck of a lookout spot."

I followed the film crew inside a Buddhist temple. Inside the air was pungent with incense, and smoky wisps filtered through shafts of sunlight that somehow streamed in through an opening at the top, a hole carved through the rocky mountain by American B-52 bombers.

A huge carved Buddha overlooked a shrine. The film crew used these sights as a backdrop for the informative narratives that North was sharing with the camera—musings about the war, his experiences in this former area of combat, and the many friends and comrades that were killed nearby.

The acoustics were great inside the temple, and after filming, and before we went back down, we all paused for prayer. Individuals in our group shared brief but meaningful petitions with God—"That this land might be healed from the aftermath of the Vietnam War."

Another prayer was, even more significant, "We pray for this country, that it will be opened to preach the gospel of Jesus Christ, and that people here will find Christ and follow Him in discipleship." When we finished praying, someone started—and the rest of us followed—in the singing of the Doxology.

Next we visited China Beach, which was stunningly beautiful. I remember thinking, *It's no wonder our soldiers and Marines enjoyed their R & R here.*

China Beach was also the title of an ABC-TV network drama from 1988–1991, starring Dana Delany, who depicted the life of an Army nurse in the China Beach combat evacuation hospital.

China Beach stretches for miles, and we could have walked north or south for hours without running out of sand. Where we *did* stop was at a cafe right on the beach, overlooking the exotic blue water and the "schools" of human fish swimming in the water.

Oliver North had brought his trunks for a swim at this historic place and had even decided to skip lunch in favor of a swim. But he didn't go swimming.

Instead about half of our group—including North—made a decision to attend a four o'clock Catholic Mass. As our vehicles pulled into the courtyard of the beautiful Vietnamese church, we could see that crowds of people had already come together and the building would soon be overflowing. We learned that three thousand people would participate during the two worship services scheduled that day.

A young priest greeted us and invited us to his office for brief conversation before the service. When we found seats inside the church, I noticed, surprisingly, that there were mostly young people and their youngsters in attendance. The reason I was surprised was because I had attended similar services in the former Soviet Union, where only older people attended.

Both countries were former Communist regimes, yet there was a sharp contrast here. The people were dressed with their finest clothes, in respect for their reverence for God. And, as I'd suspected when we first pulled up in the courtyard, the crowds had already filled the church and overflowed from every side, spilling outside where they hoped they could still be able to hear and participate.

I noticed two little Vietnamese children who were checking us out. I stooped down to their level and handed each of them a copy of the Vietnamese New Testament. As they gratefully took them, a man moved slowly to my side and whispered, "Do you have another one?" I didn't, unfortunately. It pointed out the great need in the country.

When the service started, the congregation hushed—even the little children present. The music, the priest's homily, and other parts of the service moved me deeply, and I was glad that we'd decided to skip swimming on China Beach to come here and worship.

When the time came for participation in Communion, Oliver North and David Roth were among those who went forward to the altar, and I watched as North took the wafer and bowed in silent prayer.

I wondered what was now going through his mind—he had fought as a US Marine in combat not far from this church but now had returned to this neighborhood to worship in this holy place.

I don't know what thoughts were in his head, but in my own mind I was deeply moved by the presence of God in this place and by the opportunity to worship Him.

Later, at dinner, Ollie North was sitting next to me, reflecting on the day's events, including the visit to the church. He turned toward me, and as we reviewed our visit to the sanctuary of the small church, he said reverently, "The service was the highlight of my day."

We excused ourselves to discuss the schedule for the next day. Ollie and his group had already received clearances from the Communist authorities to go to Con Thien to do some filming of a former Marine fire base in the Con Thien area. There would be no other opportunity for the crew to capture those moments, so we agreed that we'd split up.

While North and his film crew went to Con Thien, we followed through with our other plans.

Chapter Eighteen

MAKING FRIENDS WITH FORMER ENEMIES

The next morning in Vietnam came early. We had an 8:00 a.m. meeting in the Office of the Department of Health. Dr. Nguyen Van Ly (pronounced Lee) took us on a tour of the Tam Ky Hospital and then to the Thank Binh Hospital, where International Aid had recently sent a shipping container packed with medicines and medical equipment. That recent gift must have still been fresh in the minds of our hosts, as they were very gracious in expressing their gratitude.

We toured the hospitals' rehabilitation centers, and Dr. Ly pointed out that while malaria is the greatest cause of death in

Vietnam, the second greatest problem is the number of injuries caused by exploding ordnance and munitions left over from the war.

As we toured the various areas of the rehab centers, we were shown patients who had lost arms and legs to exploding munitions and mines but who were being fitted with artificial limbs and participating in all kinds of physical rehabilitation exercises. Despite their horrific injuries, these people seemed excited about changing their lives through the gifts of these artificial limbs and other aids provided by International Aid and other humanitarian and religious organizations.

Before our visit ended, Dr. Ly took us into a conference room and laid out a map of Hien District near the Laotian border. "This is a very needy place. They are desperate for medical assistance. Would you go there and see if you can help these people?" he asked.

"How far away is it, and how long would it take us to get there?" someone from our group asked, and then added, "If it's too far we may not be able to go there. Besides, since it's not on our schedule, we may run into problems with the government for changing our itinerary."

"It is true that no outside group has been allowed to go there, other than the MIA United Force teams who were invited there," Dr. Ly said. "However, *I* can get the necessary government permissions. Please, these people are desperate. I hope you will agree to see them."

Four of us agreed to go see what might be done for the desperate medical plight of the people of Hien District.

As we got more information about the area, we learned that the people of Hien District were tribesmen, and those of the

Katu tribe in particular were people once known to sacrifice other human beings and eat their flesh—and it's said that foreigners were a special "delight" and there was a special ritual for splattering their blood and painting the faces and skin of the Katu people, prior to whatever other plans they had for the hapless foreigners.[1]

We also learned that these once fierce tribal warriors once had an encounter with Christians following a missionary incursion into their area and many of them were converted to Christianity. Of course, conversion to Christianity was forbidden under Communist rule and was probably the factor prohibiting travel by Westerners to that region. Or maybe the real reason was the fact that it took four hours—each way—by four-wheel vehicles to reach Hien District.

Dr. Ly took care of the permits for our trip to Hien, and we located four-wheel vehicles to get us there and back. The roads were every bit as treacherous as we'd been told. Often they disappeared under a streambed or were covered over by landslides or mud left by rains and storm runoff. The ride was tedious and bumpy, but many hours after departing, we finally arrived at the outskirts of Hien district, home of some thirty thousand people.

In Hien we were greeted by the head of the Vietnamese People's Party and the chief medical officer, a local physician. All the people we met were friendly, and their warm smiles underscored their genuine greetings.

We were taken on a tour of their sixty-bed hospital and told of their medical needs. A lack of necessary equipment told the story of their needs. A portable US Army field table served as their only operating unit. They had no X-ray equipment, and I asked what they did when they needed an X-ray to treat patients with broken bones and other injuries or medical emergencies.

"It usually means that we have to take them somewhere else to be treated," the doctor told us. "If it's a broken arm or leg, we try to make the patient comfortable for the trip, which takes several hours, as you know, having just come that way."

The doctor next led us to the patients' rooms. To get there, we had to wade across a small stream. Inside the compound, the rooms were dark, gloomy, and drab—the floors and beds were dirty and likewise dingy. There were bars on the windows—and it made me wonder if the facility had been a former POW camp.

Beds were affixed with bamboo poles on each corner of cot-like hospital beds, so that any intravenous fluids could be hung above the patient for transfusion.

The first three rooms were for children—whose mothers were also there to feed and take care of their kids. All three little patients that were hospitalized were there because of malaria—the number one killer in Vietnam. My heart went out to these helpless little ones and to all the other patients in other rooms of the hospital, waiting for eventual healing or death.

These tribal people deserved better. I asked, "Why haven't you been able to get more help? If not from your government, what about foreign humanitarian organizations like the UN's WHO[2] operation?"

Our official government guide, Mr. Vyn, spoke up. He tried to give the matter his best spin. "Our government health efforts are very good," he said, but added, "The problem is, we are constantly overwhelmed, and the Hien District is too small to get the attention of outside help."

"What about religious organizations? Are the Hien people Buddhists?" I asked.

"No, they are not Buddhists. The people here believe in heaven," Mr. Vyn answered, and he explained how Christians had originally come to this village, settled there, and began to make converts and improve the way of life for the people.

I was excited to hear this, and I told our Vietnamese hosts, "I believe that our God arranged this special trip to visit Hien just for us. We're going to help you in the months ahead."

We went back to Dr. Vyn's office and laid out an agenda for International Aid to ship a container of medical supplies and equipment to the Hien hospital. By now, even the Communist party leader was expressing his willingness to accept help from an American Christian organization.

Ralph Plumb took advantage of their openness and boldly asked, "May I assume from your willingness to accept our humanitarian aid that you would also approve of our sending Bibles for the people, in the same container as the medical equipment and supplies?"

Unhesitatingly, a representative of the Vietnamese Foreign Department replied, "Yes!"

With this one-word acceptance and pronouncement of approval, I saw at once a remarkable, incredible step. It was something that we could not have achieved had we not traveled to Hien. That simple yes would mean the possible importation of massive numbers of Bibles for this region and even the rest of Vietnam.

On our return to Danang, we expressed our gratitude. Only God could've pulled off such a coup. This side trip was obviously a major breakthrough. When we returned to Danang, we met with Dr. Nguyen Van Ly and reported on the efforts of the trip to Hien that he wanted us to make.

He seemed pleased with the outcome. We talked about other ventures that might help seal our friendship with Vietnam.

Then I extended an invitation for him to visit the United States. "I'm on the board of trustees of the SwedishAmerican Hospital in my city of Rockford, Illinois. I'd like you to come to Rockford, as my guest, and meet with our hospital people and learn about our health system firsthand, since you are the most important person in the Vietnamese Health System, at least in this region."

Dr. Ly was excited and took no time in responding, but boldly added a postscript: "Is it possible that my good friend Mr. Dinh An could be included in your invitation?"

Mr. An, I remembered, was second in command of the Communist People's Committee. We would need his help in getting the various permissions to allow Christians to enter the country and be allowed to preach the gospel and plant churches. I said, "Of course. Mr. An is also invited to come with you. I'm sure that it will be instructive for him, too."

That new, important connection would turn out to be useful just hours later.

Dr. Ly assigned Vin Nhan, a young Vietnamese ex-army man, now an employee in the Foreign Economic Relations Department, to be my guide and take me around the city for my other meetings. I hopped on the back of Vin Nhan's motor scooter, and he drove me through the narrow streets of Danang, dodging pedestrians, bicycles, trucks, and other vehicles deftly, and getting me to my eleven o'clock appointment at the Tin Lanh Church.

Pastor Le Cao Quy was waiting outside to greet me and then took me on a brief tour of his church. "We have three hundred members," he said, smiling broadly, "and our church is one of thirty in most of the eighty-five provinces. We have ten others approved by the government, but we have no trained pastors to lead them."

"How many Christians live in this area?" I asked Pastor Quy.

"About twenty-five thousand in this region. That is why we need Bibles."

"How many Bibles, and what else do you need?" I asked.

"We can use ten thousand Bibles, ten thousand hymnals, and an overhead projector. And, oh yes, a computer," Pastor Quy replied.

I made notes of his requests and promised to do what I could to help him. Then I gave him what little materials I had left—two children's music tapes, three kids' tracts, a set of children's books, and a Superbook video. The video was an immediate hit. There were two kids, a couple of teenagers, and several adults in the church when we played the video. All were excited to see an animated presentation of a Bible story, *The First King,* come to life.

The pastor expanded his previous list to include a set of the Superbook videos. He said, "We have nothing to use to teach the children. In our country, nearly all children do not receive any advanced education. There are no high schools here. As a result, many adults cannot read or write. I would like to have a set of the videos to teach the children *and* the adults about Jesus."

"What about the possibility of our helping you start a church planting school here in Danang?" I asked.

Beaming at the question, Pastor Quy pulled out a file from his desk and showed me a request that he'd already sent to the government, a request for permission to open a four-year Bible school for fifty students.

"I sent this request to Prime Minister Vo Van Kiet, with a copy to Mr. An—"

I interrupted him. "Do you mean the Mr. An who is a senior official in the People's Committee?"

Pastor Quy looked at me quizzically. "Why, yes … do you know him?"

"Yes," I answered. "I was with Dr. Ly this morning, and I agreed to bring him and Mr. An to America next July to get a better perspective on American health-care systems. Dr. Ly gave us permission to include Bibles in shipping containers with medical equipment for the Vietnamese people. We can include the Bibles and other things that you want with that shipment. I'm certain that if I contact Mr. An, he'll approve your request. I'll also tell him that we're sending some materials for you in the other shipment."

My guide, Vin Khan, whom Dr. Ly had assigned to me, spoke up. "It is true," he said. "I was there in Dr. Ly's office when these arrangements were approved. I will be most happy to take your request to Mr. An for permission to receive the shipments of materials."

The next day, our group met up with Oliver North's film group to compare notes of our different schedules following the change in our different itineraries when the film crew went to Con Thien and our team went to Hien.

Ollie reported that his trip to the former Con Thien fire base was a highlight of his trip. "The film is a documentary of my return to Vietnam," he said, "and I wasn't sure of what we'd be able to see and shoot. But yesterday I visited the exact bunker in which I fought—the place where I was wounded in combat. I even met with some former enemies. I walked on the ground at Quan Tri where so many of my friends and fellow Marines gave their lives."

I watched his eyes grow misty as he recalled those deeply personal memories that had moved him as he'd returned to Vietnam. I felt that we all benefitted from North's sharing his feelings and memories.

For me, what transpired in my various assignments in Vietnam was a profoundly healing experience after the earlier attitudes I'd acquired after seeing the Hanoi Hilton, the US bomber that had been shot down, and the photos showing the harsh treatment of the American POWs by the Vietnamese.

The wonderful selfless dedication of Vietnamese Christians, and even the kindness of the medical authorities that we'd met with, showed me an entirely different picture of the Vietnamese people—an entirely opposite picture from those imbedded in my mind because of the war.

I met Vietnamese leaders who cared about their people. (In contrast to some leaders we ran into in other parts of the world, a few corrupt people were insincere and conniving—trying to get money or supplies from us Americans, and they were disappointed and went away grumbling when we were able to see through them and turn down their requests.)

What struck me the most was the remarkable way that God always seemed to be one step ahead of us on our trips across Vietnam. I can only describe such divine connections and appointments as miraculous. In no way could I—or anyone else—be able to orchestrate our meetings in ways that brought great blessings to us and to the people who would benefit from the food, medical, and other relief efforts. Nor could we ever be able to get Bibles and Christian materials into Vietnam without God's intervention. The leaders themselves, though still Communists, thought allowing Bibles into the country was a small price to pay for the medical equipment, medicines, and other "impossible to get" materials.

As I reflect over the past three chapters that I've written about our trip to Vietnam, I'm struck how each chapter was one miracle after another, and how all three chapter accounts of our trip were wrapped up in an incredible testimony to the goodness and greatness of God.

Only He could have pulled off such an amazing set of God-directed interventions. And He allowed me to watch it happen. Wow!

(The following Vietnam anecdote was written by Jim Rosene of Kids Around the World. It underscores the validity of the work in Vietnam and other countries around the world.)

In the fall of 1999 we were making final arrangements for a trip to Danang, Vietnam. We were working with the Southwest General Baptist District, which partnered with Kids Around the World in bringing a playground to be constructed in Danang.

There was great excitement not only that a playground was going to be built for children of the city, but that in the process, our group would be the largest group of Americans to enter Danang since the end of the Vietnam War some thirty years earlier.

All the details had been worked out—lodging, transportation, shipping of a forty-foot container, tools, and materials. We were all set. There had been some discussions with local Christian churches concerning some training of children's workers. Following that training, we planned to leave them some basic methods of teaching the Bible to children—using a Flannelgraph.

As a side note, I remember when I was first introduced to Flannelgraph. I was in grade school and walked to my friend's house, where his mom used Flannelgraph materials to share Bible stories based on the lives of great men and women of faith. As a kid I was really "wowed," and it was exciting!

But in the nearly forty-five intervening years, I'd never seen another set of Flannelgraph stories and never even thought about using them—until now. There, in Danang, I was going to use them to teach.

But a month before we were to depart for Vietnam, Denny Johnson called me and shared disappointing news. In the briefest of phone calls, Denny told me that the Vietnamese officials had met, and, for some unexplained reason, those officials decided they didn't want "Jim Rosene" to come and teach in the Danang churches.

My heart sank. I'd prepared so hard for this training; I'd developed and practiced my Flannelgraph techniques, and now—within a several seconds phone call—everything had changed dramatically.

Denny later called me back with an idea. He told me, "Jim, I've sent an email out to as many mission organizations as I could think of that have ministries in Southeast Asia. Since Vietnam has denied your coming to Danang to teach in the local churches, I asked the other Asian ministries if they had a way to use you while the rest of the Kids Around the World volunteers and leaders construct the playground."

I appreciated Denny's gesture, but it wasn't what I had in mind. I was certain that God wanted me to train Vietnamese leaders—not to be "auctioned" off to anyone who could put me to work. Not exactly a morale boost!

Nevertheless, I told Denny I'd be up for whatever the Lord put together.

Within a few days Denny received a reply from a missionary serving in Chiang Mai, Thailand. He worked with a group called Pioneers, a group we'd worked with in Sarajevo, so we were at least familiar with their work.

The missionary told Denny in his email reply, "We'd love to have Jim come and train our workers. We'll start working on it right now, and I'll have someone meet Jim at the airport."

So I began making plans to travel to Thailand instead of Vietnam. Our group's travel plans took the entire team through Bangkok, Thailand, where we stayed overnight and headed back to the airport in the morning.

I remember saying good-bye to the team as they walked through security at the airport; I had an overwhelming feeling of disappointment and discouragement. I don't remember feeling more alone than I was then.

After I landed in Chiang Mai, as I made my way toward the terminal exit doors, I discovered that there was no one there to meet me, and I had no idea who I could call. I was utterly alone.

Fatigued from the long flight halfway across the world and hungry, I sat down in a chair near the exit doors and cried out to God, "Lord, what's going on? Is it your plan to bring me to Thailand, forgotten and alone, and try to figure out what I'm supposed to do now?"

As I sat in that chair near the exit, I watched groups of people come and go, until I was the only one left in the terminal—*now what?*

It was then that I began to experience a sense of God's calming presence in this situation. Overwhelmed by this peace that flooded over me, it was as if God was saying, "Jim, sit tight. I have this situation under control. I have a plan for you, so don't be nervous."

With a calmer demeanor, I dug through my notes to find the name of the hotel where I was to stay and looked around for a taxi to take me there when I noticed a young American running toward me.

He shouted out, "Are you Jim Rosene?"

I nodded.

"I'm *so* sorry we forgot you. We were so excited to meet the new schoolteachers that arrived for our mission school that I forgot about you. I'm sorry."

The missionary continued, "We have to hurry—there's a group of children's workers waiting for you!" He helped grab my luggage, and we got into his car and drove through the streets of Chiang Mai as quickly as the traffic allowed, and we parked in front of a small storefront office.

We grabbed my bags and hurried inside. I saw a group of some fifteen young people sitting in a circle, waiting, and checking me out.

I walked into the room, sat down among the children's workers, and began teaching. I shared a brief introduction and then presented the teachers with a brief Flannelgraph lesson. That's when I noticed one of the young women crying. It rattled me—*what did I do to offend her?*

I couldn't believe it—my first Thai training event, and I made someone cry! Now my mind was flooded with all kinds of thoughts—what did I do? Did I blunder with some cultural *faux pas?* Did my American humor offend her?

Her tearful response bothered me, but despite the distraction of her weeping, I kept teaching. At the first break—actually it was for tea—I walked over to the missionary who'd introduced me. I asked him, "What did I do to make that young woman cry?"

"Oh, you don't understand," he said. "You didn't make her cry. Wait until you hear her story."

He told me, "This young woman attended a conference three years ago, and for the first time she saw a set of Flannelgraph stories. She saw how effective the stories were and instantly fell in love with the Flannelgraphs and wanted to get some so she could share the stories of the Bible.

"She also knew she didn't have any money to buy them, so she had prayed, 'Dear God, I need those Flannelgraphs for the children of my Sunday school, but I don't know how to get them. I don't know who to contact. I don't have any money, but I will trust You, God, to deliver those Flannelgraphs to me.' She told our group that she's been praying for those Flannelgraphs for three years."

I looked at her across the room. She stood there by the Flannelgraph easel, looking longingly at the colorful materials.

The missionary continued with his explanation. "And today, an American came to Chiang Mai, Thailand, to conduct a training class, and when he pulled out the Flannelgraphs—"

I interrupted his story. "—and it was the exact set of Flannelgraphs she's been praying for."

It was then that I began to understand why I wasn't able to go to Vietnam. God had a different appointment for me. He needed me to make a delivery in Chiang Mai, Thailand.

I was overwhelmed and somewhat emotional myself when after the training, I presented a Flannelgraph set of materials to the young woman who'd prayed for so long that God would bring them to her. As she wept her tears were ones of pure joy.

Later, after I tried to digest all of what happened, I prayed for forgiveness for my self-centered feelings and disappointment—for thinking only of myself.

When I thought about the lengths to which God had worked in that young woman's life—to bring her exactly what she needed to help others—it was a defining moment of true faith for me. It was then, and there, that I decided I wanted to serve God for the rest of my life.[3]

Chapter Nineteen

LOOKING FOR AN OFF-RAMP AT 90 MPH

On another overseas trip, Evie and I were traveling in Germany from Austria, eastbound on the famous German Autobahn. Our guidebook told us a lot about the Autobahn: The recommended cruising speed is 130 kilometers per hour (81 MPH), and yet, there's no stated speed limit. You're simply instructed—if you drive slow—to stay in the right-hand lane and allow other cars to pass.

Most Americans first heard about the Autobahn during or right after WWII, because we'd always heard Adolf Hitler had built the Autobahn to help move his troops across Germany. However, the truth is, the first construction of the Autobahn was done in 1931, between Cologne and Bonn, and Hitler wasn't installed as German Chancellor until 1933—two years later. So I guess we can chalk up the claim that the Autobahn was Hitler's idea as an urban myth.

As I drove my rental car fast along the divided highway, I was impressed by the quality of the construction of the road. American freeways and Interstate highways are laid out as limited access highways with wide lanes and a center divide, just as the Autobahn. Yet the Autobahn roadbeds are smooth and level—something I thought was incredible, especially after nearly a century of use!

My wife, Evie, was with me as we raced along the Autobahn. We both commented on the attention to aesthetics the road-building architects had given—beautiful scenery filled our sight lines in every direction, with fields of clover or ripening grain, and mountain backdrops.

Suddenly, as we approached a small rise in the roadway, I noticed a "rest area" on the opposite side of the Autobahn. Then, in a quick glance in that direction, I also saw an airplane on the ground, parked in the "rest area" on the opposite side of the road.

As a pilot myself, I thought the sight of an airplane on the ground alongside the Autobahn seemed unusually strange. I wondered if the pilot had run out of fuel or had mechanical trouble—maybe he'd been forced to land on the highway, and somehow he'd taxied or was towed to the rest stop.

"Did you see that?" I asked Evie.

"Yeah, it's an airplane, but I don't see an airport," she replied. I clicked the coast button on the rental car's cruise control, and the car began to slow down.

"What are you doing?" Evie asked.

"I have a strong feeling that I ought to go back to check on that airplane. Maybe I can offer some help."

"But how can you do that? It's on the other side of the Autobahn. The traffic is going in the opposite direction."

I said, "There's an exit ramp. I'll get off here, make a loop, and that'll get me on the Autobahn going the other direction. It won't take us long to get back to that rest stop where we saw the plane."

I executed the turns to leave the eastbound lanes of the Autobahn and connect to the westbound lanes, heading back in the direction from which we came. Then I accelerated to keep pace with the rest of traffic—all of it going much faster.

After a few minutes, a small station wagon came up behind us at a high rate of speed, and after getting uncomfortably close to our back bumper, it passed. I felt the *swoosh* of its draft against our car as the station wagon swerved to the left into the passing lane, and I watched as the driver signaled that he was going to return into our lane, just ahead of us.

My foot instinctively lifted from the gas pedal and poised over the brake pedal as a caution, and I was thinking—*Maybe I'll have to stop quickly*.

The driver of the station wagon was going too fast. He'd swerved to pass us, accelerated, and then tried to straighten out his car and maneuver back into the right lane in front of us. But he overcorrected, and his car shot even more to the right—straight across the right lane we were in and onto the shoulder of the Autobahn.

I braked and fell back cautiously. The other car was now hurtling toward a field—aiming for an invisible path across it—but before he entered the field, the driver hit a culvert, stopping his station wagon in its tracks.

A law of physics was broken—he'd been going too fast to stop completely—and the station wagon's speed and momentum caused it to smash through the top third of the exposed culvert and sent it through a line of bushes, after which the driver totally lost control of his car. Only a second or two after leaving the highway, the car was rolling over and over across the flat field. Both Evie and I gasped—loud enough to startle each other, not believing what we were seeing.

It happened so quickly that I hesitated about what to do. Then, instinctively, I braked hard and stopped on the shoulder alongside the highway. None of the other cars stopped—only us. Perhaps no one else had even seen what happened.

Quickly I parked, turned on the hazard lights, killed the engine, and grabbed the keys. "We've gotta see if anyone's hurt," I told Evie, who's a retired nurse.

Evie and I ran toward where the tire tracks of the station wagon led us through the field to the vehicle. It was upside down, resting on its roof. Two of its doors were opened, and the driver and his companion were not in the car.

Looking around, we saw what we took as a married couple—thrown out of the car and lying many feet apart in the grassy field. The man was not moving. The woman was badly injured but was calling out for her children—still inside the wrecked car.

Evie, the German mother, and I ran to the car, where I saw three young children. All three were trapped inside and were apparently unconscious. I reached inside, grabbed a little girl, and tried to pull her out. With some effort, she was freed, and her mother and I handed her to Evie, who took the girl away from the overturned car and laid her down safely before she ran back to help with another child.

Suddenly the mother shouted, *"Benzene!"*

I could smell gasoline and saw that a small spark had started a fire in the engine area. The mom and I worked to free the next child, a boy, and again Evie carried the child to safety, far enough away from the wreck to be out of harm's way.

Just as we pulled the last child from the crushed car and ran from the wreck toward that safe spot, the engine fire had traveled the length of the fuel line, and the instant it reached the gas tank, the car exploded in a furious fireball. As I looked back over my shoulder, the overturned station wagon was completely engulfed in flames. Fortunately, all occupants were safely out of the burning car.

With fire and smoke now attracting attention, other cars and trucks began to stop. Some drivers got out and ran over, offering help. Shortly afterward a fire engine came; then ambulances arrived, and the emergency rescue medics took over.

The authorities didn't interview us, probably because Evie and I were not conversant in the German language. So with the authorities well in charge, we got back in our car and continued our travel.

In the frenzy of that terrible accident, we forgot all about that airplane at the rest stop. Yet in retrospect, there had been people already at the rest stop, so if there had been an emergency with the plane, someone there would've helped.

However, I wondered, *What if the airplane had not been parked at the rest stop?*

And if we hadn't turned around and gotten off the Autobahn to check it out?

We wouldn't have seen the car swerve out of control
—plow through the bushes, roll over across the field
—and then finally flip over onto its top and stop and explode.

If all these events hadn't gotten our attention, three helpless children would have been burned alive when the car exploded in flames.

In the condition the mother was in, it's likely she couldn't have pulled them out of the overturned vehicle by herself—and all three of her kids could have died. Evie and I both believe that the sight of an airplane where it didn't belong caused that interruption in our travel. It was something that God did. He put us in the right place at the right time.

I've since learned that I need to trust my spiritual intuition. Through prayer and thoughtful times of reflection, I've learned to "fine-tune" that spiritual relationship that I have with God. Many times I've seen miraculous things happen as a result of following His "nudges" to change direction—and do something He wants me to do.

Sometimes God leads us to do something that will result in a "story" to share with others—in this case, God knew what was about to happen. He placed Evie and me in the right spot to save three children from sure death.

In former Communist countries, building relationships with government leaders proved critical, especially where there's a risk for pastors and other Christian leaders in current ministry. Making friends with key authorities is a way to prevent persecution of Christians. Here's one example. Hitchhiking on the goodwill we accrued by building a playground in a former Communist country, we established a Sister City relationship between that city and Rockford, resulting in an ambulance shipped over there when there were no funds in the local government's budget, and also saw to it that a home for the handicapped was established.

There are other things that can happen. An international incident took place some years after our earlier successes. A former Communist nation was caught in a dilemma reminiscent of the Cold War. The US, which leased a military air base in that country, was negotiating for an extension of the lease. Russia then applied pressure to its former satellite country, telling its leaders to reject the lease renewal with the United States and, instead, look to Russia for aid.

The resulting tension trickled down the government bureaucracy and led to a crackdown on Western influence and religious activities. A "new religion" law was passed.

Because of the relationships that had been built, no pressure has been brought upon Kids Around the World that could alter what we are doing. The elected officials have gotten to know us and to trust our good intentions.

Trust me, building relationships really works. However, it's not something I can brag about. It's all *God's* doing. These are examples of God orchestrating situations and plans to get something wonderful done.

In another instance I was on a vacation in Florida, at a party hosted by my friend Paul Kingstrom. Paul reminded me, "Denny, I know you've been praying for the Lord to lead you to a place in India where you could build a playground." I nodded and Paul asked, "Have you received an answer to your prayer?"

Kids Around the World and I had emailed several contacts, without any results. I had prayed for God to show me a spot in India—one where we could achieve the greatest effectiveness through building a playground somewhere among the 1.1 billion people living in that country.

Yet I had to admit to Paul, "I'm afraid that God still hasn't answered that prayer."

The next day it rained. I got a phone call from Paul: "Denny, my golf game's been cancelled. Can we still get together for lunch?"

I said, "Sure. I'm available."

Paul explained, "I'm having lunch with Vern Hultgren, John Ring, and another friend who just came back from India. I'd like you to join us. I was thinking, maybe these guys might have some ideas for a place to build your playground in India."

At lunch I met Bob Nelson of India Rural Evangelical Fellowship, and he told us of his work. Then, at one point, he said, "Denny, in India we have an orphanage with a thousand kids. I can't imagine any kids who need a playground more than these orphan kids do." I listened as he told me about their orphanage in the town of Repalle.

Not long after that, we worked with the city and India Rural Evangelical Fellowship and built the playground at the orphanage in Repalle, India, and followed that with a second one in the city of Rapalle—where we couldn't start construction until after moving the water buffalo out of the city park.

We worked with the local Rockford Rotary Club and developer Sunil Puri to raise the funds to make those projects happen. Yet, just as with God's detour for our trip on the Autobahn, lives would be saved in response to our obedience.

The same thing happened again. Though it perhaps was not as dramatic as the car wreck on the Autobahn, getting a playground built in a needy place in India—where desperate kids half a world away could get help—wouldn't have happened if not for an innocuous incident involving a rained-out golf game that changed everyone's plans.

That's the way God works.

Chapter Twenty

CHINA: CRACKS IN THE GREAT WALL

Bob and Faye Anderson are friends of mine who had a dream. In the mid-1980s they retired as schoolteachers in Rockford and told friends that instead of resting in rocking chairs, they wanted to go to China and teach English as a second language for Chinese students. The idea behind their new vocation was to use it as an opportunity to also answer students' questions about America and Christianity.

When they initially left for China in September 1988, Bob was sixty-six years old, and Faye was sixty-five. Their plan was to live in Xiamen, in the Fujian Province of China, a port city across from Taiwan in the northwest Pacific.

They decided to teach English as a second language to students from Xiamen University "for maybe a year, and then return to the US." However Bob and Faye fell in love with the Chinese people—especially the university students. That one-year experiment turned into a whole new career of more than twenty years in China.

They left China for periodic vacations back in the US, and for a short hiatus for their safety following the Tiananmen Square incidents of 1989, where—according to the Chinese Red Cross—between two and three thousand Chinese students and other protesters were killed. They went back in September 1989 to stay until fulfilling a dream that lasted more than twenty years. Their "second" teaching career turned out to be "a greatly fulfilling adventure."

When they came back to America, they left a number of "children" and "grandchildren" that they acquired through their twenty years of ministry. They never had any children of their own, but these "adopted" ones that they'd come to know and love more than made up for their lack of progeny of their own.

Ironically, in this land of nearly four million square miles there was a population of 1.3 billion people (1,330,044,544 according to a July 2008 estimate). Kids Around the World came to China to build its thirty-fourth playground in 2004. The site for that playground was in the growing community of Langfang, China, not far from where Bob and Faye Anderson lived and worked.

The playground in Langfang was a joint venture between Kids Around the World, the Million Dollar Round Table Foundation (which donated the playground equipment), and the Philip Hayden Foundation (which acquired the land from the Chinese government). The land was formerly a shepherd's field, and it seemed appropriate that we use it to build a playground for "little lost sheep."

The Hayden Foundation also erected a new "Children's Village"—an orphanage for children born with birth defects who were discarded by their parents. The Children's Village also has facilities for housing 150 children, a training center, and a guesthouse.

I remember when we went to Langfang to build the playground that our construction crew, led by Ralph Peterson, was apprehensive about whether it would even be possible. We didn't incur difficulties with the government or the shipping of our equipment. The problem was *weather*. In late January the weather is much like Midwestern America's seasons and temperatures.

They told us that the temperatures would likely be below freezing—which posed problems for our construction crews by preventing us from digging into the frozen soil and keeping the concrete footings from setting properly. Miraculously, when it was time to do the work, the weather cooperated—with temperatures *above* freezing, ideal for the construction.

The other problem we had was the dedication of the playground. On the day of dedication, we were warned to expect only a few people to come—due to the extreme cold weather. That was sad news for our crew—for that's how they're "paid." Their satisfaction comes from seeing the kids when they're let into the playground area for the first time. The volunteer workers were all there for the same reason: to put smiles on as many faces of as many children as possible.

At first the hearts of our volunteer workers sank when the Chinese leaders told them they wouldn't see many smiling faces this time for the new playground. However to our great surprise and gratitude, despite the frigid weather, the kids came *in droves!*—invited by the Hayden Foundation—from the village across the street from the orphanage, and the dedication was a huge success.

Later, the crew relaxed in a house provided for them for the construction period, and the extra days were spent training 169 children's workers in and around the Beijing area. One evening, in groups of four and five, they cut out Flannelgraph characters based on the JESUS film, to have characters to tell the Christmas story.

Even though Christmas had been celebrated almost a month earlier, the American volunteers had to work hard and quickly to present this holiday program. While they worked, someone spontaneously started to sing "Away In a Manger," and a moment later all were singing—some in English, others in Chinese, and still others in their own native dialects.

This training ministry of Kids Around the World used "The Story of Jesus for Children," the children's version of the JESUS film, augmented by the Flannelgraph stories created around the content of that film. The training itself was a low-key event and occurred at different locations every day. The 169 Chinese Christians attended seminars with ideas and methods for teaching kids. I was amazed at how enthusiastically they were received—but I don't know why I should be. It's always that way when we finish a training session for leaders of kids.

In China, Evie and I met a man named Liu Chen.[1] He was a pastor for one of the underground (unregistered) house church groups. We gave him Bibles that we'd brought with us to share with his people. Mr. Chen told us how he'd been imprisoned for his faith.

The charge? That he'd broken laws forbidding worship in an unregistered church. He also told us details about his sentence to hard labor: "I had to work in the sewers and clean them. Every day I was forced to work in sewage up to my waist. Each morning I had to go out and work in the stench-filled sewers."

Someone asked Lui Chen how he survived that ordeal. He said, "I would imagine that instead of a stinking sewer, I was in a fragrant garden, communing with God, and I'd sing to the Lord"—and then he sang us a sample of a hymn—his words were in Chinese, but I knew the English melody—a song that tells a story:

I'd stay in the garden with Him, though the night around me is falling;
But He bids me go, through a vale of woe, His voice to me is calling.
And He walks with me, and He talks with
me, and He tells me I am His own;
And the joy we share as we tarry there, none other has ever known.
And He walks with me, and He talks with
me, and He tells me I am His own;
And the joy we share as we tarry there, none other has ever known.[2]

God blessed and protected Lui Chen when he was imprisoned for his faith. He also permitted him to survive that terrible time and to eventually resume his ministry among the house churches.

We had come to that area as representatives of International Aid. Ralph Plumb was the director, and I was a board member of the organization. We negotiated with the Hmong leaders who controlled the region—and forged this deal: International Aid would rebuild the health clinic for the minority people of that mountain region, and in return the leaders agreed to allow the Christians to build several churches and gave their word to not persecute the Christians or harm their churches.

Agreement was also reached with the town's political leadership and Pastor Lui Chen. The clinic was rebuilt, and the churches were constructed and then filled with worshippers who were left unmolested.

The underground church is growing in China, even as the government in some regions still makes it tough for churches to get started and then begin to thrive—legally. So they meet in small groups, usually in a home. However, we work with the Chinese government leaders since we are in their country as guests.

Evie and I visited a few of these churches. As the "underground" churches are growing in China, the governments in some regions are being more open to Christians—they realize Christians are not a threat to the government, and their motives are to help and love others, as the example of Jesus laid out. Christians continue to meet in homes and approved homes.

Our American friends, Bob and Faye Anderson, told us about Lam Ma[3]—a Chinese Christian from the Beijing area who had also been imprisoned for his faith. He'd been active in establishing house churches and had been arrested. Then, after serving his sentence at hard labor, he was released. They told us,

> We had invited two Chinese university students over to watch a six-part video series about the Christian response to the theory of evolution. We had them over for dinner and invited Lam Ma to share his Christian experiences. We could tell that

> these science-based videos made an impression on the students, but we were nervous about what Lam Ma would say.
>
> We had to be careful when it came to sharing our religious viewpoints. If our students asked questions, we were allowed to answer—but we were forbidden to proselytize. So we excused ourselves after dinner and let Lam Ma explain how the Christian God created the universe and all that's in it. After listening and some more dialogue, these two students were converted to Christianity and began worshipping in one of the house churches led by Lam Ma.

Faye Anderson also said that the reason the house churches were growing so fast is that the people in those churches tell their friends and neighbors stories about Jesus and bring them to a house church. As this church grew to about fifty people, the leader would then divide the congregation into two new house churches, and the process would repeat itself.

In Lumung the Christian leadership asked us for ten thousand sets of the JESUS film Flannelgraphs. I'd brought one set with me to Beijing. That's all I could provide them at the time. I told them we'd have to find a way to import ten thousand sets into the country. Meanwhile I told them they could at least have the one I brought with me to Beijing.

Getting it to them seemed almost like a scene from a spy novel. We arranged to meet one of the Christian leaders at a table in a second-floor restaurant, a prearranged place. I put the Flannelgraph set down next to me.

The leader came, chatted briefly about the weather and asked if I liked the restaurant, then he surreptitiously picked up the Flannelgraph and excused himself. I watched as he left the second-floor restaurant area but couldn't see him as he brought it to a waiting bike on the street below.

A young man on the bike hurried away with the Flannelgraph set, or perhaps even gave it to another courier to further confuse anyone following "the American."

I was truly impressed with the house-church movement in China. Of course, we're most familiar with their explosive growth in adding to the rolls of new Christian believers. Yet most people don't realize that the house church is a place that they can go regularly to learn other things besides Christian doctrine.

Most of the Christians with whom I came in contact will not go to a higher learning institution. They'll only take instruction from a *Christian* teacher. Interestingly, though, they also learn culture in churches—music in particular, but also drama and art. They also learn sports—perhaps as a by-product of hosting the Chinese Olympic Games of 2008. The Chinese also learn by doing—acquiring leadership and organizational skills, gaining practical experience by volunteering to help others, or caring for the sick and elderly.

House churches also participate in teaching the children in China. They practice the precepts of Orality's oral-visual teaching, singing or memorizing the words of Scripture or songs. That kind of teaching is effective, and it can't easily be stopped or interfered with by political or government leaders.

I think that if the West can provide the Chinese house churches with musical instruments and electronic keyboards, that may also become important—to help the churches to create and program music that's not just interesting and fun but something that edifies and changes lives.

I learned something interesting about the Christians in China—they receive tremendous encouragement from singing hymns. I suppose that's not a surprise. I've seen that kind of encouragement all across the world, as well as in our own American churches. However, many of the Chinese house churches don't have musical instruments or musicians to carry a tune—and that makes congregational worship music more difficult.

I heard about an electronic iPod-style "hymnal player" that could be used to lead a small house church congregation in singing hymns. The device contains a thousand best-loved Chinese hymns. A house church leader turns it on and picks out a hymn, and it pops up instantly for the people to begin praising God. These hymns are a wonderful way to strengthen believers and teach them biblical truths through song.

Can hymns, storytelling, and Flannelgraphs be used in connection to their own music, the content of certain songs with themes that reinforce Christian doctrine and values? We're *already doing those things* by pairing Flannelgraph stories with other implements—like illustrated children's Bibles in areas like China, Central Asia, Romania, Philippines, and Latin America. *Why?*

The desperate need for illustrated children's Bibles and Bible stories that are not dependent upon the written word is obvious. As I've already pointed out, two-thirds of the world can't read or write in

Western ways. They have a visual-oral tradition. The tools that we're using take advantage of that visual-oral tradition.

It's important that we accelerate our efforts in evangelizing kids. The percentage of children under age fifteen is already a huge part of the population in countries across the planet, and they need to know Jesus before they become adults—because studies show that they'll be less likely to consider God, Jesus, and Christianity after they move into their teenage years.

Here's the most recent ranking of kids under age fifteen, as percentage of overall population, by area or country:

40–50 percent in Africa
35 percent in Philippines
31 percent in Mexico
21 percent in China
33 percent in Egypt
31 percent in India[4]

I remember the time that former President Nixon and Secretary of State Henry Kissinger went to China. Following those talks, China opened their nation to Westerners beginning in 1973. That's when I first began to hear about the house churches there. We were told that the total Christian population was one or two million (depending on the source of information) and was initially outlawed by Mao's Communist government when the revolution occurred.

By the 1970s, we heard estimates that Mao Tse-Tung, the first revolutionary leader of Communist China, had killed thirty to fifty million citizens in that first generation of the totalitarian regime.

Ironically, there were also estimates that *more than thirty million evangelical Christians* were meeting in house churches across China, and that encouraged those of us in the West. Amazingly, Christianity was still alive after that first generation of Communism—despite the oppression and persecution. In the 1990s it was said that the Christian population was between *fifty and one hundred million.* However, a report presented at Beijing University stated that the number of Christians in China had risen to one hundred and thirty million by the end of 2006.[5]

These numbers are astonishing when you take into account the fact that the Chinese evangelical church has existed despite difficulties for most of the past sixty years.

Estimates of Christians who died for their faith are said to be in the millions. During the Cultural Revolution, almost all the evangelical Christian Chinese leadership and local pastors were killed, imprisoned, or otherwise silenced. Amazingly, even after more than a half-century of such persecution, the Chinese church has gone from one or two million to fifty times that figure.

Someone told me that there are now more evangelical Christians in China than in the United States. Amazing things are happening there. Interestingly, we also see a new openness to Christianity in Cuba, with a change of heart of Fidel Castro, happening at the same time as the fresh openness of the Chinese government.

Chapter Twenty-One

SARAJEVO: "THIS HELL PROVES THERE MUST BE A HEAVEN"

I was going to begin this chapter by saying that I've been blessed to be able to visit many great countries and cultures in my lifetime. Yet, upon further reflection, I might need to choose a different word than *blessed* for *some* of my visits. Or maybe not.

Experiences in Rwanda, Haiti, Bosnia, the Chernobyl Exclusion Zone, and totalitarian regimes like Cuba, Pakistan, Afghanistan, and Vietnam were *interesting* and eye-opening to say the least—but sometimes the people who lived there were desperate in many ways. Still, despite some of those desperate situations in these places, I was always *blessed* in some way by going to them.

Nevertheless, we have to be wary. Those of us who are serious about changing the world in the name of our God by enlisting people to be Christ followers have to recognize that there are sometimes major foes to contend with if we want to make a difference in our world.

Missionary Ted Esler[1] is one of those who wants to make a difference.

I first met Ted when I first visited Sarajevo in the spring of 1996, when he came to get Kids Around the World president Jim Rosene, Kids' playground coordinator Ralph Peterson, and me at the Zagreb airport because hostilities in Sarajevo were still too recent and snipers and insurgents were still causing trouble. So the Sarajevo airport had yet to be reopened.

Ted met us in a blue Chrysler minivan, and I noticed that it had Minnesota license plates.

He chuckled. "Yeah, I had the van shipped over from the States and tried to get new plates when we got here, but I'm still waiting. The Bosnia government is yet to get organized."

On the ride from the Zagreb airport, Ted drove east, alongside the Sava River, and he told me about what was happening in Sarajevo. "During the war our part of town had been an early focal point of the fighting," he said. "The Serbs had captured the area around the airport and held that ground. The Muslims had taken the northern part of the city, where 'Sniper Alley' started. That's why the people started to dig trenches parallel to the apartment buildings where the snipers were, and the street, where the tanks and soldiers were lobbing in mortar rounds and other munitions, rifle fire, and grenades."

As we finally entered Sarajevo, I changed the subject—or at least thought I did: "Well, a playground here would really get people's attention."

Ted looked at me with a look that conveyed, *Wow! You guys have no clue.*

I tried to clarify what I meant to say: "Uh, I mean, I can imagine how surprised the people would be, seeing a playground where a war was going on just months earlier?"

Ted nodded. "It was a siege within a siege—everything and everybody was exposed and vulnerable. Lots of people were killed."

We went to meet with a representative of the US Embassy in Sarajevo, and he and Ted took us to the proposed site for the playground. I could see why as we drove through the street that we had some security from UN and NATO peacekeepers.

Everywhere we looked, however, there were burned-out hulks of cars, trucks, and even buses. We could still see the smoke and soot damage, with gaping holes created by mortars, and grenades cratered parts of those buildings across that avenue. They were caught in cross fire when firefights began. As if reading my mind, Ted answered the question I was about to ask—"The reason they haven't started to rebuild those homes and apartments is they're afraid the war might start again."

As the van slowed, the man from the US Embassy pointed to the edge of a large open field surrounded on three sides with buildings and a market across the street on one side. The three buildings effectively sheltered the field. As he stopped the van, he swept his arm to indicate where he was gesturing.

"This is it," he said proudly. We followed up with our own comments of admiration.

Ted said, "The Sarajevo city government offered the land for a playground, and the US Agency for International Development is willing to provide some support."

"Really—USAID is willing to help us?" I asked.

Ted nodded his head again. "It's a perfect place for a playground. By the way, have you heard where the playground equipment is? It's supposed to get here anytime now."

Usually Kids Around the World buys a complete set of playground equipment, then packs the various components and modules in crates or other packing, and finally puts everything into a cargo container about the size of a semitrailer truck to be shipped by sea container ships.

However, this time, we were shipping the equipment and tools by air. The shipment had to be packed in boxes and crates—some forty or so—which were flown to an air base used by American troops that would help get the shipment to us in Sarajevo.

Despite the careful planning, delays in shipping could cause much grief if the volunteers arrived and had to sit around for days if delivery was held up for any reason.

Ted reassured me with the answer I was waiting to hear: "The first shipments started to arrive this past week. The rest will be here tomorrow. Your team will be good to go."

"Did you have any problems getting it into the country? I mean that cargo is valued at more than a hundred thousand dollars. We've never had a problem, but—"

Ted smiled and shook his head. "Not to worry. Getting it here was an adventure, but a fun one. The US Army stepped up to the plate. They provided the overland transportations, using their trucks free of charge."

"But how did—" I started to ask.

"A while back, the US Army, NATO, and the UN implemented a plan called, 'Arms for Bosnia.' They send munitions and other supplies into the country. They use this stuff to train and arm the Bosnia army, so they can stabilize the region."

Again I asked, "But how did—" And again Ted answered the question I hadn't yet asked.

"Your stuff was packed into army transport trucks and armored personnel carriers—placed alongside machine guns, armored vehicles, and weapons were purple and yellow slides, red merry-go-rounds, swings, and all the crates of tools.

"Everything you guys packed into crates and shipped from the States—nails, hammers, screwdrivers, rakes, brooms, shovels and picks, wheelbarrows, wrenches, and an endless assortment of nuts and bolts. Everything. Also, all the crates were numbered. I was impressed," Ted said, adding quizzically, "but there was one crate that puzzled me. It had a hinged top."

"Oh, that's John," Jim Rosene said with a laugh.

"John?"

"It's a prefabricated outhouse," I added with a grin. "After we take out all the tools and stuff, we take the crate out of the truck. Inside there's a toilet, and we bolt it to what will be the bottom of the crate when it's tipped on its side. One of our guys will saw a hole in the wood below the toilet. The hinged top on the crate becomes the outhouse door, and then it's ready to set up on-site for the workers."

The next morning the army trucks pulled up to the site as we were also arriving, and the unloading happened quickly. A crowd of kids and adults stood behind our orange webbed construction fence to watch. When they saw the huge pieces of playground parts, it didn't take long for them to figure out what was going to take place in the former field.

Before the construction of the equipment could start, however, we still had to fill in some holes made during the war by mortar rounds, mines, and other explosions. A couple of local trucks were requisitioned to go get sand to dump into the holes—which had first been filled with debris picked up from all over the field. Next, the same treatment was done with the long, deep trenches that the people used to cross the city and avoid snipers and other gunfire. We used an ancient Bosnian bulldozer to push old cars, broken refrigerators, burned mattresses, and other trash into the long five-feet-deep trenches.

After that, trucks drove down to the seaside to get loads of sand to cover the debris piled into the trenches and to complete the job by leveling everything before proceeding with the playground construction. It was at this point that we ran into yet another glitch.

When the trucks dumped the sand into piles, the area was soon swarmed with men and women who showed up with shovels, buckets, and wheelbarrows. They wanted the sand to mix with bags of cement to do repairs and construction of their own following the war's destruction.

That kind of larceny seemed forgivable, but the man from the US Army Corps of Engineers told us how to deal with the scavengers: "Send the trucks to get sand from the Adriatic coast. The sand is mostly salt. If they try to use it with cement, it won't work, and they know that their labor will be in vain. They'd have to do everything over," he told us.

He added, "Be sure to let the people know. Tell them, 'This sand is from the seashore, and it's mostly salt, but good for the children when they play. It's perfect for the kids, but you'll destroy your cement work if you try to use it as a concrete mix.'"

The plan worked. Grumbling, the people left without taking any sand, and they never returned to help themselves to any of our other materials. Even when we brought in loads of regular sand to mix *our* cement for the footings and other construction, they didn't seem to want to take a chance—maybe it was also sea sand—so they left us alone.

It was a deeply emotional experience for us to build a playground for children in Sarajevo, Bosnia—on the very site where urban snipers had been shooting at civilians trying to make their way through the cities.

Earlier, when I was in Kosovo, I saw the infamous gymnasium where bullet holes garishly decorated all four walls—where countless men and boys were lined up and shot to death.

In Sarajevo I stayed in the Hilton Hotel, but guests were restricted to rooms at the back side of the hotel—the front guest rooms were still frequently targeted by snipers, and the rooms were constantly being shot up by .30 caliber rifles, .50 caliber machine gun shells, and rocket-propelled grenades.

Even little children had been targets in Sarajevo while the war raged. Adults and kids alike had to scurry behind burned-out buses or cars, hide behind walls until it was safe, or otherwise find trenches that could offer them safe passage through the gauntlet of snipers. However when we built the playground in 1996, most of the violence had ended. Still, we were nervous to be reminded that it was to be constructed on the very site of one of the most infamous and deadly shootings. We were assured that with UN, US, and NATO forces a heavy presence in the area, the children would not be in harm's way—reassurance that eased my fears.

We first had to use our equipment to fill in the trenches and remove the debris and skeletons of cars and other vehicles—targets of the snipers. As you might expect, our transformation of a killing field into a playground was dramatic and emotional for the Bosnians who attended the groundbreaking ceremony, but it was not as traumatic as their memories of the site's past. Transformed into a playground, it was a remarkable spiritual object lesson of God's victory over the darkness of war, genocide, and horrific evil.

As the playground took shape and was nearing completion, the children (and many adults) who came every day to watch from behind the orange webbed construction fence grew into a large crowd. They must have asked each other with a sense of anticipation, *When will it be finished?*

Meanwhile, while all this was taking place, another project was going on out of sight of the crowds. Dr. Jerome Weiskopf, a leading plastic surgeon from Rockford who'd done pioneering miracles in microsurgery and other advances, traveled with the team to do surgeries in Sarajevo. My wife, Evie, a registered nurse, assisted. They focused on the children as many aid and relief organizations dealt only with life-and-death emergency medical problems—a broken bone, lacerations, elevated fevers, and the kinds of things that are routine.

What wasn't routine were the huge numbers of kids who might have been injured by flying shrapnel or bullet wounds on their faces. Those wounds destroyed smiles and self-esteem, and Dr. Weiskopf and Evie knew that this was part of the treatment. They were continually busy repairing the faces of little ones, fixing the results of hurried, botched emergency surgeries done in the middle of a war in a partially protected area.

A German relief agency brought several tons of food to the construction site of the playground, where it was easy for them to distribute.

While these things were taking place, so were other activities. Several team members who weren't involved with the construction were busy visiting the local schools with their puppets program—and the kids ate it up. No one had paid them so much attention in a long time, and it had also been a long time since many of them had laughed with such spontaneous happiness. Between "shows" in the schools, our American teens handed out copies of Billy Graham's book *Peace with God.*

Finally, it was opening day. Kids listened to the brief dedication of the playground and prayer offered to underscore what was immediately understood by the crowd, both adults and kids: This was really special. From somewhere in the crowd, someone started to sing a song of "thank you" to the Americans and local Christians for this magnificent gift to them. Everyone else started to sing along and clapped enthusiastically afterward.

We had invited the mayor of the community to speak. He was followed by our new friend, missionary Ted Esler, who expressed a few words of thanks to the Kids Around the World team and then explained the motivation behind their travel halfway across the globe to do this for the people filling the playground to listen.

"The Americans came here to share out of their abundance, because God shared with them out of *His* abundance," Ted told them.

After that, the ribbon was cut and cameras flashed as the playground was officially dedicated and opened for business. A huge cheer and noisy ovation erupted from the crowd of kids—and they instantly swarmed over whatever piece of playground equipment was nearest to where they'd been standing and patiently waiting.

Over the next five days, some thirty-thousand children played on all the rides, slides, and other brightly colored equipment. They had come from all parts of Sarajevo, most by buses—and those not able to use transportation were not afraid to walk *miles* from outlying villages, just to see and enjoy the playground.

This was one of the first playgrounds built by Kids Around the World teams, and I was so moved at what took place in Sarajevo. It was such a wonderful high that it energized me all the way back to the United States. It's a feeling that happens every time we build a playground.

I also recall how blessed I was that so many families were helped by the playgrounds we also built in some of these other locations, such as refugee camps in the strife-torn Thailand, near the border area of Myanmar (formerly Burma), and other desperate places.

Even visiting all these difficult sites makes me pause to consider the possible danger or threats that might come our way, just for *visiting* such places. Places like Sarajevo and Bosnia, Rwanda, Haiti, and Afghanistan. However, by God's grace, we never faced any real danger—even though at an apartment we stayed at, as we walked up to the second floor, we saw bullet holes that had been sprayed all the way from ground level to above the second floor near the roof. During the night, we'd be awakened by the sounds of land mines exploding—as some person, or an unlucky animal—had just stepped on the wrong spot. We were sobered by knowing that people during the war had no doubt run for their lives, and might even have lost the race.

We made two trips to Sarajevo. The first one was to meet Ted Esler and visit with USAID. We'd hoped they would partner with us as a humanitarian contributor to gender peace within the community.

We told the receptionist in the USAID offices what we hoped to do, and told her something of our history of building playgrounds in places around the world where they were most needed. After the receptionist checked with the people in charge, we were told they did not have time to visit with us.

But as we exited the building and headed for the parking lot, a man came running out of the USAID office. He called to us and said, "Did you say that you have a *playground* to offer?"

We told him that was correct.

He smiled sheepishly and said, "I'm sorry we didn't pick up on that. But let's start over. We've got just the spot," and he continued to tell us about a site that was absolutely perfect. We talked some more, and then he reached out his arm to shake my hand. He said, "We'd love to partner with you!"

However, on our other trip to Sarajevo, we met with the city Muslim leadership. They had first refused to allow the Christians to even meet and "discuss a deal." They probably worried that if we built a playground we'd also set up loudspeakers and preach to the neighborhood.

The leaders finally gave in and gave us a meeting. We did our best to assure them that we had no hidden agenda or plans for religious agitation.

As we explained what we do, we could see them softening to the idea. I said to the chief Muslim leader, "We'll build a playground for you. It won't cost you anything but the land you'd donate for the playground. But there is one condition. It's an agreement that you'll allow the few Christians to meet in one of the storefront spaces, without persecuting them."

They seemed satisfied by the terms. The Muslims nodded agreeably, and so did we.

The playground was built, and kids of both faiths—Christian and Muslim—played together. Conversations between the children's parents took place at the playground—in a neutral setting where kids were happy and sharing the fun. Both the kids and their moms and dads took advantage of that neutral setting to get to know each other, as they sat on the park benches watching their children.

There were no confrontations. No protesters. No persecution. No hired goons to beat up and chase the people away. No shots fired. Just smiles, laughing shouts of joy, and shared conversation with each other—proving that they had more in common than they might have guessed.

Everywhere I go, I always come to a serious conclusion about whether we should be there at a "rough" place like Sarajevo. However, I also know that we, and scores or hundreds of our prayer partners, had all prayed about our safety first. Then, God would give us a sense of peace about going to a particular place. God always opened the doors for us to go someplace, and we always had a sense that His safety and protection would follow us.

We have constructed playgrounds and performed puppet and Flannelgraph programs for kids in schools—even in former or present Communist dictatorships and nations run by extremist Islamic fundamentalists or militant Hindus.

True Christianity hasn't declared war on any of these groups, but the leaders of each of these other groups isn't bashful about their plans to persecute—and even kill—Christians, and try to destroy their churches and the Christian faith itself, usually by extreme violence and terrorism instead of honest, peaceful, and respectful theological debate.

We are always aware of those threats to our faith and the future of Christianity. Besides making sure that we cover each project with plenty of prayer, we always take every effort to protect our teams and those national Christian leaders who work with us.

We never take chances or unnecessary risks with our people or the people whom we come to help. We pray, trust God, and let Him take care of any potential confrontations with evil. No evil, large or small, will ever be victorious over the God of the universe.

Chapter Twenty-Two

DIFFERENT WORLDVIEWS—PART I

Fanatical Islamic Terrorism Targets Christians

In my travels across the Middle East, Africa, and Southeast Asia I was aware of the terror threats of Islamic fundamentalists whose militant view of their religion sometimes led them to blow up buildings—and *themselves*—or order to kill those they called "infidels," as if it were a direct order from Allah.

September 11, 2001, while Evie and I were on the Amazon River, scouting out a possible playground site, the attack on the World Trade Center and Pentagon occurred, killing 2,752 people—four hundred more fatalities than those in the Japanese attack on Pearl Harbor that launched World War II. The 9/11 massacre prompted Americans and their allies to go to war against those who planned and carried out the homicidal acts against the US, prompting then-President George W. Bush to announce a war on terror, but many Americans couldn't make a distinction between al-Qaeda and other Islamists. Few even knew that al-Qaeda was a terrorist group.

I had witnessed the evil potential of the Islamic fanatics just eight months after 9/11. It was on a visit to Kabul, Afghanistan, in May 2002. Immediately following the 9/11 event, our nation went to war against terror in Afghanistan and Iraq—to find and destroy al-Qaeda and Osama bin Laden.

Though Afghanistan was on a war footing, one of the stops on my trip to that country was to visit and to see for myself the sadness and horror in what I'd been told took place in a Kabul soccer stadium, and another visit that—although it had its share of bad memories—left a *good* memory of spiritual triumph.

First, let me tell you of my visit to the soccer stadium in Kabul. It was built by King Amunullah Khan in 1923 to mark Afghanistan's status as a newly independent nation. But not long after its completion the stadium became the site for public displays of what the Taliban called "corporal punishment." This corporal punishment included *stonings, amputations by sword, and beheadings*. I shudder to think what took place in the other public displays for punishment.

When I was there in 2002, the stadium was empty, but it looked like a typical sports complex. Yet I knew that, although it served as a soccer stadium, the site was also a place of public executions—stonings, beheadings, hangings, executions by bullets, and various other ways of dealing with both petty and serious "crimes."

The Taliban controlled most of Afghanistan at the time, and they governed by intimidation and by applying strict Islamic Sharia laws. The Taliban followed centuries-old practices that invoked harsh public punishment of those wrongdoers. The Taliban's religious army also made the punishments very public. They were scheduled for Friday—the eve of their Sabbath—when the largest number of people would be able to watch.

Taliban fundamentalists interpreted—*(or misinterpreted)*—age-old laws of the Quran and prescribed punishments for breaking the laws of their holy book. To Westerners, the Taliban's actions hark back to the Dark Ages—a time that the Quran was drafted—a thousand years ago.

The harsh Taliban laws have not been at all moderated since the tenth and eleventh centuries—they still prescribe punishment that Westerners call barbaric. True, the Judeo-Christian Old Testament also had harsh punishment for crimes like adultery or murder, but when Jesus came to offer His life for our sins and crimes, the old laws were moderated when the New Testament brought in the element of repentance and grace to address crime and punishment.

In Kabul, even today, if a man is caught stealing, his hand and one foot are cut off as a public display of "justice." Taking that punishment a step further, a religious leader might also dramatically and violently chop off the man's hand while robed doctors "humanely" amputate the person's foot. The leader holds up the bloody hand and amputated foot as a warning to the crowd—*See what happens when you steal or rob?*

One of the most common *executions* is for sexual sin. If a man or woman is caught committing the act of promiscuity (sex with many partners or premarital sex) or adultery, they can be subject to a terrible verdict of death by severe methods.[1] In such cases the man and/or woman is usually buried in the ground—the man up to his waist; the woman up to her shoulders—and they are stoned to death. The Taliban even gives the barbaric act of stoning a benign sounding name—*lapidation.*

Other forms of lethal punishment—such as murder—are meted out as an "eye for an eye" kind of retribution. A relative of the victim gets the "privilege" of carrying out the execution. Recent death sentences included having the father of a victim shoot the killer to death. Another victim, a mother, was given the opportunity to take the life of the killer of her murdered son. The Taliban gave her a huge knife to behead a prisoner brought to the stadium—the alleged murderer. The practice is called *qasas,* meaning "religiously sanctioned slitting of human throats."[2]

In yet another situation a woman was found guilty of killing her abusive husband with an ax, but she complained that it was self-defense. Her pleas were ignored and, though she was a mother of seven, she was summarily executed by a Taliban soldier, by three shots from his pistol.

Before my visit to Kabul, a French news service reported that:

> In August 1998 the hardline Taliban publicly executed a murderer and amputated limbs of two robbers amid shouts of, "God is Great," at the Kabul stadium.

> Thousands of Taliban soldiers and citizens, including women, watched the proceedings as the murderer squatted in the center of the open stadium. After his face was covered with a mask he was shot dead by the father of the man allegedly killed by the accused earlier this year.
>
> Later a team of surgeons wearing blue surgical masks chopped off right hands and left feet of two men convicted of highway robbery. The surgeons amputated the limbs after anesthetizing the prisoners and left the severed limbs on the ground for the spectators to rush up and have a close look.[3]

According to other news reports, the Taliban leaders sometimes hang the amputated limbs from a tree or post as a deterrent to the same kinds of crime. That practice has, thankfully, been waning with the invasion of Afghanistan by the US.

However, another grisly story of fanatical Islamist extremists took place in eastern Pakistan on August 3, 2009, the exact day that this chapter was being written. The headline was:

Eight Christians Burned to Death in Pakistan After Koran is "Defiled"[4]

Writer Zahid Hussain told how an Islamic militant group burned some forty Christian homes in eastern Pakistan, while the Christians feared for their lives. Eight people—including women and at least one child—were burned inside their homes, and two others were shot to death. Christians indicated that the number of believers killed was higher than police reported.

This kind of attack by Islamic extremists is becoming more frequent and definitely more deadly since I was last in Pakistan. In recent years Christians in India have been attacked and often killed by both Muslims and Hindus.

I fear for those believers who have decided to follow Jesus Christ.

As I was putting thoughts together for this chapter, someone sent me a YouTube video that he thought all Christians ought to view. It was created by someone in Lebanon, and at my last look, the site had over thirteen million viewers. I don't know if the video[5] is still being posted, but it's the content that caught my attention.

I listened to the words of the YouTube video and felt that the narration and graphics are dramatic and unsettling. Some points are worth noting:

The *average* fertility rate for *all* the countries of the European Union is 1.38 … yet the population of Europe is *not* declining. Europe is holding its own, but that's because of *immigration.*

Since 1990, *Islamic immigration has accounted for 90 percent of all of Europe's immigration* and by 2048, these stats forecast that France will be an Islamic republic … Great Britain's Muslim population has risen from eighty-two thousand to *2.5 million,* with more than one thousand mosques.

In the Netherlands, 50 percent of all newborns are Muslims. In fifteen years, *half of the population* of the Netherlands will be Muslim. Russia has twenty-three million Muslims.…

Muammar al-Gaddafi (former Libyan leader) once said: "There are signs that Allah will grant victory to Islam in Europe without swords, without guns, without conquest. We don't need terrorists.... The 50-plus million Muslims [in Europe] will turn it into a Muslim continent within a few decades."[6]

In North America, there's a similar story. Canada had a 1.6 million population increase, but 1.2 million, most of this population increase, is from immigration.

In the US, even with the influx of Latino immigration from Mexico and other Latin American nations, the rate is the minimum to sustain an American culture. In 1970 there were one hundred thousand Muslims in America; in 2008 there were *nine million*.[7]

Studies show that within five to seven years, Islam will be the dominant religion in the world; it has already surpassed the Catholic Church, and Islam may surpass all other Christian denominations as well.[8]

Many experts think that because Christianity and Islam are often competitors in developing countries, direct confrontation might lead to eventual cataclysmic global conflict.

Muslims already represent or control about a fifth of the world's population, compared with 33 percent for Christians. Yet Islam is growing faster than Christianity, largely because of faster population growth in Muslim countries. As indicated elsewhere, because of the greater population growth rate of Muslims in many countries, Islam might surpass Christianity as the world's biggest religion.

Author Philip Jenkins gives a worst-case scenario that would include a wave of religious conflicts reminiscent of the Middle Ages. Jenkins, writing about potential future Islamic or Western conflicts, says: "Imagine the world of the 13th century armed with nuclear warheads and anthrax."[9] That strikes me as a troubling scenario indeed.

Others think such dire scenarios are less likely, but it's possible decades of friction lie ahead if Christianity and Islam compete, especially in Africa and Asia.

It's important that, instead of confrontation and conflict between Christianity and radical Islam, we simply "tell the truth." God is truth, the Bible is truth, and the Holy Spirit is truth. The fact is, the suffering of those who die without Christ will be even more unbearable when they learn that it will last *forever*.

That's a challenge to those of us who want to teach and help children across the world become followers of Jesus Christ. I was thinking about the dramatic contrast between the Taliban and al-Qaeda—and Christ followers. A recollection came to mind that was exactly that.

After I'd visited the soccer stadium in Kabul, I went to another site that gave me that different perspective of things. One that lifted my spirits. My visit was to a Christian church in Kabul. As quickly as I walked onto the grounds of this place, I was moved with feelings of faith and a sense of peace and encouragement—feelings that were deeply opposite from what I sensed in the soccer stadium.

The church I came to see was where Dr. J. Christy Wilson was the pastor. Born and raised in Tabriz, Iran, Dr. Wilson served for twenty-two years as a teacher and missionary *in Afghanistan,* where he became acting principal of a government high school. Dr. Wilson also taught private English lessons to the crown prince and conducted an English course for Afghan diplomats in the Ministry of Foreign Affairs.

Dr. Wilson also served for eleven years as pastor of the Community Christian Church in Kabul, where I'd stopped to visit. I didn't meet him, of course, because he had passed away some time earlier. Leaders in the Community Christian Church told me that when Dr. Wilson died, they left his office untouched, just as he left it.

As a follower of Christ, Dr. Wilson was a man of peace, and those two considerations made him a target of Islamic extremists. Once, during local skirmishes around Kabul, some rebels came to destroy Dr. Wilson's church, along with him and its other leaders. One of the rebels used a shoulder-fired rocket-propelled grenade launcher, with the intention of destroying the church and killing those inside. Miraculously, the RPG missed its target. First it struck a tree trunk planted near the church, and from there the grenade ricocheted off the tree, skipped over the building, and spared the church from destruction. I had the opportunity to visit Dr. Wilson's church in Kabul, where I saw the "protective tree" that saved the church.

Now, in my travels, I've seen the damage an RPG weapon can do. For the grenade to ricochet is something I'd never heard of before. If you talk to military people, they just shake their heads in disbelief. I thoroughly believe in that miracle. I think God protected the church and prepared it for its spiritual and humanitarian mission for years to come—a fitting tribute to Dr. Wilson's legacy.

What Dr. Wilson did as part of his charge as a missionary was to try to save human beings, here and now and for eternity. He's our model, and his story needs to be told.

We must refine our global strategies to reach youngsters *now* with the good news of the gospel, so that our efforts can alter the future, before our kids can be influenced by those who seek their minds and hearts. We have to be there first, determine what the world's dominant religious faiths will be like in the next twenty-five to fifty years, and contend not just for the faith of our fathers—but even more for the faith of our children.

Chapter Twenty-Three

DIFFERENT WORLDVIEWS—PART II

Hindu Extremists and Terrorist Mobs

From my ten trips to India and the study of current events, I know that India is experiencing serious religious troubles. Hindu extremists and terrorists are routinely killing Christians and Muslims. Muslims are retaliating, which only escalates the violence.

The roots of the Hindu religion go back nearly five thousand years, to Aryan ancestry, which makes Hinduism the world's oldest contemporary religion.

Ironically, Hindus make up less than 9 to 15 percent of the people who make up the population of India today. Hindus also make up one of the three small, recognized minority castes among India's other castes or classes. Yet they nevertheless have virtual control of the power structures of India: the government, army, news media, education, wealth, religion, and commerce.

The real majority of India are the oppressed and minority religions (including Christians and Muslims) and tribal peoples and outcaste untouchables (called Dalits), who are kept in subjugation through Hindu monopolies of power and a continuing violence for any who get out of line.

But even moderate, modern Hindus now question the morality of such Hindu dominance of every aspect of Indian society based on the Hindus' historical "rights" of "Brahman Power" or racial superiority. This imbalance among the various castes and classes is becoming the world's most explosive "civil rights" cause. As was the case with apartheid in South Africa, where blacks outnumbered the whites and were able to gain their freedom, many think that India seems vulnerable to a revolution. A scant minority of Hindus rule based on their *claimed* power, and some think that rule—which seems at odds with India's implied democracy—will be soon challenged.

Of India's 1.2 billion people, 52 percent make up the Backward Caste; 6 percent are Tribals; 17 percent are Christians, Muslims, Buddhists, and other religions; and 16 percent are categorized as the Untouchable Caste (Dalits)—but Hindus claim that the Dalits fall under the umbrella of their Hindu "caretakers"—or in other words, 85–91 percent of India's population are NOT Hindus.[1]

The Hindus comprise about two hundred million of the entire population. The other castes, classes, and religions comprise *one billion* people. Yet for thousands of years the Hindus have convinced the other Indian classes—through religious persuasion—that they must do as the Hindus tell them. They are not free to choose their employment; they can't get an education (except through small allotments for Dalits, Tribals, and Backward castes); they can't acquire wealth, carry weapons, convert to another religion—and they are taught from generation to generation that it is their "karma" to serve their Hindu masters.

According to Hindu religion, it seems the only reason for allowing non-Hindus to live is for them to produce and work for them. However the lower classes are beginning to challenge this rationale of their Hindu "masters" by confrontation. They have the numbers to put their own candidates up for election in parliament, but tradition and Hindu suppression have kept them uneducated, illiterate, and unorganized for centuries. Still, some Dalits, Tribals, and other castes are telling the Hindu hierarchy that since they are not considered Hindus, then they have a constitutional right to change their religion and establish their own political structures.

Dr. Paul Larsen has been studying these recent spontaneous movements of the Dalit and other lower castes as they try to disengage from Hindu domination by moving toward mass conversion rallies, where millions of various untouchable castes convert to Christianity or Buddhism. (They prefer not to become Muslims because of the terrorist reputation that that religion recently acquired after the 2009 attack in Mumbai [Bombay].)

Since 2001 mass conversion rallies have been held. Some of these caste members became Buddhists; others became followers of Jesus.

Dr. Larsen told us that in several instances, the caste leaders who converted to Christianity consulted with him and other Christian leaders about the implications of conversion, to make certain that they understand God's plan of salvation.

The caste leaders and the other caste members who decide to become Christians are mentored and discipled by educated, theologically literate Indian Christians. And they "get it," no doubt by the presence of the Holy Spirit by which they seem to be guided to faith to become a Christ follower. Dr. Larsen reports that no fewer than tens of thousands—hundreds of thousands, perhaps even a million or more—have been brought into the kingdom in this unique manner. Note how it's all coming about, for the most part, through the communication methods of Orality. Most of these converts were won not by preachers, or by curricula—but by storytellers.

These new Christians—over the past five to eight years that these conversions have taken place—have become discipled; have started to begin and then build churches and schools; and have begun to train pastors or send them to seminaries and classes—many of them helped by my good friends Dr. Lareau Lindquist, Bob Nelson, John DeVries, Dave Stravers, Dennis Mulder, Jim Green, and Steve Douglass.

The eager Indian converts have outpaced such traditional missionary efforts as conversion and discipleship. Why? Is it really working? Will this turning to Christianity be such a threat to Hinduism that the religion will eventually topple from power?

Only God knows.

After ten trips to India, I believe that Hinduism is quite nervous that India's "majority of minorities" will demand freedom and independence from the virtual slavery of the Hindu traditions and established power centers.

Can Christianity help pull them out of their subjugation and rise up, just as blacks in America were freed from slavery because Christian churches lobbied against it before, during, and after the Civil War—and more recently, just as blacks threw off the yoke of apartheid in South Africa? Let's pray it'll be so.

Dr. Vishal Mangalwadi is a renowned Indian Christian scholar who has published more than a dozen books on Hinduism and the West, including *The Quest for Freedom & Dignity*. He has written what the Dalits at the end of the twentieth century began to declare:

> Hinduism was the cause of India's oppressive backwardness. The Dalit analysis is now winning the day. This view, that Hinduism's oppressive structure results in a backward society, was in fact, the viewpoint of the 19th century missionary movement. But during the 20th century, the [Christian] Church rarely said that the Hindu worldview, which had shaped India for 3,000 years, was responsible for its misery. The reason for this lack of moral clarity is simple: the liberal, syncretistic Christians were looking for light in Hinduism, so they didn't want to criticize it. The evangelicals were simply seeking souls … (generally speaking) [and] they lacked intellectual training, social vision, or prophetic courage to speak the truth.

> The truth is that oppression is evil. This truth has penetrated the masses through modern education, free market economy, the information age, and—most supremely—democracy. And this truth is now tearing apart India's ancient religious civilization.[2]

Do Christians have an answer to this dilemma of how to help modern Indians see Hinduism for what it is—a religion that virtually enslaves nearly two-thirds to three-fourths of its people?

According to Dr. Vishal Mangalwadi, Christians hide the solution under a bushel. He said, "India is looking for a new worldview on which to build a new India."[3]

In the wake of mass conversions and anti-Hinduism rallies, truth-seeking Dalits, Tribals, and other oppressed people of India are truly seeking answers. Dr. Mangalwadi said, "As I talked to many of them I discovered that one of their basic questions was: *Does God exist?* They saw Neo-Buddhism as 'rational' because it does not *depend* upon God or miracles. One Backward caste activist gave me a little booklet in Hindi entitled 'If There Were a God …' I am not aware of any Christian booklet in Hindi that argues *for* the *existence of God.*"[4]

Still, many of the anti-Hinduism castes are taking serious note of Christianity, and there is a growing trend toward Christian conversion, but those conversions have also fueled anti-Christian violence by Hindu militants.

Most troubling is the fact that these Hindu militant sects should, by any reasonable guidelines, be described as terrorist groups.

Within just the past few years, some *tens of thousands* of Christians and Tribals have been overtly persecuted—in Assam, Manipur, Orissa, and other Indian states where militant Hindu mobs have attacked Christians and burned their villages. In these terror acts, women and female children were raped—as husbands and fathers were forced to watch the atrocities before *they, too,* were beaten and/or killed.

The increased violence is usually caused by Hindu extremists who are angry at Christian conversions; they see the growth of Christianity as a serious threat that will ultimately destroy Hinduism.

The Hindus are stepping up their offensive strategies. Perhaps as many as eight different states in India have passed anti-conversion laws—and India already passed tough laws prohibiting foreign missionaries from coming to India to seek converts to Christianity.

When such anti-conversion laws are passed by state governments—run by the Hindu majority—and then, when Hindu militants consistently carry out a systematic campaign to eradicate Christians from the land, those strategies collapse. Persecution and killings do not stop the Holy Spirit from wooing converts despite militant opposition—converts are made *because* of Hindu terrorism.

Kids Around the World works with the Evangelical Fellowship of India, having been introduced to us through Dr. Lareau Lindquist of Barnabas International. EFI assigned Ben Toshi to Kids Around the World to train children's workers how to use Flannelgraphs to help Indian children hear, know, and love the stories and lessons of the Bible.

David C Cook is also a partner of Kids Around the World, and has introduced a new program to help teach orphans in some eighteen thousand orphanages in India. The program includes lessons based on Bible stories, and materials for character building and coping with practical issues of life. Cook also introduced in India a sixteen-page *Story of Jesus,* using "comic book" illustrations from the Action Bible, which Cook also publishes.

According to Dr. Richard Howell, president of the Evangelical Fellowship of India, "Every Christian denomination has been attacked—our schools, our colleges, our orphanages. Everything that Christians own … have been attacked."[5] More recently he reported, "With two to three incidents of violence in the community each week in 2011, Christians continue to face the worst ever persecution."[6]

With the threat of class genocide, Christians have identified with the Backward castes, Tribals, Dalits, Muslims, and other minorities being attacked by Hindu terrorists, and they've created a virtual coalition through solidarity with these other groups.

Dr. Richard Howell is quoted in a newspaper article: "What the Dalits are saying to the Christians is, 'Stand with us, and oppose the oppressive caste system perpetuated by Hinduism.'"[7]

A spokesperson of the All India Christian Council added, "Christians [are showing] … solidarity with the anti-caste message."[8] That may be because Christians are also becoming a persecuted group in India.

The state of Orissa in India has experienced some of the worst violence and persecution against Christians in India's recent history. Orissa is also the site of the slaying of Australian missionary Graham Staines and his two young sons—ages six and ten. The three were burned to death as they slept inside their vehicle after a Bible study class. The incident received global coverage and brought wide condemnation from world leaders.[9]

Christians were also targets of terrorism from Hindu militants in Mumbai (Bombay), where Hindu thugs broke up a Christian prayer meeting, attacked the pastor, and violently assaulted the men, women, and little children who were in the service. The pastor and a four-year-old girl were among the many who sustained wounds and other injuries for refusing to chant slogans praising Hindu gods and recant their Christian conversion.

At least one good thing has resulted from these attacks—more people have been converted to Christianity, due in part from the Christians' responses to their attackers. Bible distribution agencies in India have seen great results as people wonder what is so intriguing and mysterious about Christianity that gets the Hindus so worked up—and then get Bibles to see for themselves what it's all about.

In India I met with Dr. Bill Scott and his wife, Joyce, visiting their offices and watching them meet with the children of the area. What an awesome work of love! For years these children have been reached by programs that reach out to *thousands* of kids. With songs, stories, skits, games, Mailbox Club, and Bible dramatizations, many of the children listen and are introduced to a loving Savior.

Another recent phenomenon in India is the virtual explosion of mass conversions. Dr. Paul Larsen, who travels to India regularly, has witnessed many mass conversion rallies and similar recent events that were spearheaded by leaders of the lower castes and Dalit "untouchables" to repudiate their bondage to Hinduism.

Dr. Larsen told of one recent trip: "We joined more than thirty adults and young people from the US who came to India to wash the feet of the poorest of poor. These lower caste members and untouchables wept as men and women alike had their feet washed by Christian Indians and American believers.

"The event was covered extensively by the Indian national press and television. One newspaper carried my remarks to the crowd verbatim. One newspaper closed a lengthy article this way, 'It is sad that in beautiful India, Americans must come to wash the feet of the poor to show us that one God has created us all equal!'"[10]

The conversions to Christianity are happening across India despite the violence and terrorism of militant Hindu mobs. The most wonderful outcome is that untold thousands have received eternal life, something that they've never had the chance to hear about until recently.

Dr. Larsen also said, "It's as if there is a Spirit too great to be contained by threats and suppression, and it's my opinion that these are spontaneous events that are generated by the Holy Spirit, and—based on recent events—it's possible that within the next decades, hundreds of millions of India's poorest and disenfranchised citizens become Christ followers."[11]

Hundreds of millions of India's citizens are becoming Christ followers?

It's an idea that is hard to grasp. Yet we are already seeing significant examples of it taking place in that homeland of more than a billion souls.

And if such an explosion of conversions among seeking souls in India will shake and transform the nation, imagine what possibilities lie ahead when India's neighboring nations see it happen! The "great awakening" that takes place in India will be witnessed by *other hundreds of millions* of watching souls.

God willing, the same miraculous work of God will also resonate in the hearts and minds of Indonesians, Tibetans, Cambodians, Vietnamese, Filipinos, Malayans—even the people of China to the east, and Pakistan, Afghanistan, and the watching millions of the Middle East, on the western borders of India.

My prayer is that this "great awakening" *will happen soon*—and it's my hope that it'll *begin with the children*. American agencies can help with stories from the Bible, building schools, and teaching kids to read and write, and instill in each one not only a Christian faith but the morality and character that Jesus taught.

Hinduism has made it a point to keep the lower caste Indians from becoming educated and able to provide for their families—things that should be civil rights in a nation that calls itself a democracy. Hindu dominance has resulted in the situation that as many as half a billion souls are illiterate and unable to receive the gospel message through literature.

Dr. Larsen makes an interesting point: "In November 2001 one of the first major conversion rallies was planned. The government tried to stop it, but it took place—not with the huge throngs that were projected, but still thousands of non-Hindu people showed up.

"I think it was a spontaneous work of the Holy Spirit. I also noticed that following this period, many American Christian television programs suddenly appeared on television satellites reaching India day after day with their messages. Many of the poor and lower caste people have access to TV sets and watched these programs. They may be illiterate, but many understood the speaking voices, and when the caste leaders called for these huge conversion rallies, many may have responded because of the tipping points of those events."[12]

There's a huge case for helping India with Orality-style programs that communicate directly and in the native dialect of the listeners. The needs of the lower and poorer classes underscore the dramatic and urgent need for these programs. If the Hindu government fails to provide the rights to education and freedom of religion, then perhaps Christ followers must take the initiative for those responsibilities.

Orality programs can lead to understanding the gospel, and Orality can help explain the truths of the gospel to children through simple God-centered stories. We can encourage new converts by helping them start schools to teach themselves not just to read and write, but to hear the stories of the Bible and understand how to be a Christ follower—and that kind of person can change a culture and a nation.

I believe that this strategy is not only possible, but it's likely to happen. It will begin through the universal use of Orality-based Bible stories and programs for the two-thirds of the world who cannot or choose not to read.

Chapter Twenty-Four

DIFFERENT WORLDVIEWS—PART III

"All children are atheists."—Paul-Henri, baron d'Holbach (1723–1789)

Baron d'Holbach, an eighteenth-century philosopher, said, "All children are atheists—they have no idea of God."

Similarly, George H. Smith wrote: "The man who is unacquainted with theism is an atheist because he does not believe in a god. This category would also include the child with the conceptual capacity to grasp the issues involved, but who is still unaware of those issues. The fact that this child does not believe in god qualifies him as an atheist."[1]

On the subject of these two observations, I was surprised to run across an article written by a respected Oxford University scholar that contradicts these statements noted above.

Martin Beckford wrote for a British newspaper about his interview with Dr. Justin Barrett, who reported on scientific experiments that suggest that "children are 'born believers' in God and do not simply acquire religious beliefs through [adult] indoctrination."[2]

The *Telegraph* article also states that Dr. Barrett believed that young children have faith *"even when they have not been taught about it by family or at school,"* and he argues hypothetically that children living and growing up on their own deserted island would ultimately come to believe in God.[3] (To see the full article, please refer to note 2 above in the notes section at the end of the book.)

The point of the article was that children with normal developing minds are open to believe in a supernatural creation and intelligent design.

The idea that children are born with a predisposition to believe in God is quite a contrast to the quote of the eighteenth-century philosopher who claimed that "all children are atheists." For hundreds of years, that quote has been a rallying cry for atheists.

Atheism as an "accepted" philosophy was kick-started in societies of the nineteenth century by Karl Marx and Friedrich Engels, both of whom argued that belief in God and religion are tools for those in power to oppress and control the working class.

There were other voices promoting atheism, especially within what was called the French Enlightenment. One of those voices was the Marquis de Sade. De Sade encouraged sex and violence as a way of avoiding what he called "Christian slave-morality."

That viewpoint was picked up by the "hippie revolution" in America and Europe during the 1960s and 1970s. In de Sade's worldview, anything and everything was permitted—since, according to this worldview, there was no God to prevent humankind from doing as they please. Those who follow de Sade's example delight in saying that the philosophy proves that God doesn't exist.

Other offshoots of this nihilistic worldview were promoted by those who followed this dogma, translated from German—a quotation of Max Stirner: "What you have the power to do, you also have the right to do."

That idea, fostered by early European athcists, was embellished by Friedrich Nietzsche, who was probably the best-known European atheist—remembered as the philosopher who influenced Hitler. Nietzsche coined the phrase "God is dead" and must have undoubtedly believed that Judeo-Christian morality was a "cosmic crime against life"—forbidding different kinds of individual behavior as sinful. Nietzsche considered himself above traditional moral rules about how people express themselves—especially in such areas as sexuality, violence, and cruelty.[4]

Nietzsche believed that traditional morality was a weakness and even devised a "morality for the strong." The tenets of "moral" code were cruelty and the will to even destroy what he called "inferior" human beings—a concept that Hitler took to enormous lengths during the Holocaust and World War II.

Marx and Marxist-Leninism

A similar strand of atheism that used violence and dominating other humans was Marxism and Marxist-Leninism, which systematically used violence to create a Communist society.

Marx's totalitarian Communism (and disciples Lenin, Stalin, Hitler, and other regimes) used Nietzsche's nihilistic ideas to launch an atheistic revolution that swept through the entire twentieth century. These men didn't believe it was immoral to commit violence and cruelty on "weaker" societies and ethnic groups, because Christian morality was an "irrelevant ideology," and the totalitarian regimes sought "greater good" from the ideas of Nazi, Communist, and secular humanist revolutions.

The events following 1917—the Russian revolution, Hitler's Third Reich in the 1930s and 1940s, and the rise of world Communism in the 1950s—all were examples of where atheistic, amoral, and immoral philosophies can lead.

Beginning in the twentieth century, atheism was promoted under the guise of secular humanism. Beginning in the field of education, it expanded into other fields, such as the US bureaucracy and branches of government. The US Supreme Court interpreted that references to God and Christian principles were not to be promoted in the schools, as—according to a humanist rallying call that began some sixty years ago—a wall of separation should divide society from Judeo-Christian precepts.

In recent years modern atheists have done their best to eliminate Judeo-Christian tenets and morality from the schools (and just about every other area of society). But it's that blow to our children's education that troubles me most. Atheism is surely behind this embargo to keep God and Christian morals out of the schools, but I still hold out hope.

I take great pleasure every time I visit a foreign land and see that it's Christianity—not atheism—that has made the most strides in winning the minds, hearts, and souls of most people. Everywhere I go in the emerging nations of India, Africa, China, South America—statistics prove the atheists are wrong. Christian influence is growing around the world.

True, atheists have made *some* progress promoting their philosophies in America in recent years, but only when they compare their "progress" with earlier results. If they compare their efforts to what's happening through the activities of evangelical Christianity, atheism is losing ground. This impotent "religion" is still light-years behind the curve.

As evidence that something is happening, a few Christian leaders from around the world gathered in Florida in January 2009 for a meeting of the Call2All North American Global Congress,[5] to brainstorm strategies on: *How to reach the more than two billion people who have never heard of Jesus or have never been challenged to follow Him.*

The Call2All North American Global Congress convened pastors, organizational presidents/CEOs, and ministry leaders to pull together ideas and resources with the aim of sharing the gospel with *everyone in the world.*

Philadelphia Inquirer writer Paul Nussbaum—some three years before the Call2All meeting—made note of the obvious global change in Christianity. He cited statistics that, in the latter half of the twentieth century, dramatic changes have taken place within evangelical Christianity. Nussbaum says evangelicalism "is leaving home."[6]

Nussbaum stated, "In 1960, an estimated 50 million evangelical Christians lived in the West, and 25 million in the rest of the world; today, there are an estimated 75 million in the West, and *325 million in the rest of the world.*"[7] That's the reason that Kids Around the World is stepping up its efforts to train children's workers and give them the "tools" (Flannelgraphs and puppets) to help them more effectively reach kids.

Other evangelical agencies have estimated that there may now be even more Christians in China than in America. Nussbaum also confirms that fact and adds: "Most evangelicals now live in China, South Korea, India, Africa and Latin America, where they are transforming their religion … [by] infusing it with local traditions and practices. And, they are even sending 'reverse missionaries' to Europe and the United States."[8]

It's true. South Korean churches have sent twelve thousand Christian missionaries to other countries.[9] Only US churches send more missionaries overseas. And my friends Dr. Paul Larsen and Dr. Rochunga Pudaite have told me that the Evangelical Free Church of India and other Christian churches in India are sending missionaries to other Asian countries.

Africans, South Americans, and Asians are outperforming the West by advancing evangelical Christianity. As new evangelicals overseas expand their influence and territory, they're often confronted by other religions—most often Islam, militant Hinduism, and even atheistic government regimes (as in North Korea, China, Cuba, and other dictator-run totalitarian countries).

However, evangelicals are still among the fastest-growing segments of Christianity.

John H. Orme, the late executive director of the Interdenominational Foreign Mission Association (IFMA),[10] an alliance of evangelical mission groups, said the old citadels of Christianity could learn from the new evangelical movements of the rest of the world. Before his passing in 2006, Orme said, "I wish the Third World would have more effect on us. The church in the developing world is much more alive to the working of the Holy Spirit."[11]

(That might be why a recent runaway best seller is Francis Chan's book *Crazy Love,* published by David C Cook.)

A century ago, fewer than 10 percent of Africa's religious groups were made up of evangelical Christians. Today it's nearly *50 percent.* That's a huge increase from 1900 to now—with more than 350 million believers today. One African nation, Uganda, has nearly twenty million Christians and is expected to have fifty million by 2050. Other African congregations have grown so big that their churches are running out of space—a great problem to have.

Western preachers use advertising and pleas from the pulpit to get people to show up. In contrast, the congregations of African churches are sometimes so great that their pastors ask their people *to attend only twice a month*—to give others a chance to worship. Central and South America are witnessing an explosive growth of Pentecostal churches. A study by David Martin also shows that, recently, millions of South American Catholics have become evangelical Protestants.[12] In Brazil there are fifty million evangelical Protestants compared to a few decades ago when there weren't even enough to count.

So Why Do Atheists Hate Evangelicals?

It began with the explosive growth of evangelical Christianity during the Cold War. Soviet nations were steered by atheist ideology and were ruled with an iron fist. However, when I visited Russia and former USSR satellite countries after the collapse of Communism, I was struck by the difference. Atheism had been all but kicked aside along with the Communists.

When I was in Moscow's Red Square, we even found a Christian church inside the Kremlin walls. The early Communist regime had taken over the Kremlin after the revolution of 1917 but never destroyed the Christian influence of the buildings. Ceilings and walls are still painted with the original art of Bible stories—the creation, Adam and Eve, the Old Testament heroes, and the New Testament gospel stories of Jesus and His disciples; what I'd call an Orality form of communicating Christianity.

Inside the Kremlin, at the very heart of Communism's atheism, were murals, frescos, and resplendent panes of colored glass—all stories from the Bible. I was filled with a strong feeling of how God overrules tyrants, false religions, and lies. These fantastic, artistic, and holy expressions of biblical stories as a means of communication stand also as a dramatic statement of the impotence of atheism!

Is Atheism Dying?

Even in Cuba, when I visited in 1992, the ruling Communist party had changed the country's constitution. The revolutionists had referred to Cuba as an "atheist" nation when it changed the constitution, but more recently it was changed to a "secular" nation—a dramatic reversal of perception and attitude. Some say that it was this backing away from atheism that led to the visit by the late Pope John Paul II just six years later.

The 1990s—when Soviet Communism collapsed—brought turmoil in Cuba. The Soviets could no longer subsidize the Cuban economy. However, Cuban Christians recognized the problem and stepped in to help.

In the 1990s, there had been a resurgence of evangelical churches (and house churches), so it was natural for Cuban Christian groups to step in whenever and wherever they could to ease hunger, care for the needs of the sick and elderly, and volunteer relief aid following disastrous storms.

Although Cuban officials probably wouldn't publicly admit it, Cuba clearly benefits from the relief and development work of its churches. In the fall of 2008, Atlantic hurricanes destroyed $10 billion in property. Immediately after each hurricane, Cuban churches mobilized and tapped "their growing network of resources to feed, shelter, and care for the homeless and hungry."[13]

It got to the point, at least from my perspective, where Cuba was doing well and was better off *without* the former Soviet subsidies.

I also saw an openness and cooperation firsthand after Cuba changed their constitution from "atheist" nation to "secularist"—and when I visited Cuba a second time in 2000, this time I met Fidel Castro, who came to an evangelical church to speak.

Castro, who was educated by Catholics, said publicly, "Communism has not worked here in Cuba," and he criticized Iran's leadership for dealing harshly with Israel.

We'd gone to Cuba to get permission to construct three playgrounds—in Havana, Matanzas, and next to the seminary near

Havana. However, the US Consulate office denied permission for us to construct the playgrounds in Cuba, based on the US sanctions. They told us that we couldn't "do business" with the Cuban government.

Likewise the Castro government took the position that they'd approve the playgrounds, "But not if we have to work with Americans."

So we got a bright idea. We approached the United Nations, which steered us to their UNICEF office. UNICEF agreed to sponsor our playground projects, and they went to both the US Consulate and the Castro government separately. It wasn't long before UNICEF provided us with all the necessary visas, documents, and government approvals—and the three "UNICEF" playgrounds were constructed in Cuba.

One of the locations where we built a playground was at a facility that housed kids affected by the nuclear accident in Chernobyl, Ukraine. These were kids who suffered from radiation poisoning and cancer from the aftereffects of the Chernobyl nuclear disaster. Part of Russia's subsidy for Cuba was in exchange for Cuba taking care of these kids. Castro's Cuba provided housing and medical facilities for the kids to recover in the tropical sunshine and fresh air. Our volunteers received great satisfaction knowing they had brightened the lives of these former Soviet citizens suffering from radiation poisoning.

Concurrent to building the three playgrounds, we also provided Flannelgraph materials and training to four hundred children's workers, working with Jose Lopez, secretary of the Council of Churches in Havana.

Jose also worked closely with the Bible League, getting approval to bring into Cuba an Illustrated New Testament, a comic-book–style version of the Scriptures, produced by David C Cook.

Our training of the four hundred Cuban workers—each of whom held weekly worship and presented Bible stories for as many as fifty kids in a class—was provided from the day the playground was dedicated. It was to be a place of belonging and believing for *thousands of kids* who now see and hear the gospel instead of Communist dogma.

According to *Christianity Today,* Cuban evangelicals report that the days of the former persecution of believers by atheist hard-liners has ended and discrimination is easing.[14]

With Russia pulling away from its foreign aid and subsidies to Cuba following the collapse of Communism, evangelical and Catholic churches are increasingly filling that void.

We also saw the expansion of Christian evangelism taking place as we traveled to Honduras, Ecuador, Chile, the Amazon, and other parts of Central and South America. When we traveled there to construct playgrounds, we trained and equipped national teachers and lay leaders with the same follow-up stories and materials for these Christian workers as we do everywhere we go.

These workers use Flannelgraph stories to explain to children what it means to follow Jesus. So there was an opportunity for our Christ-centered materials to present biblical truths presented by Christian teachers and workers.

Incidentally, does anti-religious school curricula affect the kids in schools in countries like the United States and Canada? According to one source,[15] the answer is a resounding YES:

The Percentage of Teens Who Identify as Christians Is Shrinking

	1984	1992	2000	2008
Roman Catholic	50%	41%	39%	32%
Protestant	35%	28%	22%	13%
Other faiths*	3%	10%	14%	16%
No faith at all	12%	21%	25%	32%
* *Includes: Islam, Buddhism, Judaism, Hinduism, Sikhism, Aboriginal.* Source: Project Teen Canada.				

Notice that the number of young people who identify themselves as Christian has been declining significantly over the past generation. And those teens who claim themselves as "other faiths" or "no faith at all" have increased significantly.

No doubt there are a number of reasons for that, but we can assume that one is a secular society trying to negate the influences of the church and parachurch organizations in their attempts to help youngsters and teens to become Christ followers.

So we are always encouraged when we can do storytelling for so many kids in various countries—including our own—and to train teachers to multiply our efforts exponentially. That may be one of the reasons that Christianity is increasing worldwide.

In my opinion, atheism is missing a key ingredient in their approach to promulgating their point of view. If, as they say (as in the quote at the beginning of this chapter), that all children are atheists, why is it that so many kids, when exposed to the gospel of Christ, are open to and accept the truth of the Bible so readily? I think that it's because children long for a place to belong, and Christianity offers them that opportunity; they intuitively are drawn to God.

In China, atheism is the *de facto* dogma of the Communist state. Even though the Chinese constitution guarantees freedom of religion, Christians must worship in churches operated by two state-controlled organizations—one for Protestants, the second for Catholics. However, there has been explosive growth of the Christian church movements, including many more Chinese churches. Despite government prohibitions in some regions, many people are choosing their own churches—even though technically, those churches are illegal.

In September 2009, a Christian megachurch in northern China was shut down by hundreds of police who attacked the church, breaking windows, smashing furniture, and confiscating computers, Bibles, and church collections.

Following the attacks, the pastors were arrested and imprisoned. An unknown number of church members were hospitalized with serious injuries, and it's said that many others were arrested and taken away.

The Golden Lamp Church usually ministers to some fifty thousand worshippers in their eight-story complex. Months later, the gates to the church's facilities were still locked and guarded by a police presence posted on the edge of the church grounds.

CBN news reported, "The closure of the mega-church is a sign that the Beijing government is trying to reign in the rapid spread of Christianity over the Communist nation. Church leaders have called the crackdown the harshest they have seen in many years."[16]

Yet despite such limitations imposed by the Chinese government, there are now at least *one hundred million Christians* in China who worship in evangelical and Catholic churches. And author David Aikman observed that, at current growth rates, China will in a few decades become the largest *Christian country* in the world.[17]

In Korea, Christians outnumber Buddhists, and there are a number of megachurches with more than ten thousand members each—and one Full Gospel Church has *seven hundred and fifty thousand members.*

The Catholic Church in the Philippines reports that there are currently sixty million members in the nation—and expects to double that figure to one hundred and twenty million by 2050.[18]

So, as to the culture clash between atheism and Christianity, it is no longer, "God is dead," as Nietzsche long ago proclaimed. Someone recently wrote a wry headline that makes a good epitaph: "God is not dead. Nietzsche is!"

Chapter Twenty-Five

KEEPING YOUR LIFE TOGETHER WHEN YOUR WORLD IS FALLING APART

The previous chapters may seem to be a digression from the central theme of Orality and the strategies of the twenty-first century to communicate to those who cannot, or choose not, to read or write.

But by presenting these chapters, we want to show how Christ followers are being challenged by ideological and religious confrontations by extremist Islam, atheism, militant Hinduism, and aging Communism.

There are also schisms within the various Christian denominations and sects that can be threats to those who try to set the example for discipleship of Christ followers. Sometimes those who call themselves Christians discover that their enemies in the faith are other Christians. This is an age-old problem that goes back to the time of Jesus.

Group dynamics force churches to compare themselves to other churches. Most of the churches that Jesus addressed in Revelation 1–3 were self-satisfied and "doing their own thing." Only two churches of the seven (Philadelphia and Smyrna) were commended. This goes to show that the majority isn't always right. It's always possible to be doing better than some other guy, but still not doing our best and even perhaps missing the mark!

But unfortunately—in an age of "easy belief" and "salvation without any demands"—many people are confused about their place in God's view of humanity. Even those who claim to be Christian believers sometimes cause grief and confusion. Many are, in truth, stumbling blocks to faith and do harm by hindering others seeking to follow Jesus Christ.

If people truly understand what Jesus says in His Word about what it means *to be a Christian*—they'd see that being a Christian in name only will *not* get them into the kingdom. Nor will they get into the kingdom by simply attending church with others who claim to be Christians—in the kingdom of God on earth.

These observations are about what it means to be a *Christ follower* and what the Word of God tells us what a Christian truly is. He describes people seeking truth together, where Jesus is in their midst, to bring godly understanding through the Holy Spirit. That's the model for becoming a Christ follower.

John wrote, "In the beginning was the Word, and the Word was with God, and the Word was God" (John 1:1). A word is part of language and expresses human thoughts—*if* both parties understand that language.

In the context of Orality, words are usually an aural expression of complex language—but it can just as well be symbols, drawings as printed impressions on a cave wall, scratches on a rock, or impressions on paper. All are means of communications that make human beings distinct from the other animals on earth—but the remarkable thing is, *human beings can also understand the words of God* as presented in the Bible.

Even people who can't read those words from the Bible can—when someone who *has* read those words comes along to bring them to life. Sometimes in various countries where Kids Around the World conducts training, Christian nationals use visual pictures to substitute as representations for words. They provide the visual representation as "words"—words that are printed photos in a book, or drawings fastened onto felt to tell a story on a Flannelgraph.

Too many people believe that God once spoke to mankind in a book called the Bible but that for a couple thousand years since that revelation, He has been silent. They don't see the Bible's relevance today.

This may come as a surprise, but God has never stopped speaking.

If we assume a study of His Word, the Lord comes personally into our midst to explain it and teach us its truth.[1] And the Holy Spirit indwells us and teaches us.

Regular attendance at church and listening to sermons don't, by themselves, make disciples. Rather, personal study of the Word with another person, with Jesus in your midst, and having the Holy Spirit speak the words and thoughts of God to you directly, results in a deeper understanding of what it means to be a disciple or Christ follower.

Perhaps it's the "house church" that's the model church for the future. In the house-church setting, programs and building are no longer as important to bring people together to learn from God's Word.

Doing what Jesus described—"For where two or three come together in My name, there am I with them"—is to discover that *God speaks to us directly.* What He says to you may even be different from what He says to someone else—even though both of you hear or read the same words. It's these resulting thoughts, illumination, conviction, and understanding that make His Word so unique, revelatory, and personal. What's critical is *how* God reveals the intended meaning of the words of the Bible *to you* personally.

When sincere people seek Christ, they often make an earnest effort and a good start, but the majority (as in the parable of the sower) fall by the wayside. The main problem is they're not *rooted and grounded in the Word.*

We are called out of this world (away from the pressures of and conformity to the world), and only when we get away from the influence of the world can we get into a personal and intimate relationship with God through the study of His Word. However, in the context of the visual-oral learner, our familiarity with the "Word" (of God)—where Word means Story—would be more easily understood as "God's Story."

By doing this study of God's Story with another believer, we can experience Christ in our midst as we read or hear His Word. *This ongoing process of studying and reading the Word together deepens our understanding and ownership of the Word,* and it has four considerations.

1. Hear His Word/Story.

Jesus said to His listeners, "Anyone with ears to hear should listen and understand" (Mark 4:9 NLT). That admonition by Jesus appears several times in the Gospels of Matthew, Mark, Luke, and John, as well as Revelation. There's a universal inclusiveness intended in Christ's injunction. The "hearing" is for everyone. Everyone is supposed to listen for God's voice. There's no excuse for not listening to Him speak through the Scriptures (His Word). It begins with Christ's call to listen and understand.

2. Keep His Word/Story (That Is, Don't Lose What You Hear).

For the one who hears His Word (His Story), there's an expectation of action and accountability. We are to *keep the words* of Jesus as written in the Bible and spoken to us. God's Word tells us, "All Scripture is inspired by God and is useful to teach us what is true and to make us realize what is wrong in our lives. It corrects us when we are wrong and teaches us to do what is right" (2 Tim. 3:16 NLT). If we ignore the Word or refuse to obey His Word that's given to us, I believe we call into question the reality of our response to Christ's call to be His followers. If we haven't moved *out of the world* and walked *into His kingdom,* we're probably not obeying Him (Matt. 7:21 NLT).

If we allow the Lord to work through us, we can become like the early disciples and apostles recorded in the book of Acts (in their response to their call to follow Jesus).

3. Experience the Implication of the Word/Story Sincerely.

If we hear His Word but don't keep (obey) it, we're like the apostate churches described in Revelation 1–3. If we deny or disown Christ, we're "missing the mark" through sin and are being disobedient.

The apostle Paul described hearing and obeying God's Word as *a walk of faith into Christ's kingdom, that's expressed by a transformed life,* qualities that Paul called the fruits of the Spirit: love, joy, peace, patience, kindness, goodness, faithfulness, gentleness, and self-control (Gal. 5:22–23).

I can relate more to the apostle Paul—I think he was more like us. He describes himself as the "chief of sinners." Paul said, "But God had mercy on me so that Christ Jesus could use me as a prime example of his great patience with even the worst sinners. Then others will realize that they, too, can believe in him and receive eternal life" (1 Tim. 1:16 NLT). Paul also encourages us that we can transform our lives and turn our backs on sin, *if we so choose.*

4. Share the Word/Story with Others.

Following Jesus' resurrection, two of His disciples were walking along the road to Emmaus. The disciples were disheartened following the events of the Lord's crucifixion. Suddenly as they walked, Jesus appeared to them and began to explain the Scriptures to them. Not until they reached their destination did they recognize Jesus (Luke 24:35).

When they discovered who He was, in their excitement, they rushed back to Jerusalem to tell the others. In the same way, when Jesus comes to us and reveals Himself, we're *changed* by Him and given a new life with new instructions and new goals.

That's when He sends *us* out to "go *tell* others"—to tell them the stories of Jesus. These "others" need to have the same opportunity to respond to Christ's calling as we've had. We are to *put into practice what we have heard.*

Following Christ by walking *into* His kingdom (while at the same time *walking out of* the realm of the world—or "Babylon," as He calls the world) proves that we've understood His call. This action initiates a relationship with Jesus Christ, and our lives begin to model a life that He describes in the Bible.

The exciting point is that *our* relationship with Christ is the same kind of relationship that He had with His disciples. He calls us in the same way that He called them—"Come, follow me," and *belong* to Him.

Jesus' call is simple. He asks us to follow Him, and when we do, He makes His teaching clear and enables us to integrate it into our lives.

We don't need to complicate this simple process. His Word/ Story says, "Ask me and I will tell you remarkable secrets you do not know about things to come" (Jer. 33:3 NLT).

Our role is to become the "calling upon Him" ones—as well as "called out" ones. That's how we *continue to learn from Him.* After He's taught us, we await His orders to go out into the world to extend the same invitation to others.

The end of the book of Mark records Jesus' commission to His disciples. He told them, "Go into all the world and preach the good news to all creation" (16:15). Matthew also records Jesus telling the disciples to go into all the world to preach and teach, but he adds, "Baptize people in all nations so that everyone can be saved" (Matt. 28:19, author's paraphrase).

I think it's interesting that not everyone is called to be a missionary or a minister, yet Jesus calls each of us to share the gospel with others.

As we come into His "school" to learn, we are taught *to help others learn also;* "go therefore and disciple all nations" (the rest of mankind) to choose to follow Christ. Jesus calls all the people of "the world" to leave that realm and enter into another realm, His incredible kingdom.

People balk when asked to change their name and identity when they come into this new name. There is great significance in being a "Christ's one" (Christian) since our new name is God's name. We will probably be called by that name by others.

> Then Jesus said to his disciples, "If anyone would come after me, he must deny himself and take up his cross and follow me." (Matt. 16:24)

When we receive Christ into our lives, we identify with the Almighty God. Are we willing to do that?

Perhaps you've already chosen to do so—or, if not, are you willing to choose to do so now? It was for this reason that God sent Jesus to our planet (John 3:16–17). God made us in His image and likeness and has an eternal purpose for us. That purpose is to answer Christ's call and help others to do the same. This is what God intended from the beginning of time. *This is the time-tested formula for how to "grow a church."*

Yet if we choose to respond to Christ's invitation, we must be willing participants. He won't force a person against his or her will to do so, but if we agree to follow Him, Jesus Christ offers the inner strength to make that most important journey that anyone will ever have to face in life.

Jesus Christ answered our question, *How can I keep my life together when my world is coming apart?* He said, "Seek first the kingdom of God and His righteousness, and all these things shall be added to you" (Matt. 6:33 NKJV). However, in the seventh chapter of Matthew He also says, "Enter through the narrow gate. For wide is the gate and broad is the road that leads to destruction, and many enter through it. But small is the gate and narrow the road that leads to life, and only a few find it" (Matt. 7:13–14).

Chapter Twenty-Six

ARE WE A LOST GENERATION?

Those of us alive on planet earth today have entered a new century as well as a new millennium.

Does anyone know where we are going?

Does anyone even care anymore?

Why should anyone *care* what happens when or if a person spends time seeking God and His purposes?

What is also apparent in many of our churches is that the line between church and culture is blurred. Differences or distinctions between Christians and the secular culture simply don't exist. For example, according to Dr. James Dobson, the incidence of divorce is as prevalent in churches as in the rest of society.[1]

To back up this premise, a Christian research group discovered that *there are no real apparent differences in behavior or lifestyle between Christians and non-Christians.* Nearly the same percentage of Christians and non-Christians watch movies and listen to pop music every week, buy lottery tickets, watch cable TV, have filed a lawsuit, have watched porn in the past three months, register to vote, and have sought counseling help or have taken drugs for depression in the past year.

The harsh reality is that *there is no practical difference between Christians and non-Christians in most culture or lifestyle areas.* Church members are just as likely as their "worldly" neighbors to be alcoholics, commit adultery, cheat on their taxes, steal from their employers, abuse their children, disobey traffic laws, and in other ways miss the mark as far as living up to godly standards of behavior.

Is it time to write an obituary for the church?

As can be expected, a number of secular social scientists are already declaring that the church is dead. However, even some of the best *Christian* thinkers are predicting an uncertain future or a gloomy end for the Christian church in America.

Our churches have been decimated by divorce just as devastatingly as ordinary non-churched American families have. Churchgoing mothers have to work outside the home in one-parent families and traditional two-parent families, just as non-churched families. Some churchgoing dads support two families and have to work at two or more jobs, just as their non-churched counterparts.

Contemporary people, whether they go to church or not, generally feel helpless, lonely, and needy. Yet frequently they don't turn to their church because of its institutionalized nature or self-serving programs that often offer no encouragement—nor practical help to the specific needs of non-Christians or hapless church members.

However, even when churches *do* address real needs, it's often within a context of our *culture* rather than religious tradition. A former pastor of a sizable evangelical congregation has confided that much of his counseling is with church members who are having extramarital affairs and with those who are sexually abusing their own children!

In that and so many other respects, there's really no difference between church members and nonbelievers. The apostle Paul recognized the same problem in the first century. He told the Christians at Rome, "Therefore, I urge you, brothers, in view of God's mercy, to offer your bodies as living sacrifices, holy and pleasing to God—this is your spiritual act of worship. Do not conform any longer to the pattern of this world, but be transformed by the renewing of your mind. Then you will be able to test and approve what God's will is—his good, pleasing, and perfect will" (Rom. 12:1–2).

Unfortunately, the church of our era has—in all too many cases—become an organization with man-made benefits to its members, rather than an organism offering divine life and relationships. The objectives of such churches are often worthy. Church leaders are sometimes "purpose-driven" instead of "Christ-following." They talk of goals, objectives, and agendas, instead of making priorities for changing lives.

The trouble is, with the blurring of the lines between Christianity and culture, the apostle Paul's admonition in Romans 12 no longer attracts as many people as Christ's followers. Such a commitment is too much for many who are attracted to the world and its ways.

Christians all over the world today seem to be suffering from an identity crisis. Perhaps you are one of those asking, "Who are we really?"

It took many trials and struggles for the apostle Paul to discover and develop his own identity. At first Paul (who was first called Saul) was like most other people—he saw Christianity as a religion and not *a way of living*. It took a divine appearance by Jesus Christ to convince him to abandon his old belief system and follow Christ.

Not everyone has such an experience. This is complicated by the fact that even when Christians confront unbelievers in order to convert them, the unbelievers are not asked to change very much. They are often permitted to maintain their lifestyles and belief systems and just tack on the label *Christian* when it suits them.

If it's true, as those studies say, that there are no real differences between Christians and unbelievers, then how can we know that we're truly Christ's followers?

How do we know that those to whom we present evidence of God's love and presence will or won't become believers and become followers of Jesus Christ?

Jesus was very clear about the distinctions between the world and His kingdom. He said, "If anyone would come after me, he must deny himself and take up his cross and follow me" (Matt. 16:24).

Ironically, the Bible tells us that Jesus went to "publicans and sinners" with the good news of the gospel. That's probably because they already knew that they were sinners! Every time He went to the *religious leaders* to speak, they wanted to argue with Him or even excommunicate or kill Him.

At some point in a person's life, he or she may have discovered that family, friends, or the church was giving mixed signals about what it is to be a Christian. A person must decide for him or herself how to get at the source for the truth about the Christian life for a practical understanding of who or what the church *is*.

Samuel Chiang reports that of the 4.35 billion people who are visual or oral learners, nearly 1.5 billion are young children between the ages of eight and fifteen. Chiang also wrote of this incredible illustration of what could happen if we were to switch our methods:

> Many [evangelical] organizations have seen increased effectiveness in many regions of the world. For example, one organization did a comparison of "before" and "after" effects of Orality training. The results were startling: in a five-year period 50 non-literates took an average of 2.67 years to lead 815 people to Christ, [during which time they] planted 22 churches.
>
> After they were trained in visual-oral methods to tell 85 Bible stories that were accurate and culturally relevant, the same 50 non-literates led 9,122 people to Christ, and planted 370 churches—*in one year!*[2]

Using visual-oral strategies to make ten times the disciples in just a year is remarkable. Grant Lovejoy observed that such learners use forms of communication that are familiar—to those within a culture—offering them stories, parables, ancient proverbs, plays and dramatic presentations with which they are familiar, songs, chants, and poetry or fables.[3] In such a culture the visual-oral strategies really work.

In the illustrations above, by using the methods of Orality, results increased tenfold in a year. Let's hope that Christian organizations will consider these options, especially with kids.

Some of our Christian colleges and seminaries are taking notice of Orality and its explosive success in reaching people for Christ. Dr. Jerry Cain, president of Judson University in Elgin, Illinois, told me recently that Judson now has a curriculum of storytelling.

Jim Rosene also recently told me a story that connects what Judson University is doing with something that the school's namesake ties in with Orality. Jim said:

> Eight years ago I found myself in Thailand, at a United Nations High Commissioner for Refugees (UNHCR) refugee camp. I was there to train a Christian Burmese teacher how to use our Flannelgraph stories to win his people to Christ. After our session, he shared a story with me about Adoniram Judson (for whom Judson College was named) who went to Burma (now called Myanmar) after being expelled from India. Judson was a Baptist missionary from America who labored with great success for almost forty years in Burma.
>
> Adoniram Judson went to the Burmese tribe near the border of Burma and Thailand and used oral methods to present the gospel to the tribal

> people. He had an interpreter, who took Judson's stories and translated them into Burmese history and traditions and shared Jesus Christ's history and how He came to die for their sins.
>
> Judson was successful in winning followers, but so were his interpreters. Later, these new Burmese Christians crossed over into Thailand and presented the same gospel message—except that Judson didn't go with them: They shared Christ on their own.
>
> Today, nearly two hundred years later, there are Christians in Thailand as a direct result of Judson's presenting Christ to them through visual-oral methods. Surprisingly, some four to five churches were planted back then, and they are still very much alive today, growing by the same methods as Judson used to win Burmese tribal seekers. When I heard about how these tribal people kept the chain from breaking by winning others generation to generation, I was amazed, and it helps me to see the potential that we have.[4]

Jim's assessment is correct. I'm also a great believer in the visual-oral methods that Judson used to win the hearts of Burmese tribals—and that can win the hearts of nonbelievers today. These methods are intrinsically no different than they were for Adoniram Judson.

Kids Around the World has changed some of its *methods* within the past five to ten years. Yet our mission will not change—only our methods and strategies have changed. We use playgrounds, puppets, and Flannelgraph Bible stories as a means to reach those who cannot practically be reached by literate-based methods.

In recent times we've sometimes partnered with other organizations to use social or humanitarian relief to help the people who in turn will listen to the stories and watch the Flannelgraph presentations. When we help others in this way, we don't just give them a *story* to tell others. We also minister to their human needs.

Jesus set an example for us. He was known and revered during His earthly lifetime as the Great Healer, yet He never veered from His mission—Jesus told parables and talked with people like the woman at the well, Nicodemus, the religious leaders in the temple, and sinners and tax collectors.

And, yes, when He healed the sick, there was another purpose involved besides making someone well and whole—because in the process, Jesus created an event that became a story to tell others—and to demonstrate His power and deity. Jesus' mission was to obey God and to follow the plan given to Him by His heavenly Father.

Why are stories important?

By now I think you know. I've "only" mentioned it a dozen times or more in these chapters: *Only a minority of the world's population is literate.* Some of these population groups are literate in just a single language or dialect. So there is a great chasm of understanding if we continue to use *only* the printed word to reach them. We can *never even keep up with the increase in population* if that's all we do.

We need a tenfold increase in our efforts every year. The way to achieve that is to use visual-oral methods—by teaching people from their cultures to teach their own clans, tribes, and communities—by using memorized Bible stories, Flannelgraph presentations, and music or drama from their own history and traditions, but set in the biblical stories that they can tell and retell.

It's our prayerful desire to make sure that the hundreds of millions of "kids around the world" who have never heard of Jesus will be brought into the kingdom of Christ while they are yet young—for there's an encouraging statistic that we face if we do it now: 75 to 90 percent of children who are presented with the gospel while they are yet children will likely respond positively.

However, once they reach adolescence, those numbers reverse, and most kids will not become followers of Jesus once they reach the ages of twelve to fourteen. We have quite a challenge before us, but we also have a great God to lead us into those harvest fields.

Chapter Twenty-Seven

TEACH CHILDREN ABOUT HEAVEN

We need to tell the kids about heaven.

As I've been working on the material I want to put into this book, this chapter on heaven is imperative. But how can we begin to describe heaven? As far as we know, those who go to heaven don't return to earth, so it's impossible for someone (except Jesus) to tell us what heaven looks like.

The truth is, heaven and hell are real, and in the social circles of young people, they never hear much about either place—except in the realm of entertainment. The latest trend seems to be about demons, avatars,[1] and vampires—creatures with supernatural powers who interact with humans. Two of the most advertised films of the past several years are *The Twilight Saga: New Moon* and *Avatar,* a film by veteran filmmaker James Cameron (whose budget for the film ballooned from three hundred million to *half a billion dollars).*[2]

A top-grossing motion picture at the end of 2009 was *The Twilight Saga: New Moon,* a blockbuster that broke box office records with more than *a quarter billion* dollars in just the first three weeks of its release—on a production budget of "only" fifty million.[3]

Avatar grossed $212 million in its first two weeks of release and was expected to surpass *The Twilight Saga: New Moon*—but it was a toss-up for final accounting as entertainment industry reports indicate that *Avatar* is likely to bring in more than *$1 billion* in receipts.[4]

The Twilight Saga: New Moon is based on the four-book Twilight "vampire" series, written by Stephenie Meyer. All four of these novels smashed records on the various best-seller lists. Although she has "only" sold about forty-two million books so far, the author nevertheless surpassed records that until now were "owned" by J. K. Rowling, author of the phenomenal Harry Potter series—with its own supernatural antagonists.

As of August 8, 2011, *Harry Potter and the Deathly Hallows—Part 2* earned an astounding worldwide box office gross of *$1.3 billion,* making the film the third-highest-grossing film worldwide of all time.[5]

Supernatural demons, wizards, false gods, "creatures from hell," and vampires are the current rage among today's adolescents and teens. What bothers me about all these films is that the focus of vampire and "hell" movies is totally opposite of what we're trying to do to get kids to learn.

There's so much false information about the supernatural beings of these books and movies, that it weighs heavily against a "fair and balanced" presentation. We see plenty of beings from hell or the nether lands—but where are the glimpses of heaven?

In fact I don't ever recall hearing many *sermons* about what heaven is like. The few sermons I've heard in describing heaven focus on the scenes that are described by John in the book of Revelation—featuring "streets of gold" and other incredible physical manifestations of precious stones and metals. Other, nonbiblical descriptions include harps and angels in the clouds, and other cliché depictions. What do we truly know about heaven?

My complaint is that ministers aren't preaching sermons about heaven so we can learn more about God's promised paradise. It's a shame that we don't hear about it.

We need to describe heaven, so our kids and grandkids can look forward to it in great anticipation. Muslim believers make a big thing about heaven. I have visited several mosques in the Middle East. The Arab descendants of Abraham and Ishmael continually talk about and even describe heaven in great expansive narratives.

Yet in contrast to the Islamic faith, most Christians don't give much attention to heaven.

We hear about Islamic extremists or terrorists who are presented with such a fantastic presentation that the listener can even project himself or herself into the descriptions. The visions are so powerful they can even motivate a young person to strap on a bomb and walk into a crowded market to blow himself or herself to pieces.

Think of how powerful a description of paradise is for a Muslim to willingly do such a terrorist act. The greatest repeated example of

Islam depicts heaven as a place for great pleasure—of great feasting and looking forward to the sexual pleasure of seventy lovely virgins. To impoverished young men who've never had a decent break in their lives, this false promise must be highly motivating.

However, Christian theology offers those who seek to follow Jesus a promise that we can be saved from eternal death in hell and have a wonderful eternal life with Christ in *our* paradise. That promise of heaven is a convincing reality that leads many to repent and turn to Christ.

In my role as chairman of the Chaplain's Committee for SwedishAmerican Health System in Rockford, Illinois, I see this experience on a regular basis. Patients, when coming to the hospital with serious, life-threatening illnesses, are nearly always frightened.

True, they're worried about their health, of course—especially the life-threatening injury or illness that brings them to the hospital. However, many times, they don't fear death. *They're afraid of hell.* And their uncertain hospital stay puts that issue ahead of everything else.

Death can be a frightening matter—especially for the person who doesn't know if he or she will go to heaven or hell—if they die in the hospital.

The odd thing is, most Americans already believe in both heaven and hell, even if they don't go to church regularly. I suspect that their absence from church triggers that terrible fear because of their careless living. Many won't be able to avoid hell, and they have no assurance they'll be going to heaven. So hospitals are often the place where people take an urgent spiritual inventory.

For the many who face that kind of unknown, I'm glad that SwedishAmerican has a staff of chaplains to help people who are brought to a hospital.

But what about those who don't survive long enough to consider that frightening choice? What if there's no time to see a chaplain or a minister or priest?

Shouldn't our *churches* be explaining what eternity will be like—telling folks the difference between hell and heaven? Shouldn't people be able to, *before* they're dying, hear more about what heaven is going to be like?

I especially thought of kids when I was reading the statistics about what they're being fed through cultural influences—in movies, books, TV, Internet chat rooms, and music—and what they're being told in schools.

Those stats about kids, especially the one I cited earlier—that our kids will have already made their most serious decisions before age fourteen—motivate me to tell my kids and grandkids about heaven and how to get there.

I trust that you've provided your kids and grandkids with opportunities to learn about heaven, so they make their choice of where they'll spend eternity. We can't choose for them.

That discussion—just because it's a serious one—doesn't have to take on a "fire and brimstone" approach. If you haven't talked to your children or grandchildren about heaven, and your pastor hasn't preached about what heaven will be like or what heaven offers the believer, you should consider reading one of Randy Alcorn's books.[6] He has clearly defined adult presentations about heaven, but has also written *Heaven for Kids.*

Alcorn, in his introduction to that book, wrote:

> It might surprise you to discover that many people find no joy when they think about Heaven. Wondering why? They don't look forward to going there because of what they believe Heaven is like.
>
> Gary Larson showed a common view of Heaven in one of his *Far Side* cartoons. In it a man with angel wings and a halo sits on a cloud, doing nothing, with no one nearby. He has the expression of someone stuck on a desert island, bored because he has absolutely nothing to do. A caption shows what he's thinking: "Wish I'd brought a magazine."[7]

To clear up that universal misconception of what heaven is like, Alcorn answered the question, "Do I really need to think about heaven?" He answered with these excerpts:

> Pretend you're a part of a NASA team preparing for a five-year mission to Mars. After a period of heavy-duty training, the launch day finally arrives. As the rocket lifts off, one of the other astronauts says to you, "What do you know about Mars?"
>
> Imagine shrugging your shoulders and saying, "Nothing. We never talked about it. I guess we'll find out when we get there." Think that would happen? Not likely, right? Part of your training would have prepared you for where you would be living

> for the next five years. You'd have talked about Mars 24/7, wouldn't you? *After all, that's where you were headed!...*
>
> So if Heaven—or as the apostle Peter calls it, "the new heavens and new earth"—will be your home someday, wouldn't it be great to learn all you can about it now?[8]

These questions set up the presentation of heaven in Alcorn's books, especially those written for children. He lays out ideas of what heaven may be like, with descriptions of "the new heavens and new earth." Here are some of those questions and answers that are found in the Bible:

> What happens after we die?
> In heaven, will we have real bodies? What will they be like?
> What does it mean to have eternal life?
> What will life in heaven be like? Will heaven be boring?
> Can we be sure we'll go to heaven instead of hell?
> If we go to heaven but some people we love go to hell, won't we be sad in heaven?
> Will animals (and pets) be in heaven?[9]

When we get older, our questions about heaven are different from when we were children or young adults. As we age we tend to think about things such as freedom from disease and avoidance of unforeseen calamities. While mature adults focus on the things that *won't* be in heaven, children are more preoccupied with the things that *they're involved with at the time*—kids imagine heaven as a place for playing, being with their friends and pets—and if they'd grow up in heaven if they die as kids. Youngsters tend to address the practical concerns and involvements of their lives, and that's what they do as they think about heaven.

But most kids—and many adults for that matter—still don't have much preoccupation with heaven. Usually their thoughts of heaven are predicated by fears of dying or separation from their family and friends. The rest of the time, most people just have an uncomplicated fantasy about heaven—the kind of abstract thinking that comes from the stereotypes—like the one of heaven being a boring place where you'll live forever without anything to do but play a harp and sit on clouds. The few who *do* give some real study to the subject of heaven are primarily motivated by their own worries about what happens when they die.

Children may have some of the same concerns, but they like to think about all the *possibilities of heaven* rather than just the generalities or bland expectations. I think that's why Alcorn's books are so helpful. He builds on *what kids wonder about* but hardly ever verbalize in public—for fear of looking silly for asking something like, "Will my dog be in heaven?"

A friend of mine recently overheard a conversation between three senior citizens, and the subject of their conversation was *their pets.* Two of them had pet dogs, and the third person was a cat owner. The conversation centered on the fact that all three pets—like their owners—were in the latter stages of life.

One dog suffered from cancer and crippling arthritis. “We still go for walks,” his mistress told her friends, “but now Maurice [her dog] can only walk partway. After he does his business, I pick him up and put him in his stroller to go home. He really likes his stroller.” Then, her eyes misted as she said softly, “He’s still responsive, but”—she paused, then blinking back tears, she said in a whisper—“it won’t be long before the vet will have to put him to sleep.”

The other two pet owners nodded their heads understandingly. Their pets were also living on borrowed time. Then the first woman asked her two friends, “Do you think Maurice will go to heaven when he dies?”

There was silence after the question, and then the first woman said, “Just kidding.” The other two chuckled nervously. Then the first woman added, “I hope Maurice *will* be there when I go, though.”

I’ve seen people like that—pet owners who give their pets human qualities. They seem to hold out hope that heaven will have a place for dogs and cats. Grandchildren hope that their dogs, turtles, and hamsters will also be in heaven along with Maurice and Tabby.

Personally I think that it’s consistent with God’s love for us to have animals in heaven.

I read the New Testament Gospels about the character and acts of Jesus—how He related to children and adults and how He took a particular interest in children. The kids are depicted in the Gospels as playful, trusting, happy, and confident.

Theologians may be more inclined to tell us about heaven in terms that relate to God, rather than us humans. It’s true that heaven will be a place where we will worship God in person and enjoy His presence and character. However I think—besides those worshipful qualities—that heaven will be as Jesus said in John 14, a place where there are many rooms/houses for each citizen of heaven. "If it were not so, I would have told you," He reminded them (John 14:2).

If Jesus thought enough of those who'll be with Him in heaven—for whom He will prepare a place—why couldn't He also provide the companionship of a beloved pet as a resident of heaven, just as an adult human resident of heaven will share the companionship of a former spouse, family member, or close friend in heaven?

Wouldn't it be reasonable for a child received into heaven to be made at home with his pet? Well, I'll leave it to the theologians to cite scriptural answers to such questions and leave my words on this matter to be more like a kid's "common sense" than religious dogma.

Surely such scenes would be wonderful. Jesus told His disciples that He was going to create "new heavens and earth," and I'm certain that He's able to even outdo the original creation of the "old" heavens and the "old" earth—with astonishing surprises for our senses.

I have my own imaginations about what the "new heavens and new earth" are like. Wouldn't you expect the new heavens and new earth to be something familiar—like the beautiful landscapes of earth—only more magnificent?

I imagine mountain vistas with snow-covered caps, wide lakes surrounded by tall pines, sandy beaches and palm trees with a soft lapping of the ocean waves, or even a simple park with a bench nearby to watch laughing, playful games taking place—or if you preferred, silence for meditation (except for the singing of birds). You can probably come up with your own descriptions of the new heavens and new earth. We know that God has a love for blue and green colors. In His first creation, He used blue in the skies and in the seas. And green is abundant in the grasslands, forests, and farmlands. Those colors and *your* favorite colors will be used in heaven.

The Bible tells us that when we go to heaven, we'll have new bodies—but the Bible doesn't say much as to whether the new bodies will be supplied with the same senses we have on earth. The joys, pleasures, and happiness that we experience on earth usually involve our senses—so why wouldn't God allow us to inhale the fragrance of flowers, hear the songs of angels and birds, take in the sights of majestic and unbelievable sights, and touch and taste these beautiful things? If not, why not?

Author Randy Alcorn listed a number of things that he suspects we'll see in heaven:

> Arts, music, and entertainment.
> Games, play, and sports.
> Improving your knowledge by learning new things.
> Hobbies—like making furniture, arranging flowers and gardening, etc.
> Extraordinary means of travel—with a possibility of even exploring the universe.
> Time travel?—why not?[10]

Why not, indeed? Are any of these incredible things too bizarre to be possible in heaven? Do any of these things pose a problem, or are any too difficult for God?

Alcorn reminds us that our God is a God "who is able, through his mighty power at work within us, to accomplish infinitely more than we might ask or think" (Eph. 3:20 NLT).

Alcorn added, "That means there is *no end* to how much more God can do than we could ever expect. Wow!"[11]

Reading Randy Alcorn's books about heaven makes me wonder why so few preachers offer sermons about heaven and hell. I believe that if congregations had storytelling—pictorial presentations that portray clearly the events leading up to the good news about heaven, don't you think it'd increase the population of heaven? I do—I think it'd also have an impact on society and culture for the "here and now."

In my opinion, there need to be *more sermons on heaven*—so that *more people* will be excited about going there. To meet the need of the two-thirds of the world that can't or won't choose to read and write, we need to use the Orality (storytelling) techniques to describe heaven.

Think of all the creative and artistic methods that would dramatically enhance our imaginations of what it will be like in heaven—with art, music, drama, dance, games, storytelling, and other exciting considerations. We should let the children describe their ideas of heaven—as they'd imagine it. Does it really matter if it turns out to be a bit different? As a matter of fact, it'll probably be even better than they imagined!

More sermons about heaven might motivate and change those who claim to follow Christ but ignore Jesus' commandment to "go into all the world and preach the gospel to every creature" (Mark 16:15 NKJV) and to "make disciples of all the nations" (Matt. 28:19 NKJV). As Christ followers, we're expected to help fulfill the Great Commission by telling others about Jesus and giving our time or money to make sure the gospel will be preached throughout the world, especially to the children.

One of my persistent efforts is to pray for Christian churches and their congregations—wherever they might be across the world. I want to see American churches—as well as churches in India, China, Indonesia, Korea, South America, Africa, and Australia—make every effort to fulfill the Great Commission.

At the same time, we must do our best to make certain that *we each* do our very best to fulfill *our part* in the Great Commission, and *to make sure that children all around the world are included in that global outreach and invitation to be with Him in heaven.*

Chapter Twenty-Eight

THE THIRD LAUSANNE CONGRESS ON WORLD EVANGELIZATION

In October 2010 the Third Lausanne Congress on World Evangelization was held in Cape Town, South Africa, and Jim Rosene of Kids Around the World attended. He was a committee chair of the Children's Task Force of International Orality Network (ION), on behalf of the evangelization efforts for the largest age demographic—*children*. I attended as well, along with Cris Doornbos, president of David C Cook.

The 2010 Congress, held in collaboration with the World Evangelical Alliance, convened to confront the critical issues of our time—other world faiths, poverty, HIV/AIDS, and persecution, among other issues that relate to the future of the church and world evangelization.

At Lausanne III, at Cape Town 2010, I participated in the formation of strategic partnerships, joint venture plans, and creative ideas for operations that make it possible for more men, women, children, and young people to hear and respond to the gospel.

The most powerful moments of the first day—and perhaps the entire conference—was when a teenage girl from North Korea spoke about her life. Her mother died of leukemia while giving birth when this teenager was a very young girl. Her father was a high-ranking government official and part of the inner circle of Kim Jong Il, the dictator of North Korea. But for some reason her father was to be imprisoned by Communist officials, and he fled to China with his then six-year-old daughter.

Now the six-year-old girl is a young woman, telling the crowd at Lausanne III, at Cape Town 2010, how her father was brought to a Christian church in China by a Chinese believer, where he subsequently found Christ.

However, her father was later betrayed, and the Chinese government arrested him and sent him back to North Korea, where he was sentenced to four years in a Communist prison for political and religious reasons.

The Korean girl explained what happened next. She said her father simply disappeared. She'd tried to contact her father but had yet to hear from him or even find out where he is. She presumes that an executioner's bullet took his life or that he died in prison.

Meanwhile she was adopted into the family of a Chinese pastor, where she also became a Christian—but recently she left China after seeing a vision of Jesus in a dream calling her to go back to North Korea to serve her people.

As she told the audience her plan to return to North Korea, the entire audience seemed to stop breathing at the same time—four thousand people catching their breath in unison at the terrible thought of the risk she had just shared with them. But she was not deterred.

She spoke softly, poignantly, and with emotion. Her words were clear and went straight to the hearts of the audience. She spoke for less than ten minutes, then she bowed in the Oriental tradition and quietly walked backstage. After a few seconds of stunned silence, there was an explosive standing ovation—two minutes of sustained clapping—directed to that little eighteen-year-old girl who was trusting Jesus to be with her when she goes back to Pyongyang, the capital of North Korea, her native land.

Before that young girl's emotional but courageous testimony brought the audience to their feet for sustained applause, she thanked God for His grace to her and her North Korean family. She told us how God had given her heart a burden for her own people and asked for our prayers for them—for North Korea.

She was so inspiring. Her simple, emotional words were worth the entire trip for me, just to hear those few minutes of heartfelt testimony.[1]

The audience wouldn't stop clapping. They knew collectively and intuitively that God had anointed her. As the applause continued, someone escorted her back out onto the stage. Shyly, looking toward the floor, she gave a polite bow again and left the stage. She absolutely stunned the entire audience.

We all made a promise to pray for this young woman especially, but also for her atheistic nation of North Korea. It made me think of the difference that Christ made in the life of that young woman when a Chinese Christian family took her in as a girl. That girl is now a teenager. She had the boldness, determination, and willingness to risk her future, and perhaps even her life, to tell her story and the Bible's stories of Jesus. It was a powerful challenge to those of us who heard her testimony in person.

That young woman's "Real Story," told with passion, will be remembered—told and retold by the four thousand people in the audience that day in Cape Town. As the girl walked shyly toward the podium from curtains at the back of the stage, the leader merely said to her, "Tell me a story," *and she did.*

Chapter Twenty-Nine

FACING THE FUTURE

In the preface to this book, I laid out ten statements addressing the major content objectives that we wanted to present. What follows is a response and summary of material presented in this book with the hope that it will inform your thoughts regarding these new ideas of Orality and the need to minister to children to have a more vibrant and expanding church in the future. Here are those original ten statements and also the responses:

- ***Two-thirds of the people living on earth either can't read or choose not to learn that way.*** Most of the nonliterate people are under the age of twenty-five, and an ever-growing majority are school-age children. Evangelizing and discipling children is the best way to get them to become Christ followers. It doesn't seem like a big deal—using pictures and telling a story—but sometimes it is. The fact is, kids love stories, and because they're kids, they are at the age and frame of life where a good story can make the difference for them that results in a changed life. Understanding how the world and its children learn can and should make a difference in how you teach and train them. It's a process just like the one you use to instruct and disciple your children, your church, and your community. The nonliterate two-thirds of the world is now hearing about Jesus, and these people need us to use our storytelling techniques and principles to help them change and shape their lives.

- ***Orality (storytelling) is the way to reach those people.*** Orality is the way that most of the rest of the world learns. There are already agencies and organizations using these new methods and ways to communicate biblical truth effectively, and as a result, the number of converts to Christianity is growing exponentially around the globe. Jesus knew the importance of storytelling. When He went to the mountainside where thousands gathered to listen to Him—the greatest teacher known to man—lives were changed forever. He told them a parable—a story—and that was not something new. The adults understood His stories, and the children loved them as well. Yet Jesus also knew that some people needed to read the Torah. He taught them from the Scriptures when He went to the temple. Moral principles and guidelines for following God's commandments were the eternal implications for life, but the majority of people in Jesus' day received this learning from stories and parables—from the greatest storyteller who ever lived.

- ***Orality is best described as storytelling: the way the world learns.*** Orality is all around us—we even practice it every day. We sit around the living room, in the family room, or at the dining room table and tell stories (about our day, our work, our day at school, our experiences, and the things we'd encountered or learned that day)—and we share them with our kids, parents, and friends. When we go out to restaurants, we also share stories while we wait for our food to come. Even artwork on the wall tells a story without words. There might even be a TV set nearby to tell us "stories" of the day. Or we might go to a play or a concert to hear a story set to music, drama, or dance. Even our prayers are spoken to God in story form.
- ***Why is it so important that we understand Orality and use it more?*** Because it's so effective in reaching kids. It's the best way to communicate ideas and beliefs to them when they are

young. Studies show that most people come to know Christ at an early age and so can get to understand what it means to follow Him as they make a personal decision for Jesus before the age of fourteen. If kids don't understand good moral teaching and have an understanding of God's love and grace by ages twelve to fourteen, fewer than 25 percent will decide "later" to follow Jesus Christ and live the life that He outlines in His Word. Consequently, because the statistics are so stacked against them, these kids who do not make a decision to follow Christ will—statistically—*never* make that decision.

- ***Who is doing the job of reaching kids?*** There are many great organizations working to change lives. The local church is one of them. Many churches send out young people on short-term overseas mission trips, and in their local communities they do a wonderful job with tutoring and presenting VBS programs, street ministry, and similar programs. Navigators, Awana, Child Evangelism, and other parachurch organizations specialize in evangelizing and ministering to kids. I was glad when God gave us the vision to create an organization that we named Kids Around the World to focus on teaching and discipling children. I've seen children's workers in some of the countries in which Kids Around the World has worked. Building playgrounds is only part of our mission. The less visible efforts involve training Christian volunteer workers to teach kids about Jesus, and training local Christian leaders to do the same. I've seen the responses of these local leaders when they complete the training that we give them using the Flannelgraph materials and a set of teaching pictures. They literally weep for joy for having the experience of teaching the stories of the Bible—using pictures, a voice, facial expressions, and their hands as the tools to help change the lives of kids they teach.

- ***Orality is a strategy that Kids Around the World uses to win youngsters (and their parents) to Christ.*** When we build playgrounds, it's a wonderful gift to a community. Not just the opportunity for kids to play, but to provide a chance for them to hear about Jesus through our storytellers and lead them to a decision to follow Him that often lasts a lifetime. Even the older kids (teens) hang around and listen. Sometimes moms and dads who brought the kids to the new playground (or who curiously watched it being constructed) listen to the stories and watch the joy and wonder on the kids' faces as they interact with the storytellers.
- ***Building playgrounds is a nonthreatening way to break the ice in other cultures.*** Working

with foreign politicians and local authorities, Kids Around the World makes friends not just for building a playground, but gaining approvals and official permission to conduct ministry outreach in their cities and villages. It's this ministry outreach, with an emphasis on evangelizing and making disciples and leaders, that is the mission of Kids Around the World. In 1994 we built our first playground in Brovary, Ukraine. In January 2006, we celebrated our one hundredth playground (in the Dominican Republic). Our two hundredth playground was completed in July 2011 in Guatemala. At the time of this writing we have completed 208 playgrounds.

- ***Churches seldom invest enough resources into children's ministry, whether in the US or abroad.*** Kids are often the forgotten demographic when it comes to evangelism, yet as we know, statistics show that kids who make a decision to follow Christ will likely do so before they reach the age of fourteen, and few will do so later. However, in many if not most churches today, funds are lacking for ministries for kids; churches must fight for their very survival. So when the budgets are reviewed, sometimes there's only enough to keep the lights on, pay the pastor, and fund only the basics. Money for children's work is put at the end of the line. Most small churches can't afford a children's worker or fund Sunday school material or the Vacation Bible School sessions for the summer recess. All these children's ministries come with a bill attached. Yet it's the kids who will ultimately make the decisions for Christ in the churches—kids are that church's future. That's why even during the poor economic cycles, many churches nonetheless make children's ministries a priority.

- ***Many churches do not understand the importance and value of "belonging" and the effectiveness of "storytelling."*** Seeking ways to make kids feel wanted, loved, and important is critical for setting the stage for the storytelling to bear fruit. Most of us are typical parents, concerned about our teenagers—who their friends are, where they're going, and what they're doing. At that stage in life, teens typically have already formed their group of friends and established their own moral framework. By then, they've already decided whether to invite Christ into their lives or not. So the time to change the course of their lives is when they're small children. To that end, the church needs to provide fantastic programming, the best teachers, and the best learning tools. Kids will always pour themselves into singing, dancing, expressing themselves with pictures and drawings, and acting out their passionate ideas in drama and musical groups. Parents need to bring them to church, encourage Christian friendships, and give them a solid loving family structure and an oral-visual demonstration of Christ's parental love. Kids need to understand and experience the need to feel they "belong." Adults may miss this; the church might miss this. Youngsters and even teens learn best when they are in their "comfort group" and trust the one telling the story. Kids will either join a "good gang" or a "bad gang." It's their nature to *belong* to one or the other. Just be sure to steer your children to play with kids with good moral standards similar to those that you have. Allowing kids to know and become friends with church kids helps too, and provides opportunities for kids and their friends to enjoy parties at home with family and friends (or at the church) to help them reinforce that sense of "belonging." The next step of child discipleship is the matter of "becoming" more like Jesus, followed by "behaving" according to biblical precepts and principles.

- ***Not enough churches and Christian agencies are telling kids about heaven—"the place where they have an opportunity to spend eternity."*** Heaven is something Jesus promised His followers, and children were a key audience for His parables and stories. We need to model our storytelling with patterns set by Jesus as a way to win followers—just as He did. The church and Christian families may be overlooking a huge opportunity by ignoring what heaven is like—and giving kids hope. I think that's mostly missing in the overall outreach of Christianity. Most other religions of the world give emphasis to rewards that are waiting for their people in the afterlife. Sometimes I feel that as Christians we do a poor job in describing the fabulous and unimaginable life and scenes to come. The hope of heaven is something we should not miss sharing with our children, for if we fail in that responsibility, they may never commit themselves to Christ and the hope of heaven. Jesus said that for those who choose not to "belong" to Him, the result is they will not be able to go to heaven. He said, "For God loved the world so much that he gave his only Son, so that every one who believes in him shall not be lost, but should have eternal life. You must understand that God has not sent his Son into the world to pass sentence upon it, but to save it—through him" (John 3:16–17 PH).

I end my stories here, and if my mom and dad were still with us, I think they would be pleased to know that we just built a playground at the former Blackhawk Court projects (now named Orton Keyes).

Just for the kids—and it took place where it all began when I was just six years old. No doubt there were many who listened to the stories and responded to them, particularly the kids from the projects.

At the same time, I know that there are still other kids who will trust Christ, as Jesus presented Himself in John 3, if they get the chance. Many more will have their own stories to share. I believe there are plenty of such stories to be told. My prayer is that we all make certain that we will all be in heaven to enjoy and share in those common conversations based on our experiences here on earth.

And yes, I believe there will be a time for telling stories in heaven—maybe even around a table with a cup of coffee and a piece of cake. In fact, the results of our storytelling here on earth will be the frosting on the cake.

For contact or information about Kids Around the World:

Kids Around the World
2424 Charles Street
Rockford, Illinois 61108
1-815-229-8731

www.kidsaroundtheworld.com

For contacting Dennis Johnson:
Email: dennyjohnson@me.com

NOTES

Preface:

1. Source: International Orality Network.

Chapter One: Small Beginnings

1. Now called the Orton Keyes Housing Development in Rockford, Ill.

2. "Making Disciples of Oral Learners" (lecture, 2004 Forum for World Evangelism, conveners Avery Willis and Steve Evans, © 2005 Lausanne Committee for World Evangelism).

3. Ibid.

Chapter Three: Rips in the Iron Curtain

1. Developed by Dr. Jerome W. Berryman. More information at http://www.godlyplay.org.

Chapter Six: Groups Love to Hear a Story Too

1. Jay Kesler, *Maybe If We Try* (Rockford, IL: Quadrus Media, 1984), VHS.

2. Ibid.

3. Steven Douglass served Campus Crusade for Christ International for thirty years prior to succeeding Dr. Bill Bright as president. John Ortberg Jr., is senior pastor of Menlo Park Presbyterian Church in California, and his education includes a master's of divinity degree and doctorate in clinical psychology from Fuller Seminary; he is a nationally known minister and best-selling author. Dr. Gary Smalley is one of the best-known authors and speakers on relationships, and he has fifty-two best-selling, award-winning books to his credit. Evelyn Christenson, a pastor's wife and internationally acclaimed author, was a national women's chairman for the Baptist General Conference when she began seminars and wrote a number of books on the power of prayer.

Chapter Seven: Belonging, Becoming … and Then, Behaving

1. "Tutsi Bishop Brings God's Word to Hutus," *Washington Times,* February 5, 2009, http://www.washingtontimes.com/news/2009/feb/5/forgiven-not-forgotten/?page=all#pagebreak.

2. Ibid.

3. Sudip Mazumdar, "Man Bites 'Slumdog,'" *Newsweek,* February 20, 2009, http://www.thedailybeast.com/newsweek/2009/02/20/man-bites-slumdog.html.

Chapter Eight: What Works in "This Day and Age"?

1. Avery T. Willis Jr., was a pastor, missionary, seminary president, and a popular author and speaker. He served as senior vice president of the Overseas Operations for the International Mission Board of the Southern Baptist Convention, where he administered the work of 5,600 missionaries. Dr. Willis also served as the executive director of the recently formed International Orality Network, as well as a member of the steering committee for the Call2All Movement, until his passing in 2010.

Chapter Nine: The Oral Majority

1. *Webster's New World College Dictionary,* s.v. "orality."

2. Samuel Chiang, "Essential Elements of the Great Commission: Priority 2; The Orality Reality: Reaching and Discipling Oral Learners," 2009.

3. Erich Bridges, "Worldview: Reaching the 'Oral Majority,'" *Baptist Press,* October 7, 2004, http://www.bpnews.net/bpnews.asp?id=19311.

4. Ibid.

5. Some languages are dying off as others are being discovered (according to Wycliffe Bible Translators).

6. Watkin Roberts was converted in the great Welsh Revival (1904–1905), left his work as a "chemist" (pharmacist) while still in his early twenties, and went to India as a missionary. In 2010, the Hmar tribe that was initially reached by Roberts and was evangelized over the past one hundred years celebrated a Centenary of his coming to northeast India in 1910. Dr. Paul Roberts of Toronto, Ontario, Canada, the son of Watkin Roberts, flew to northeast India for the celebration of his late father's life.

7. Joe Musser, *Fire on the Hills* (Tyndale House Publishers, 1998) and a major motion picture, *Beyond the Next Mountain* (Global Films), based on the life and work of Dr. Rochunga Pudaite, founder of Bibles For the World, Inc., Colorado Springs, CO. (For information on the book or DVD of the film, visit their website at www.bftw.org.)

8. Paul Koehler, *Telling God's Stories With Power: Biblical Storytelling in Oral Cultures* (Pasadena, CA: William Carey Library, 2009).

9. Dr. Paul Larson, an article from a series of emails and conversations with the author. Used with permission.

Chapter Ten: Discipling Kids Through Simple Theater

1. *Wikipedia,* s.v. "Flannelgraph," last modified November 8, 2010, http://en.wikipedia.org/wiki/Flannelgraph.

2. *WikiHow,* s.v. "How to Make a Flannelgraph," last modified January 22, 2010, www.wikihow.com/Make-a-Flannelgraph.

Chapter Eleven: Storytelling As Evangelism

1. Michael Cassidy, "Evangelism as Storytelling," June 3, 2008, *Lausanne World Pulse,* http://s222745089.onlinehome.us/news/view?id=79.

2. Ibid.

3. Leighton Ford, *The Power of Story: Rediscovering the Oldest, Most Natural Way to Reach People for Christ* (Colorado Springs: NavPress, 1994), 6–7.

4. Cassidy, "Evangelism as Storytelling," *Lausanne World Pulse.*

5. Ibid.

Chapter Twelve: Start at the Beginning—with Children

1. Samuel Chiang, email to the author. Used by permission.

2. The source providing us with this information attributed it to a study from Baylor University School of Medicine.

3. Ibid.

4. J. Madeleine Nash, "Fertile Minds," *Time,* February 3, 1997, http://www.time.com/time/magazine/article/0,9171,985854,00.html.

Chapter Thirteen: The Need to Help Children Get to Know God

1. George Barna, *Transforming Children Into Spiritual Champions* (Ventura, CA: Regal Books, 2003), 19.

2. See *National Institutes of Health* and *National Association for Educational Progress.*

Chapter Fourteen: When Good Meets Evil

1. Kids Around the World developed visual Flannelgraph stories for kids in Sierra Leone, Africa. They warn kids about AIDS and teach lessons from the Bible in a comfortable setting of friends learning together.

2. Associated Press, "Somali Refugees Enter into Djibouti," *Washington Post,* March 19, 2010, http://www.washingtonpost.com/wp-dyn/content/video/2010/12/25/VI2010122501870.html.

3. "UN Warns World's Slums Grow Despite Rapid Economy Growth," *Daily Herald,* March 19, 2010, http://www.thedailyherald.com/international/4-international/1715-un-warns-worlds-slums-grow-despite-rapid-economy-growth.html.

4. Ibid.

5. Charis Gresser, "Millennium Goals," *The Financial Times,* October 14, 2010, http://www.ft.com/cms/s/0/6f42bfea-d65a-11df-81f0-00144feabdc0.html#axzz1XC7au1Ve.

6. Ibid.

Chapter Fifteen: Churches in the Twenty-first Century

1. A. W. Tozer, *The Pursuit of God* (Camp Hill, PA: Christian Publications, 1982), 11–12.

2. "Awana at Home," Awana, http://awana.org/athome/awana-at-home-statement,default,pg.html (accessed September 6, 2011).

3. Patrick Johnstone, August 2004, quoted in Dan Brewster and Patrick McDonald, "Children—The Great Omission?" Viva Network, http://www.celebratingchildrentraining.info/secure.php?module=download.php?id=3.

Chapter Sixteen: Vietnam 1993—Ho Chi Min City

1. The others in our group will be introduced in the next chapter.

2. In Vietnam, "North" is a euphemism for the former demilitarized zone in North Vietnam.

3. His real identity is not revealed to protect his privacy and safety.

Chapter Seventeen: Oliver North's Return

1. Author's note: The following chapters about Oliver North are a good example of visual-oral communication. They're "stories within stories," as that's how the people in these stories experienced them. Those who retell a story become visual-oral storytellers. So, although this book is intended for literate learners, the content can be adapted as stories for visual-oral learners and oral speaking societies, which underscores the point about visual-oral learning.

2. John Cushman Jr., "Washington Talk; 5 Young Lawyers Who Would Be Heroes … and a Marine Who Wears a Hero's Ribbons," *New York Times,* July 7, 1987, http://www.nytimes.com/1987/07/07/us/washington-talk-5-young-lawyers-who-would-be-heros-marine-who-wears-hero-s.html.

3. Oliver North and David Roth, *One More Mission: Oliver North Returns to Vietnam* (Grand Rapids: Zondervan, 1993).

4. "Remains Are Found In Vietnam; They May Be Those of US Servicemen," *Buffalo (NY) News,* January 14, 1993, http://www.highbeam.com/doc/1P2-22487151.html.

Chapter Eighteen: Making Friends with Former Enemies

1. R. L. Mole, *The Montagnards of South Vietnam: A Study of Nine Tribes* (Rutland, VT: Charles Tuttle, 1970).

2. World Health Organization of the United Nations.

3. Jim Rosene, communication with the author. Used by permission.

Chapter Twenty: China: Cracks in the Great Wall

1. His name has been changed to protect his identity.

2. C. Austin Miles, *I Come to the Garden Alone (In The Garden),* public domain.

3. His name has been changed to protect his identity. Story is used with permission.

4. United Nations Department of Economics and Social Affairs (DESA) 2006 Revision.

5. *Wikipedia,* s.v. "Christianity in China," last modified September 16, 2011, http://en.wikipedia.org/wiki/Christianity_in_China.

Chapter Twenty-One: Sarajevo: "This Hell Proves There Must Be a Heaven"

1. Author and missionary Ted Esler's recollections of this story are in his book, *Overwhelming Minority* (Orlando, FL: BottomLine Media, 2006). Some of his material is included in this chapter with Ted's permission.

Chapter Twenty-Two: Different Worldviews—Part I

1. "Execution by the Taliban," *New York Times,* January 16, 1999. http://www.nytimes.com/1999/01/16/world/execution-by-taliban-crushed-under-wall.html.

2. "Now We Have Revenge," *Associated Press,* April 24, 1998, http://www.militantislammonitor.org/article/id/1653.

3. "Taliban Publicly Execute Murderer; Amputate Two Robbers," *Agence France-Presse,* August 14, 1998.

4. Zahid Hussain, "Eight Christians Burned to Death in Pakistan After Koran is 'Defiled,'" *Times,* August 3, 2009, http://www.timesonline.co.uk/tol/news/world/asia/article6736696.ece.

5. "Muslim Demographics," YouTube video, 7:31, posted by "friendofmuslim," March 30, 2009, http://www.youtube.com/watch?v=6-3X5hIFXYU&feature=channel_video_title.

6. Ibid.

7. A current debate on US immigration estimates that some 12 to 15 million immigrants from Mexico, Central and South America, Africa, Asia, and the Middle East have crossed the border illegally. An argument is made that the US was founded as a Christian nation, and the Catholic religion of "Christian immigrants" (both legal and illegal) may be less of a problem than a burgeoning Islamic influx that includes fanatical Islamists.

8. "Muslim Demographics," YouTube video, 7:3`, posted by "friendofmuslim."

9. Philip Jenkins, *The Next Christendom: The Coming of Global Christianity* (New York: Oxford University Press, 2002), 13.

Chapter Twenty-Three: Different Worldviews—Part II

1. Information taken from a schematic chart created by Noel Bechetti, North American representative for Truthseekers, International, http://www.truthseekersinternational.org/meet-the-truthseekers-2/. Used by permission.

2. Vishal Mangalwadi, *The Quest for Freedom & Dignity* (Mumbai: GLS Publishers with Partnership Publications, 2001), page number unknown, http://listserv.virtueonline.org/pipermail/virtueonline_listserv.virtueonline.org/2002-November/004320.html.

3. Ibid.

4. Ibid.

5. Christian World News, "Christian 'Untouchables' Describe Attacks By Hindu Militants in India," *CBN News,* December 26, 2008, http://www.cbn.com/cbnnews/shows/cwn/2008/December/Indias-Christians-Face-Historical-Attacks-/.

6. John Malhotra, "EFI Records 64 Incidents of Persecution This Year," *Christianity Today India*, August 10, 2011, http://in.christiantoday.com/articles/efi-records-64-incidents-of-persecution-this-year/6542.htm.

7. Alex Buchan, "India's Christian Leaders Brace for Anti-Caste Rally," Compass News Direct, March 10, 2003, http://www.worthynews.com/1753-india-s-christian-leaders-brace-for-anti-caste-rally.

8. Ibid.

9. "Hindu Given Death for Killing Missionary," *New York Times,* September 23, 2003, http://www.nytimes.com/2003/09/23/world/hindu-given-death-for-killing-missionary.html?ref=grahamstaines.

10. Dr. Paul Larson, communication with the author. Used with permission.

11. Ibid.

12. Ibid.

Chapter Twenty-Four: Different Worldviews—Part III

1. George Smith, *Atheism: The Case Against God* (Buffalo, NY: Prometheus, 1979), 14.

2. Martin Beckford, "Children Are Born Believers in God, Academic Claims," *Daily Telegraph,* November 24, 2008, http://www.telegraph.co.uk/news/newstopics/religion/3512686/Children-are-born-believers-in-God-academic-claims.html.

3. Ibid.

4. Friedrich Nietzsche, *Also Sprach Zarathustra* (New York: Penguin, 1978).

5. Call2All is a movement organized by the Global Pastors Network—founded by the late founder of Campus Crusade for Christ, Bill Bright—to complete the Great Commission.

6. Paul Nussbaum, "Evangelical Christianity Shifting Outside West," *Philadelphia Inquirer,* February 20, 2006.

7. Ibid.

8. Ibid.

9. Norimitsu Onishi, "Korean Missionaries Carrying Word to Hard-to-Sway Places," *New York Times,* November 1, 2004, http://www.nytimes.com/2004/11/01/international/asia/01missionaries.html?_r=1&scp=1&sq=koreans+evangelizing+muslims&st=nyt.

10. IFMA has changed its name to CrossGlobal Link.

11. John Orme, quoted in Nussbaum, "Evangelical Christianity Shifting Outside West."

12. David Martin, *Tongues of Fire: The Explosion of Protestantism in Latin America* (London: Blackwell Publishers, 1993).

13. Timothy C. Morgan, "Back to Cuba," *Christianity Today,* July 9, 2009.

14. "More Freedom But Not Free," *Christianity Today,* July 9, 2009.

15. Project Teen Canada Survey Series, directed by Dr. Reginald W. Bibby, http://www.ptc08.com/english.html.

16. "Chinese Police Attack Mega-Church, Jail Pastors," CBN News, December 11, 2009, http://www.cbn.com/cbnnews/world/2009/December/Chinese-Police-Attack-Christian-Church-Jail-Pastors-/.

17. David Aikman, *Jesus in Beijing: How Christianity Is Transforming China and Changing the Global Balance of Power* (Washington, DC: Regnery Publishing Company, 2004).

18. Paul Nussbaum, "Evangelical Christianity Shifting Outside West."

Chapter Twenty-Five: Keeping Your Life Together When Your World Is Falling Apart

1. "For where two or three come together in my name, there am I with them" (Matt. 18:20).

Chapter Twenty-Six: Are We a Lost Generation?

1. James Dobson, quoted in Jay Kesler, *Maybe If We Try* (1984; Rockford, IL: Quadrus Media, 1984), VHS.

2. Samuel Chiang, quoted in Dorothy Miller, Timothy Church Planters Training, 2008.

3. Grant Lovejoy, *All That May Hear,* Orality Multiplex Position Paper for Lausanne Cape Town 2010.

4. Jim Rosene, communication with the author. Used by permission.

Chapter Twenty-Seven: Teach Children about Heaven

1. An avatar is a Hindu deity that comes to earth as an animal, man, or other creature. The word is also used by computer users who want anonymity for their online browsing, and so they select an icon to

represent them as their virtual avatar without giving away their real identities in chat rooms and other sites.

2. Michael Cieply, "A Movie's Budget Pops From the Screen," *New York Times,* November 8, 2009, http://www.nytimes.com/2009/11/09/business/media/09avatar.html?pagewanted=all.

3. Box Office Mojo, *"Twilight,"* November 21, 2008, http://www.boxofficemojo.com/movies/?id=twilight08.htm.

4. Box Office Mojo, *"Avatar,"* December 18, 2009, http://www.boxofficemojo.com/movies/?id=avatar.htm.

5. "Movie Budget Records," The Numbers, http://www.the-numbers.com/movies/records/budgets.php (accessed September 19, 2011).

6. Randy Alcorn, *Heaven* (2004) and *Heaven for Kids* (2006) both by Tyndale House Publishers.

7. Alcorn, *Heaven for Kids* (Carol Stream, IL: Tyndale, 2006), xxiv–xxv.

8. Ibid., xx–xxii.

9. Ibid., table of contents.

10. Ibid., table of contents.

11. Ibid., 164.

Chapter Twenty-Eight: The Third Lausanne Congress on World Evangelization

1. The Korean girl's testimony is on video at http://conversation.lausanne.org/en/conversations/detail/11671.